Artificial Intelligence, Mixed Reality, and the Redefinition of the Classroom

About The Futures Series on Community Colleges

The Futures Series on Community Colleges is designed to produce and deliver books that strike to the heart of issues that will shape the future of community colleges. Futures books examine emerging structures, systems, and business models and stretch prevailing assumptions about leadership and management by reaching beyond the limits of convention and tradition.

Topics addressed in the series are those that are vital to community colleges, but have yet to receive meaningful attention in literature, research, and analysis. Futures books are written by scholars and practitioners who deliver a unique perspective on a topic or issue—a president or higher education consultant bringing expert and practical understanding to a topic, a policy analyst breaking down a complex problem into component parts, an academic or think tank scholar conducting incisive research, or a researcher and a practitioner working together to examine an issue through different lenses.

Futures books are developed on the premise that disruptive innovation and industry transformation are, and will be, an ongoing challenge. Gradual improvement is, understandably, a natural preference of leaders. It will not be enough, however, to position our colleges for the future. The future will be about transformation and, to perform optimally, our colleges will need to become capable of large-scale change. As leaders come face-to-face with digital forces and rapidly changing social, economic, and public policy conditions, they will have no choice but to get ahead of change or relinquish market position to competitors. Futures books are a vehicle through which leaders can learn about and prepare for what's ahead. Whether it's through analysis of what big data will mean in the next generation of colleges or which business models will become the new normal, Futures books are a resource for practitioners who realize that the ideas of out-of-the-box thinkers and the innovative practices of high performing organizations can be invaluable for answering big questions and solving complex problems.

Books in The Futures Series on Community Colleges

Developing Tomorrow's Leaders: Context, Challenges, and Capabilities
By Pamela Eddy, Debbie L. Sydow, Richard L. Alfred, and Regina L. Garza Mitchell
This book provides a template for leadership development in the community college sector. The theme of the book focuses on the need to move beyond hierarchical leadership to networked leadership that taps talent throughout the institution. The transformational change required in the two-year sector demands new approaches to leading, including tolerance for risk, use of data analytics, and a focus on relationships. New and alternative means for leadership development are presented.

The Urgency of Now: Equity and Excellence
By Marcus M. Kolb, Samuel D. Cargile, et al.
The Urgency of Now asserts that in addition to being granted access to the community college, all 21st-century students need uncompromised support to succeed. Success means demonstrating relevant learning for transfer and employment and timely completion of credentials. Looking to the future, the authors contend that community colleges, both by their past successes and future challenges, are at the epicenter for determining the essential ingredients of a new student-centered system that guarantees equity and excellence.

Unrelenting Change, Innovation, and Risk: Forging the Next Generation of Community Colleges
By Daniel J. Phelan
In this book, thirty-five-year veteran Dan Phelan shares key insights from his personal and professional journey as a transformational, entrepreneurial community college leader. The book's wisdom and insights are amplified by observations gleaned from interviews and visits with dozens of leading practitioners. Drawing upon his sailing experiences, Phelan argues that leaders should stop playing it safe in the harbor because the real gains driving institutional and student success are found in uncharted waters. *Unrelenting Change, Innovation, and Risk* dares community college leaders to innovate and provides them with a tool kit for understanding changing conditions, assessing risk, and successfully navigating change.

Financing Community Colleges: Where We Are, Where We're Going
By Richard Romano and James Palmer
Grounded in an economic perspective, *Financing Community Colleges* helps college leaders make sense of the challenges they face in securing and managing the resources needed to carry out the community college mission. Finance has perpetually been an Achilles' heel for leaders at all levels of management. With the premise that leaders are better at winning battles they know something about, this book equips leaders with an understand-

ing of the fundamentals and the complexities of community college finance. It tackles current and emerging issues with insight that is analytic and prophetic—a must-read for current and prospective leaders.

Previously Published Books in The Future Series on Community Colleges

Minding the Dream: The Process and Practice of the American Community College, Second Edition, by Gail O. Mellow and Cynthia M. Heelan
First in the World: Community Colleges and America's Future, by J. Noah Brown
Community College Student Success: From Boardrooms to Classrooms, by Banessa Smith Morest
Re-visioning Community Colleges, by Debbie Sydow and Richard Alfred
Community Colleges on the Horizon: Challenge, Choice, or Abundance, by Richard Alfred, Christopher Shults, Ozan Jaquette, and Shelley Strickland

Artificial Intelligence, Mixed Reality, and the Redefinition of the Classroom

Scott M. Martin

Series Founding Editor: Richard L. Alfred
Series Senior Editor: Debbie L. Sydow
Series Editor: Kate Thirolf

ROWMAN & LITTLEFIELD
Lanham • Boulder • New York • London

Published by Rowman & Littlefield
An imprint of The Rowman & Littlefield Publishing Group, Inc.
4501 Forbes Boulevard, Suite 200, Lanham, Maryland 20706
www.rowman.com

6 Tinworth Street, London, SE11 5AL, United Kingdom

British Library Cataloguing in Publication Information Available

Library of Congress Cataloging-in-Publication Data

Names: Martin, Scott M., 1964–, author.
Title: Artificial intelligence, mixed reality, and the redefinition of the classroom / Scott M. Martin.
Description: Lanham, Maryland : Rowman & Littlefield, [2019] | Series: The futures series on community colleges | Includes bibliographical references.
Identifiers: LCCN 2019008401 (print) | LCCN 2019018715 (ebook) | ISBN 9781475847291 (Electronic) | ISBN 9781475847277 (cloth : alk. paper) | ISBN 9781475847284 (pbk. : alk. paper)
Subjects: LCSH: Education, Higher—Effect of technological innovations on. | Artificial intelligence—Educational applications. | Community colleges—United States—Planning.
Classification: LCC LB2395.7 (ebook) | LCC LB2395.7 .M319 2019 (print) | DDC 371.33/4—dc23
LC record available at https://lccn.loc.gov/2019008401

To those who have had the greatest impact in crafting and defining me as a student, teacher, scholar, husband, father, inventor, and author.

Morris Moshe Cotel, whose calming presence and contemplative words shared with me during my composition lessons were the most reassuring sights and sounds I received every week. He taught me the skills to consider the unconventional, to always second guess myself and others, and to envision and indeed contemplate that which I have no ability to see nor hear—whose philosophical approach to life I have never been able to imitate, but the effort to imitate still lives in me daily.

Grace Margaret Martin, by sheer example instilled in me that persistence, resoluteness, and stoicism never implies the absence of love. That forgiveness for the sake of others is in the recipe for goodness, and that I would discover the other ingredients through purposeful acts and deeds of thankfulness.

Vera Anna Lichtenberg, whose patience and tolerance the past thirty-one years has been humbling. Her wisdom and intelligence, always offered wrapped in selfless intent, and always for the sake of others, still astonishes and inspires me on a daily basis. And no matter how many impediments I may have erected from time-to-time, she has always been undeterred, able to dismantle them with her unwavering and endearing love.

And I wish to thank the Lord, for forgiving so many of my follies, more than I can count.

Contents

List of Figures

Introduction

Primarily raised by a divorced single mother who never finished undergraduate college, and having five older brothers and sisters who never demonstrated much interest in scholarly pursuits (and, therefore, chose alternative professional pathways), I had no academic role models in my youth. To follow her older brothers, my mother, always the maverick, departed the University of Minnesota after a year of study to join the Lady Marines during World War II. My father never finished high school but was a veteran of both World War II and the Korean War. So, before my father abandoned my mother when I was eight years of age, I did have two leadership and bravery role models, just not academic ones.

My parents grew up during the Great Depression, and the discipline to survive and the stoicism that resulted from that experience was inhaled in my childhood household. My mother used to tell me her family responsibility was to pick up coal from the railroad tracks that fell off the passing steam trains, used to heat their cold wooden house through the long Minnesota winters. If no coal was found, there was no heat for her home that day. Wood was rationed to heat the cooking oven. Her older brother's responsibility was to hunt and fish for food. An unsuccessful fishing trip through the ice of a lake, or no deer or birds to be found, would mean there would be no food to eat. It was very much a binary way of life.

By funny coincidence, stories such as these would surface shortly after I would request a new toy, a pair of shoes, or clothes that weren't always hand-me-downs. As my mother reminded me more times than I could count, "I cried because I had no shoes, until I saw a man with no feet." So, how did I become the first in my family to enter the storied gates of higher learning and succeed in my scholarly pursuits? I snuck in the back way.

When I was a youth, the educational chant for success was reading, writing, and arithmetic (the three Rs). Now of course it's science, technology, engineering, and math (STEM), STEAM (A for arts), or STEM + H (H for health), ad nauseam. In my public schools, I did well on the reading and writing part—math, not so much. However, during my middle and high school math-class experiences, I did notice an interesting pattern. Year after year, attending five different schools over six years (two junior high schools and three high schools), every one of my math teachers seemed particularly challenged when it came to exhibiting passion and excitement about the subject, any real interest in answering my questions, or in providing alternative pedagogical approaches or methods to solving a problem if the first approach wasn't successful. Extreme indifference seemed to describe the pattern.

None of my other teachers of other subjects exhibited these traits. I'm sure there are passionate math teachers out there, but in my experience, it was always just my math teachers who exhibited indifference. My last math course I took as a junior in high school was Algebra I, part 1, and I was pleased to finish my math career in this course by earning a D, an acceptable grade to me, and happy to never enter another classroom filled with such apathy for life.

However, along with my other secondary academic studies, I did discover I had an unusual talent for music. In addition to playing first chair in all the school marching and concert bands, I played lead trumpet for the Washington Redskins Marching Band in Washington, D.C., at the old R.F.K. Stadium. We were not paid but received two free tickets to sell or give to whomever we wished. In high school in Littleton, Colorado, I was chosen to study French horn privately at the University of Denver, and I performed as principal horn in the Denver Chamber Orchestra. I also learned to play flugelhorn, baritone, Renaissance recorder, Revolutionary War fife, a bit of cello, and of course the piano. However, my real love was composing music. Probably when I should have been doing homework, I wrote trumpet sonatas, orchestral suites, chamber music, symphonies, and string quartets, all before graduating high school. A conservatory would be my higher educational pathway, and music composition would be the key that unlocked the elusive gate.

Coming from limited means, I piled on loans and scholarships and off I went. The immense cultural change—for example, one of my peers was a noble from Scotland—took a tad bit of personae modification and study habit adjustments, but I eventually settled into the routine of successful undergraduate studies. One day, during my work-study hours at the recording studio editing audiotape, my supervisor told me about a new joint Johns Hopkins University and Peabody Conservatory audio engineering degree program beginning the following year. He also mentioned he thought I would be an ideal candidate. This new program would allow me to maintain my undergraduate composition major and double major in this new domain of recording arts and sciences, *and* the inaugural class would have access to immense scholarship support! As we were concluding our exciting conversation, and he was walking away, my supervisor also said, "and by the way, since it requires electrical engineering, you'll need to take several years of calculus; it'll be easy."

In the summer before I began this new additional academic journey, with the help of my fiancée, I began to teach myself algebra all over again. Between composing music and my work schedule, I cracked open books on algebra and then geometry. By late July, I began my personal study of trigonometry, and then precalculus, alone surrounded by multiple books and my notes.

For those of you reading this who are a tad under forty years of age, in the mid-1980s, there was no web browsers, YouTube videos, Kahn Academy, free massive open online courses (MOOCs), or math tutorials. There were just dusty books, which you had to get up and go to the library to check out or buy at a bookstore.

The fall began, and after I became accustomed to the pace of Hopkins-style math courses, I didn't just excel in the discipline; I routinely achieved higher scores on exams than engineering majors! Math was fun, and my now wife became quite bored listening to me discussing how to potentially solve various differential equations with Laplace or Fourier transforms. And yes, I did also discover the parallels between the logical patterns in both math and music—the discipline I mastered so much earlier in my life.

In retrospect, this is when I considered the teaching profession as a professional option. If I could teach myself to love a subject I so deeply despised, perhaps I could do the same for others.

Thirty years later, as a somewhat excessively involved father raising three boys, I also noticed how they all struggled with, and in turn hated, math. Year after year, I attended most of their junior high and high school back-to-school nights to meet their teachers. I also attended the occasional meetings with math teachers, program chairs, and principals over this and that math performance issue. But I also provided academic help—the tutoring and educational guidance they needed—so I could become the academic role model for them I never had. As my older two sons are now succeeding in their higher education chosen majors, both successfully taken calculus, and my youngest son is now eyeing several different college majors as an upperclassman in high school, I reflected and noted an eerily similar pattern.

Every math teacher I met or emailed as now a father, and whom my sons seemed to experience in their classrooms as apathetic, exhibited no passion and excitement about the subject, any real interest in answering my sons' questions, or in providing alternative pedagogical approaches or methods to solving a problem if the first approach wasn't working. I even discovered a history of multiple mistakes on math-preparation materials given to my sons to help them study for math tests, and consistent errors in exam answers and scoring calculations.

Again, I know there are many excellent and passionate math teachers out there in the world, but my sons and I missed out on ever connecting with one unfortunately. In our experience, despite the different time, different public schools, and different generation, surprisingly nothing seemed to change.

Although most of this book focuses on new learning approaches and technologies, teaching comes first, as this book presents new innovations from the perspective of a teacher. Without the successful practice of teaching, very little learning will take place. Although I've received immense satisfaction as an administrator founding multiple degree programs, departments, schools, institutes, and research centers over the past thirty years, my greatest joy is derived from the classroom. Imparting knowledge and knowledgeable experiences upon each new class of distinct and diverse learners is the greatest challenge, but also the greatest reward, and what keeps the teaching profession exciting and motivating year after year.

Regardless of subject matter, nothing is as professionally and personally elevating as being able to adjust and successfully mix and match your teaching style and pedagogical methods year after year to a whole new class of students with different learning styles, levels of motivation, knowledge foundations, and even personality traits that hopefully allow everyone a personal pathway to succeed. Although it is not always possible, when it does happen, it's most gratifying.

To me, the greatest reward a teacher can ever receive may come years and years later after engaging with a learner. Perhaps one student sends you an unsolicited note out of the blue that simply says, "thank you." What you did in the classroom changed their life for the better, and you as their teacher and mentor made a positive impact that stayed with them over time.

This book opens with a foundational chapter that includes a brief review of the origins of teaching and learning models molded from early Christian seminary university paradigms founded in early Europe and later in the Americas. The first chapter includes insights demonstrating how we learn, why we learn, and when we learn and includes the economics of learning, or how the business of education has always occupied a central role in education through time.

The next chapter, written by Chris Jennings at Google Analytics, provides an overview of the history of technology within the practice of teaching and learning, and affords an astute overview of the ubiquitous learning management system (LMS) and online learning in general. The chapter closes with a summary examination of games in learning and the gamification of education.

In chapter 3, I offer a synopsis of the importance of data as a critical resource required for a deeper exploration of the practice of teaching and learning, the issues of ensuring data equity, and I discuss several new fields of study that use educational-related, and not-related, data sets to peek inside the lives of the learner.

The next chapter offers a laymen's explanation of artificial intelligence, or more applicable today, machine learning, and its current applications to online learning. The chapter concludes with an overview of my artificial cognitive memory map invention, which is admittedly a few years off from being realized but is none the less an exciting proposition. This chapter is probably the most complex to digest, but I strived to make it accessible as possible to the reader without losing my obvious enthusiasm about the potential within.

Chapter 5 taps upon the prospective impact virtual reality and augmented reality may have on teaching and learning in the near future but also outlines the challenges facing its successful integration to activate the learning process. In this chapter, I also discuss the effects blockchain technologies may soon have on institutions of education, specifically to protect a learner's data from all the data-intrusive innovations I excitedly drew out in previous chapters. This last chapter concludes the book with a new cognitive model I've designed that proposes one architectural pathway to potentially achieve artificial general intelligence (AGI), human intelligence parity of sort, but specifically conceived as a model for an archetype artificial intelligence (AI) teacher. Yes, we cross over a bit into science fiction, but with conversational AI bots we interface with on websites and in our homes becoming more accurate by the day, is it such a stretch to envision a domain-expert AI teacher with the same attributes I outline within this chapter right around the corner?

It is my hope that this book doesn't just inform, educate, and entertain the educator, student, administrator, and college board member but also helps facilitate discussion and action. It is my hope that educators who read this book are inspired to take incremental risks to help change the outdated, century-old teaching and learning models still in use today. Retail business models have transformed from a department store front to a web store front. Finance and banking have changed from a scaling branch model to cloud-based online banking model, as well as allowing consumers to pay their charges at a retail checkout register with their mobile phone. The consumer transportation and the hotel industries will never return to their sedentary business models after the creation of the ride-sharing and short-term home-sharing mobile apps. The higher educational business model, sans a few experimental college examples and a handful of private, online-only colleges, has stoically remained resolute to any large-scale change.

In chapter 4 of this book, I pose the following question: With their tradition for risk-taking, philosophy of innovation, and financial heft, what would happen to higher education if, for example, Apple, Google, Facebook, or Amazon decided to build a series of universities across the United States? If any one of these tech leviathans seriously entered the higher education market, would that entry finally become the impetus for transformation, or would it then be too late?

These market-sector global leaders would not enter the education market because it's so potentially lucrative, as say, the mobile phone or entertainment-streaming submarket. In 2017, Harvard and Oxford combined generated $8 billion in revenue, a number that includes their endowment investments returns.[1] Apple generated $52.9 billion of gross revenue in just three months in 2017.[2]

No, the only reason they would enter education is that community colleges and universities are not producing the graduates with the skill sets, knowledge, and talent these goliaths require from new hires. Moreover, not only is higher education not transforming their teaching and learning models to meet the changing academic—or dare I say it, "training"—requirements of the new economy, but also they are not transforming fast enough to meet the prerequirements of the new demographics that define their student body.

As I touch on later in this book, the traditional university resident population will decline in the next five years, as first-time learners, historically underserved populations, and foreign-born learner demographics rise. Each of these demographic segments will require a specialized learning plan and academic and counseling support structures that most colleges and universities are ill prepared to offer or provide.

This book does not presume to contain all the new promising higher education teaching and learning innovations on the horizon. Nor does this book promise to offer all the passageways to apply and integrate the new innovations it does reveal. This text hopefully offers an inspirational framework of what exists now and what will exist soon: new tools, techniques, technologies, and pedagogical models that could potentially improve the educational experiences for our future learners. And it aspires to inspire the professor, chair, dean, and college board member to hopefully say, "Let's give it a try—our students deserve it." Perhaps after we see transformation in higher education, these new tools, techniques, and learning models will slowly become available to the secondary school teachers of the future, and someday somewhere a grumpy math teacher may echo, "I'll give it a try—my students deserve it."

> What we need to do is always lean into the future; when the world changes around you and when it changes against you—what used to be a tail wind is

now a head wind—you have to lean into that and figure what to do because complaining isn't a strategy.

—Jeff Bezos[3]

NOTES

1. University of Oxford, "Financial Statements 2016/17," https://www.ox.ac.uk; Harvard University, "Harvard University's Financial Results for Fiscal 2018," https://finance.harvard.edu.

2. Apple, "Apple Reports Second Quarter Result," May 2, 2017, https://www.apple.com.

3. As quoted in interview with Joanna Stern from *ABC News*. Joanna Stern, "Jeff Bezos: A Down-to-Earth CEO Reaching for the Stars," *ABC News*, September 25, 2013, https://abcnews.go.com.

Chapter One

Education

Education is a subject which has been exhausted by the ablest writers, both among the ancients and moderns.

—Noah Webster, "On the Education of Youth in America" (1788)[1]

Before we are able to understand and prognosticate where the future of teaching and learning is headed, it is important to first look back and understand the roots and foundation of how we arrived where we are today. Rather than add to the already extensive list of original research, publications, and documentation about the history of education, this chapter takes a different approach. It explores how teaching and learning evolved to become a formalized institution in its own right in our society. Furthermore, this chapter summarizes the historical role of the teacher and briefly outlines the evolution of teaching over time.

Next, we shift our focus to the learner and explore basic biological theories of how learning may occur from simple external stimuli to larger metacognitive capacitance, and then examine the critical importance of environmental influence on the learning process. Finally, we peel back the layers to unveil how technology has led to disruptive innovations across education and explore design concepts that can improve learning technologies to better match human cognitive processing. This chapter delves into the ways in which instructional and learning technologies may be better designed and implemented to not just scale domain knowledge but also improve academic performance and outcomes for a greater number of learners.

HISTORY: ORIGINS, SOCIAL STRUCTURES, AND MASS EDUCATION

Historically, the opportunity to be mentored, taught, or educated depended on social differentiation. As some social groups expanded and gained power through conflict or sublimation, they developed structured institutions to support their own purposes. Dominant societies created self-serving political, legal, economic, and divine institutions, and used another institution—education—to perpetuate and improve upon the others.[2] The origins and purpose of education within the Western Hemisphere may be examined from several perspectives. For example, varying viewpoints suggest that education served to strengthen connections between religious and political universalisms; it groomed better workers, soldiers, and citizens; it shaped learners to comprehend formal values and rituals of society; and it taught learners about their relationship to authority, be it divine, political, law, or economic.[3]

As economically successful societies grew, their social complexity became compounded by war, famine, and disease. Dishevel threatened to fragment the institutions and social cohesion, requiring the expansion of the institution of education to serve more individuals to develop the cognitive skills and knowledge to repair and preserve the nation-state. As sociologists have explained, "The imputed functional requirement of a differentiated society for cognitive or moral competence creates a need for mass schooling to provide knowledge of the structure and adherence to the norms that support the structure."[4] In short, this argument suggests that mass education acts as glue to maintain order in society.

In the early American colonies, with newfound independence and associated isolation from Western European trade, mass education became imperative to survival. The founders recognized and articulated this urgency. However, the expectation to serve the nation-state was still couched in education's purpose. As Noah Webster wrote in "On the Education of Youth in America" in 1788, "It is an object of vast magnitude that systems of education should be adopted and pursued which may not only diffuse a knowledge of the sciences but may implant in the minds of the American youth the principles of virtue and of liberty and inspire them with just and liberal ideas of government and with an inviolable attachment to their own country."[5]

In "A Bill for the More General Diffusion of Knowledge" in *Notes on the State of Virginia*, Thomas Jefferson called for the expansion of primary to secondary education for the lower-class masses within the new republic. He envisioned school districts across the nation that focused on reading, writing, and arithmetic and that would be free to attend for three years. He then envisioned the best students at those schools being able to attend further schooling in other subjects (such as Greek, Latin, geography, and advanced mathematics) all at the public expense.[6]

Thomas Jefferson was mostly a singular voice in the new republic for support of nation-state-funded institutes of public education, not just as a mechanism of social differentiation from the European elites, but also as an imperative vehicle within the republic's social structure to equalize economic opportunities and to assert social cohesion. With Jefferson's persuasive arguments in letters and speeches to his colleagues, his plan of free public education was only made possible with a slowly growing and aligned treasury, expanded across the colonies.

For some sociologists and economists, however, the expansion of institutions of "free" education was nothing more than an expansion of social welfare. From their viewpoint, expanded educational opportunities to the masses did nothing more that sustain the social structure of authority and formalize inequality. Mass education would never reach all the masses, and the appearance of equality was an illusion in an unequal society.[7]

Fast-forward to the industrialization era of the mid-nineteenth century. In the United States and in Europe, especially in the United Kingdom, mass immigration, migration, and urbanization strained the institutes of social structure. With this social transformation, outdated laws, ill-suited regulations, and limited state and religious public charities were overwhelmed by abject poverty, crime, disease, and haphazard and corruptible labor laws.[8] Industrial capitalism disrupted the means of mercantile production on a scale and at a tempo that left the nation-state ill prepared to integrate its functions into its standing social structure. Cities that contained new social subgroups required additional housing, food, health care, and an educational framework. Industrialism sometimes provided imperfect housing and sustenance for their laborers but little more.

The nation-state did not accept the role of public welfare provider easily, as the limited coffers of the institutions would require the titled and political class to devise a new tax structure aimed directly at their industrialist's benefactors. A truce of sorts would occur, and the welfare state would be funded between the public and private spheres of power, spanning the institutions of government, economics (industrialists), and the divine.[9]

Speaking of the influence of the divine, the first universities established in the colonies were Harvard (in 1636) and William & Mary (in 1693). Harvard was chartered by its royally governed state legislature, and William & Mary was chartered by royal decree.[10] In both cases, they were primarily established to provide a school of divinity to educate a new class of clergy that would be needed in the new world.

Secondarily, they also offered schools of philosophy, languages, arts, and sciences. With one foot firmly planted in the divine and secular, on balance, this educational experience may or may not support the existing institutional power of the privileged, be it divine or political. Yale's origins (founded in 1701) are no different. Founded by a group of Puritans that fled Anglican

England, Yale's early mission was to instruct youth in the arts and sciences and fit them "for Publick employment both in Church & Civil State."[11] The founders of Princeton (in 1746) were Presbyterian pastors who wrote to each other as they struggled to establish a university mission: "Though our great intention was to erect a seminary for educating Ministers of the Gospel . . . we hope it will be useful in other learned professions—Ornaments of the State as Well as the Church."[12]

By the late nineteenth century, the institutes of politics, divinity, and economics struggled to manage the influx of nondifferentially migrating and immigrating populations into cities. Societal institutions were challenged to maintain any resemblance of social structure.[13] Although industrial capitalism did provide a steady stream of taxes to the institutions of the nation-state, and provided employment opportunities for the educated and established differentiated, and the nondifferentiated, student/migrant alike, it also demanded a rational, disciplined, and mobile workforce.

Individuals and their families left their homelands and communities for work, but in doing so, increasingly found themselves detached from their previous social structure, including their own differentiated social groups and subgroups that shared familiar rituals and history. Institutions had to develop public and private systems of support to accommodate those who were displaced and distressed.[14] Existing private hospitals, schools, and universities, previously established to serve the offspring of the leaders of the institutions, could not accommodate the growing numbers of people immigrating into new societies. Central and state-level bureaucracies were invented to broaden the collection of taxes, regulate behavior, provide basic health care, and determine punishments for social disruption.[15] By the early twentieth century, publicly funded reformatories, penitentiaries, hospitals, mass public schools, and colleges had been established across most cities and states in the United States and in Europe.[16]

As sociologists have explained, if one dominant group is confronted with social problems exhibited by a neighboring subdominant social group, new powers must be created by the dominant group's institutions to erect social controls and block the spread of unrest. In some cases, this may include expanded education with mandatory attendance.[17] Institutions of law, religion, economics, and politics believed that mass public education could solve many social ills found within the nondifferentiated social groups. Mass education could offer pathways to assimilation for immigrant adults and lead to future success for their children. An educational structure may even help reduce crime and poverty.[18] So, in addition to augmenting the differentiated role of a learner, and helping establish dominance of one group over another, education could help repair and maintain social cohesions *and* legitimize the overall structure of society to serve authority.[19]

This historical overview comes down to this main point: in the modern nation-state, mass education, or equality of opportunity, has become the mechanism that has defined the differentiated. Next to inherited wealth or nationality, for individuals in highly structured social systems, education may be the most important signifier of their social group status.[20]

Public higher education, and specifically the role and purpose of community colleges, share many similar discontinuities outlined above and suffer unique challenges as well. Public community colleges near large market economies compete for resources against their well-funded neighbors: the public university and local public secondary schools. While the primary and secondary school is tasked today with curbing unsocial behavior, and asserting social cohesion, it is the community college's charge to truly differentiate the individual by providing the skills and knowledge for professional success in a competitive market economy, thereby legitimizing economic and political institutions. This is no small assignment, given that public community colleges in the United States and trades schools in Europe are the initial destination of most adult immigrants seeking to differentiate themselves upon relocation.[21] These are individuals who seek out opportunity and mobility and take the risk of entering a new social structure, in many cases conducted in a different language, and with different institutes of authority, for the sake of greater economic opportunities.

As economic opportunities for immigrants and a new demographic segment of learners have evolved to meet an ever-changing market economy, so too must the academic offerings of the community college. In 2017, for example, immigrants that earned some college credits or completed an associate's degree in a technical field held only a 10 percent employment advantage over immigrants without a high school diploma but earned more than double the median income.[22] Indeed, community colleges help open the door to membership into a new social order through teaching new knowledge and skills, and providing the licit framework for full civic participation in a new nation-state.

LEARNERS

As I outlined in the introduction to this book, the practice of learning is highly personal, and in many cases intimate. It's intimate in that to acquire knowledge (from reading, hearing, smelling, or touching) one must overcome a form of cognitive resistance. I don't mean the apprehension or insecurity of physically sitting in a classroom with peers, with the associated angst from societal, cultural, or tribal critique of dress, odor, or physical traits. And I don't mean the logging into an online class, negating these in-person social group gauntlets, but now concerned if our technology will work, when and if we should contribute to an online forum discussion, and if and when we may be interrupted by family or work colleagues.

I'm referring to the indiscernible shield that stands between aspiration and the actualized self—an unwillingness to test the convoluted intertanglement of our emotions, ego, and perceived weaknesses that may classify for us our limited aptitude. I'm also referring to the subconscious and sometimes conscious cognitive resistance that limits new neural pathways from forging in our prefrontal cortex or hippocampus and that may represent new knowledge. Learning is an intimate experience and, therefore, like all intimate experiences, may take time to build to overcome cognitive resistance.

To learn requires the suspension of cognitive resistance, and the keys to achieve this differ greatly for every learner. As psychologist Peter Michaelson has described, for some people the difficulty of learning may be due to (1) inner conflict that produces anxiety, procrastination, and indecision; (2) psychological defenses such as cynicism and passive-aggressive reactions; (3) an unwillingness to consider new ideas; (4) a passive tendency to allow good intention and willpower to collapse; (5) a narrow focus on minor details or secondary issues that obscures the larger learning goals; (6) a strong identification and comfortability with our old, limited self; (7) a stubborn unwillingness to do what's in our best interests; or (8) an unconscious determination, even compulsion, to produce self-defeat and self-sabotage.[23] One underlying constant in almost all of the above keys may be the overarching limiter: fear.

Most individual learning theorists and cognitive scientists will have a different explanation of how humans learn, because each theory relies on a varied schema that attempt to define either the functions of the brain or the functions of the mind. Distilled to its most basic biological description, learning could be outlined as any process that occurs in living organisms that leads to permanent capacity change.[24] Generally, capacity change must occur from an internal source—maturation, disease, or aging of cell structures, or external sources, such as stimulation of the biological senses that signifies awareness/dissociated learning, or context/content learning.[25] Figure 1.1 outlines the two types of biological capacity changes that signify basic learning.

Memory systems, or memory maps, as described in greater detail in chapters 4 and 5, are also critical to learning. Two distinct systems of external cognitive learning that map to internal cognitive memory functions have been defined as declarative and procedural learning (declarative, nondeclarative). Declarative learning refers to knowledge acquisition of facts and content; procedural learning refers to knowledge acquisition of skills and experiences.[26]

In most cases these systems are distinct in psychological definitions but indistinct as capacity changes, and are coupled during a learning event. Taking a seat at a desk in a lecture hall can be considered procedural (habit).

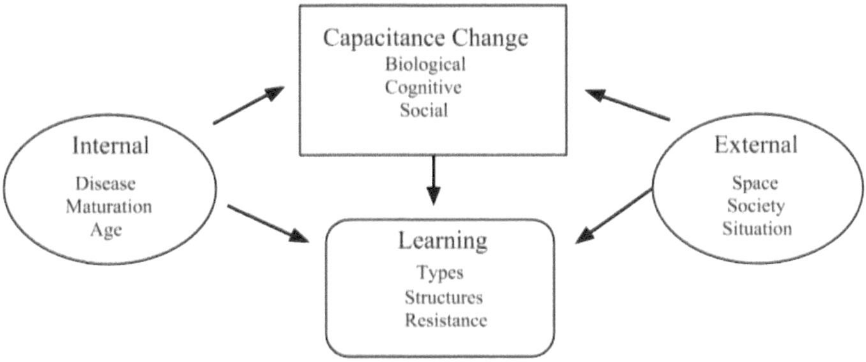

Figure 1.1. Basic biological learning schematic

Taking notes of a lecture is a form of semantic memory acquisition. Subconscious acquisition of the light in the lecture room, hum of an air conditioner, smells from a seatmate eating lunch while note-taking are an example of episodic memory procurement (subliminal stimuli), but episodic memory occurs simultaneously with semantic experiences, both being encoded in our memory map together.

Our learning style, interests, and motivation evolve and change, affected by age and maturity, and prejudiced by both internal and external stimuli, but it is the environments in which this learning takes place that has the greatest overwhelming influence.[27] Externally structured learning spaces, such as physical classrooms or occasionally online learning platforms, are designed to meet both instructional requirements and organizational limitations. But all environments also induce psychosocial responses from learners that affect cognitive learning behaviors.[28]

Good instructors arrange chairs and tables or assign learners to different seat locations in a classroom to place learners in an arrangement they believe best engages them to complete a particular task. Lecture rooms are designed so every learner can see and hear a lecturer, but not necessarily to optimize content engagement. As discussed later in chapter 4, mass lecture halls were designed from an economic standpoint—to allow universities to scale their curricula to a greater number of learners, but not necessarily to foster a better learning space pedagogically. In contrast, many biology classrooms arrange a small number of learners around lab tables that facilitate teamwork, engagement, and safety.

Although there are any number of variables involved in facilitating learning engagement that may lead to greater academic outcomes, three primary factors tend to be constant: subject-matter interest, academic challenge, and perceived control of the learning process.[29] To inspire and further motivate a learner, a teacher may have his or her class engage in tasks or assignments that may be intellectually interesting and challenging.

Obviously, an instructor can't always assign academic material that is of interest to all, but they can manipulate the task design as a challenge, and parcel components of the task so they can be accomplished in short periods of time. When such a designed task is accomplished, metacognitive self-appraisal improves, the perception of control of the learning process increases, and the triumph may result in new subject-matter appeal. Successful task and assignment design and administration can lead to improved learner engagement, demonstration of confidence, and overall self-satisfaction with the learning process.[30]

Culture and the community within the structured learning environment are factors in learner engagement as well. Placement of chairs and tables, objects in the room, and images on the walls of classrooms and lecture halls reveal the cultural context and social structure in which the learning will takes place. Posters and images representing one political party in lecture hall walls can invigorate some learners but intimidate others and undermine active subject-matter engagement for both.[31] Depending on the course context, posters and images of scholars presenting one ethnic culture or race may also elicit the same results from learners with different cultural or tribal heritage.

Instructors' subconscious cultural, economic, ethnic, sexual, or racial bias may also enter the structured learning space and alter learner outcomes. While bias may be subtle or unintentional, examples of teachers calling on mostly males or females to answer questions, not asking English-as-a-second-language (ESL) learners to read their history essay in class, or mostly assigning math-intensive projects to Asian students may have a negative impact on overall learner engagement. Even though subconscious bias exists and may put certain learners at a disadvantage, across-the-board performance expectations from every learner in the same structured learning environment is, however, not uncommon.

Adhering to the responsibilities assigned to education within the nation-state, a teacher must also convey the rules and responsibilities, explicit and implicit, expected in a classroom and that mirror those expected from the learner's role as citizen and contributing member of their social group. Rules guide learners about what physical actions they can take, when they may speak, and what is appropriate for them to say.[32] Learners and teachers also carry their own cultural and social practices into a structured learning environment. If the classroom structure does not resemble learners' social group norms, authority structure, or external cultural environment, and it may be in fact the opposite, they may be more deprived and disadvantaged compared to the more assimilated learner.[33]

Adult and adolescence learning is also affected by their childhood learning experiences, whether culturally intentional or the result of a disadvantaged environment. Young learners that didn't experience a parent or guardian that engaged them via verbal communication that builds vocabulary, and that mostly learned from creative play and then observing and interacting with social groups, may be less inclined to volunteer to speak up in class, even though an answer is known. In addition, childhood biophysical influences also affect later adult learning. Negative impact to early cognitive neurodevelopment that may also affect later neuropsychological performance can occur from poor nutrition, extended sleep loss, and exposure to environmental toxins, common in impoverished communities in both Western and in third-world countries.[34]

Lastly, cognitive social emotional states of a learner also greatly affect early childhood and young adult declarative memory neural pathway expansion, critical to hippocampus and prefrontal cortex development. Learner emotions and learning success have proven to be coupled during the knowledge-acquisition process and to sway confidence and motivation.[35] Emotions may also define aspects of learner engagement, as they may be more interested in subject-matter content they feel "good" about because they completed a related task or surpassed a self-controlled academic challenge. Likewise, a learner may feel emotionally and socially deflated if fear and nervousness become a barrier to successful academic engagement.[36]

An ideal structured learning environment is one where instructors provide an equitable space for learners to share ideas and offer comments, where answers may not be correct or always relevant but where each contribution is valued and publicly recognized as such.[37] In an equitable structured learning space, a teacher not only helps and guides struggling learners to reach the median goals of the collective but also opens pathways for them to comprehend the realistic efforts required to reach the upper tiers of achievement within their socially structured learning environment.

Finally, a model learning space is one where learners freely help, influence, and adopt and help shape social group norms. It's where an instructor offers an informed critique of contributions made and where evaluations are presented as evidence of accomplished learning steps, functioning both as an assessment tool and as an instrument to foster subject-matter interest, to challenge to reach higher goals, and to enforce self-satisfaction.

TECHNOLOGY

> Books will soon be obsolete in the schools. . . . It is possible to teach every branch of human knowledge through the motion picture. Our school system will be completely changed in the next 10 years.
>
> —Thomas Edison, 1913[38]

Technology adapted to support and augment teaching in formal learning environments may be traced to the early twentieth century, when audiovisual films and projectors were first adopted in the classroom. Although eventually, film content was created specifically for educational intentions, the technology of the camera and projector was not intended to be used in the classroom and were developed primarily for entertainment, military, and other commercial purposes.

As is the case until very recently, technology used to assist with classroom instruction, for various economic and financial reasons, was originally developed first for other more lucrative markets, and adopted and adapted for teaching and learning later. With the passage of the National Defense Education Act in 1958, a U.S. response to catch up to the Soviets after the Sputnik launch, technology vendors could target the better-funded public school and higher education markets with specific instructional technology.[39] These two approaches of technology use in education, one adapted for use and one specifically designed for education, can be summed up in two definitions of instructional technology: multimedia, such as televisions and projectors that originated from the communications revolution, and hardware and software that originated from the silicon chip revolution that is used in conjunction with traditional classroom teaching and learning tools such as textbooks, paper handouts, and chalk and blackboards. Moreover, instructional technology can be defined as designing a learning experience using both human and nonhuman technological resources that includes objectives, learning goals, assessments, and evaluation techniques, based on learning (science) research results for more effective instruction.[40]

Early examples in the United States of instructional technologies designed and developed in concert with teaching and learning goals and objectives in mind occurred in the late 1960s, funded by the passage of the Elementary and Secondary Education Act (1965, ESEA), again spurred on by the success of Sputnik. In addition to funding the development of assessment and evaluation tools to measure the performance of schools, ESEA eventually provided grants to establish a series of twenty research and development laboratories, placed strategically across the country, many near standing universities.

These new educational-focused research and development (R&D) labs were charged with developing not only new educational products but also new tools that could measure academic performance from primary and secondary learners in their districts.[41] Although only a few of the original R&D labs still exist, their founding led to both specialized education-focused graduate schools and programs, and new formative and summative methodologies for assessing and evaluating the impact of educational technologies and instruments on the learning process.[42]

Education technologies may augment and facilitate many modes of learning: active, repetitive, self-regulated, group, peer-to-peer, social emotional, and personalized learning. Research has demonstrated that learners may better comprehend and remember an explanation when it is presented in words and images than when presented in only words.[43] However, learning technologies that include words and images that are designed to match our metacognitive processing and memory acquisitions functions tend to be more successful than those that don't.[44]

Poorly designed images, combined with text, and video clips on a computer screen may produce cognitive overload: when a learner's cognitive processing ability exceeds a learner's cognitive capacity.[45] One cognitive theory of multimedia, or multisensory channel learning, has been defined by Allan Paivio in 1986 as a dual coding system that defines human cognition as specialized for dealing with both nonverbal objects (symbolic) and language (verbal). And each coding channel has finite processing ability and is subject to cognitive overload.

Richard Mayer and Roxana Moreno have expanded this coding theory to include Alan Baddeley and Graham Hitch's working-memory and long-term memory theories to describe not only how learners process and classify media, words, and language but also how we may store this information in our long-term memory. In chapter 4 we reference the Baddeley and Hitch and Mayer and Moreno multisensory channel learning theories again, and cite these influences in designing my own Knowledge Acquisition System (KAS) employed to create a new artificial-intelligence memory map structure. Furthermore, I also allude to Paivio's theories of cognitive dual-channel processing of information and memory storage when identifying essential functions and nonessential functions when designing an AI instructor in chapter 5. Figure 1.2 provides a block diagram outlining a revised version of the Mayer and Moreno Cognitive Theory Model of Learning with Media, including potential future olfactory and gustatory sensory inputs.

When using and designing learning technologies, individual learner capacity and cognitive overload should be of critical concern to an instructor. It is quite common for poorly designed user interfaces (UIs) of software applications, education-related websites, and learning management systems to offer an overload of images, text, and video that can easily cause learner cognitive overload. Even e-books now offer numerous drop-down menus, search boxes, and right or left side panels filled with images and word definitions distracting the reader from the literary content.

One solution is for an instructor to balance or "offload" demand from one channel to the other during learning. A notorious example would be of a screen imbedded with a video alongside descriptive text, whereby both information sources require processing from the visual channel, potentially causing visual channel cognitive overload. One simple remedy of this potential

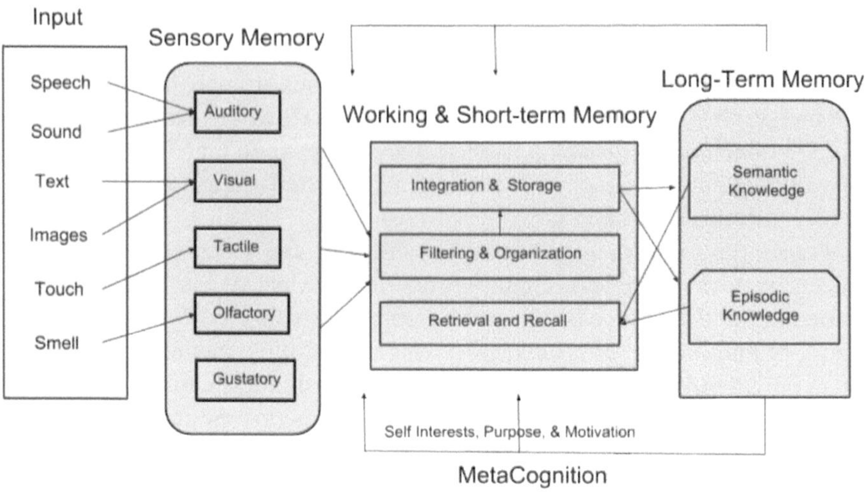

Figure 1.2. Cognitive theory of multisensory semantic and episodic learning

visual channel cognitive overload is to present the words as audio narration, sending this information to the ears for audio processing, so the eyes can process only the video information, thereby off-loading some of the visual cognitive processing.[46]

Lastly, as can be seen below, Mayer, in "Multimedia Learning" (2002), offers some design principles to adhere to, based on his research, for successful presentation of multimedia-multisensory demanding content that conform to metacognitive processing and knowledge-acquisition processing:

- Multimedia Principle: Students learn better from words and pictures than from words alone.
- Spatial Contiguity Principle: Students learn better when corresponding words and pictures are presented near rather than far from each other on a screen or page.
- Temporal Contiguity Principle: Students learn better when corresponding words and pictures are presented simultaneously rather than successively.
- Coherence Principle: Students learn better when extraneous material is excluded rather than included.
- Modality Principle: Students learn better from animation and recorded narration than from animation and on-screen text.
- Redundancy Principle: Students learn better from animation and narration than from animation, narration, and on-screen text.
- Pretraining Principle: Students learn better when training precedes rather than follows a message, meaning that when students receive pretraining or

advance information about a subject, they are able to build mental models of expectations, thereby filtering the cognitive load when postulating a potential solution.
- Signaling Principle: Students learn better when training is singled rather than nonsingled, meaning that when learners are aware of what expectations are desired within a learning experience, they are better able to allocate cognitive resources appropriately and reduce cognitive load.
- Personalization Principle: Students learn better when words are presented in conversational style rather than formal style, meaning that when words are presented from a computer in a conversational manner, students are more likely to accept the computer as a social partner, and therefore try harder to comprehend the given messages.

These principles are critically important to consider when designing new learning content for 3-D immersive virtual learning spaces, such as virtual-reality (VR) and mixed-reality (MR) environments, as cognitive and sensory overload could easily be reached because visual and audio channels of information are not generally self-controlled or regulated. In addition, the density and speed of information transfer offers limited off-load options and could impede learning and undermine intended usefulness of the learning environment.

Finally, and more complex for a successful instructor, a learner's cognitive capacity may be fluid and influenced by fluctuating levels of motivation, aptitude, emotional state, artificial stimulants, disease, diet, or lack of sleep. These cognitive capacity oscillations may require an instructor to occasionally adjust knowledge transfer rates and make greater periodic personalization modifications to match a learner's metacognitive state on any given day.

When designed to match human metacognitive processing and knowledge-acquisition models, instructional or learning technologies may allow greater subject-matter comprehension and improved long-term memory storage for a larger number of learners. Many well-designed learning technologies also stimulate active learning, that is, they stimulate visual, aural, and kinetic channels (procedural) of cognitive processing and memory allocation to better engage a learner, rather than simply functioning as semistatic content-delivery platforms. Examples can take the form of collaborative learning (on-site tools and online platforms), experiential learning, or self-regulated or multiplayer serious game play (tabletop or digital). Immersive technologies, such as VR, can also offer environments to help facilitate all three.

Adapted from Mayer and Moreno's (2003) research, and from the National Academy of Sciences Engineering, and Medicine's *How People Learn II: Learners, Contexts, and Cultures* (2018),[47] the list below outlines common traits discovered within successful learning technologies environments that facilitate active learning experiences, and may be considered a framework for future design considerations:

- Design Interactivity: Action and response design; that is, for every action from a learner in an active learning technological environment, there must be a response, indicated visually or aurally or both.
- Domain Feedback: A successful technological active learning environment provides performance states, cues, and status.
- Content Choice: Choice of content paths and temporal benchmarks motivates and engages a learner.
- Alternative Representations: Active learning technologies should present access to different perspectives, approaches, and method for solutions. This design trait allows for a learner's fluctuating cognitive capacity.
- Peer and Instructor Interactivity: All successful active learning technologies require communications channels for real-time learner-to-learner and learner-to-teacher interactivity.
- Adaptability: Active learning technology environments should be able to customize and personalize domain content to match a learner's cognitive capacity, performance and motivation levels, and interests.
- Nonlinear Content Access: Active learning technologies should allow learners to access and engage nonsequential domain content. This option offers learners control of their learning environment and facilitates learning self-regulation and intelligent adaptivity.

We explore these learning concepts more in chapters 4 and 5 with the call for greater learner interactivity within current and future online learning platforms. Learners that can interact within their virtual learning environments, whether with objects, peers, or teachers, are better engaged in the learning process, as we read here, because they match and stimulate multiple channels of our metacognitive processing functions that improve overall knowledge acquisition.

Lastly, active learning technologies also reinforce the psychological concepts of embodied and situational cognition. Bodies move around and interact with their environment, and therefore, the brain as the controlling instrument of the body must be influenced by the body's movements and interactivity with its environment. Phrased another way, a learner's metacognitive activity does not singularly occur in the mind but is shaped by its body's relationship to the environment around it; cognitive activity, and therefore cognitive capacity, is formed from both the mind and the body's situated environment.[48]

Until James J. Gibson's article on cognitive perception of motion and movement in 1954, the cognitive sciences examined sensorimotor and central cognitive processes as two distinct fields. Gibson proposed environments that supported cognitive perceptual learning and suggested that any interactivity from one system with another requires conditions that enable that interaction from both, a new subfield he later defined as ecological psychology.[49] While there are multiple movements of thought that have spun from Gibson's theories over the years, Margaret Wilson summarizes many of the common elements found in most definitions of embodied cognition below:

- Cognition is situated. Cognitive activity occurs in the context of a physical environment, and it fundamentally involves perception and interactivity.
- Cognition is time sensitive. Cognition must be viewed in a temporal framework—the time duration of the interactivity with the environment affects function impact.
- We off-load cognitive work onto the environment. Because of cognitive capacity limits, we exploit the environment to reduce the cognitive overload.
- The environment is part of the cognitive system. The information flow between mind and world though body is so complex that it is not sufficient to study the nature of cognitive activity alone.
- Cognition is for action. The function of the mind is to guide body actions, so cognitive perception and memory functions must be studied in terms of their contribution to situation and embodied comportment.
- Off-line cognition is still body based. Even when decoupled from the environment, the activity of the mind is grounded in evolved interaction with the environment, and is still influenced by past sensorimotor activities.[50]

The theories of embodied cognition reinforce active learning pedagogies, as learning that involves sensorimotor activities *and* central cognitive stimulation together, and may offer improved knowledge-acquisition coding and long-term memory storage. Technologically enhanced environments that require even slight physical interactivity to accomplish a learning task may even mimic a previously learned nonacademic chore triggering a familiar cognitive process that may reinforce a learning experience. The design of instructional and learning technologies that can adhere to Mayer and Moreno's active learning design principles that imitate the elements found in the theories of embodied cognition, as outlined by Margaret Wilson, may hold the greatest promises to scale and advance successful learning experiences to a greater number of learners.

WHY THIS MATTERS

Teaching and learning has evolved to its preeminent state within social structures through necessity. This evolution has continued, and more responsibilities have been given to the institutions of education to train and educate a growing global population and mold each member of this population into differentiated consuming and producing citizens. Moreover, the institutions of education, from mass K–12 school systems, community colleges, and public four-year universities, have been newly tasked with adopting new populations of learners requiring greater resources and additional teaching requiring new unique skills and abilities. These new learners compound the challenges of shaping and educating the future citizen, for to do so requires extensive supplementary tools, new methodologies, and greater personalization.

While not necessarily a panacea to solve and address all the complex issues of a strained mass public education institution, technological teaching and learning tools and platforms that match and complement scientifically researched cognitive models of human learning may offer some relief. Teaching and learning technologies that can adapt and adjust to a learner's cognitive style, aptitude, alternating motivation levels, and fluctuating cognitive capacity may offer the greatest hope to not only meet the learning needs and requirements of a disparate populous but also off-load some of the personalized learning requirements that teachers do not own enough time to sufficiently deliver. As educational organizations have been required to scale their facilities and resources to meet the demands of a growing diverse population of learners, perhaps cognitive-designed teaching and learning technologies hold the greatest promises to finally offer the ability to scale actual teaching and help shape the future citizen of the twenty-first century.

NOTES

1. Noah Webster, "On the Education of Youth in America," in *A Collection of Essays and Fugitiv Writings on Moral, Historical, Political and Literary Subjects* (Boston, 1790; repr., Federalist Papers Project, 2013, https://www.thefederalistpapers.org), 5.
2. Charles H. Winters, "Theological Education in the Next Decade," in *Realities and Visions: The Church's Mission Today*, ed. Furman C. Stough and Urban T. Holmes III, 125–33 (New York: Seabury, 1976).
3. Ibid.
4. John Boli, Francisco O. Ramirez, and John W. Meyer, "Explaining the Origins and Expansion of Mass Education," *Comparative Education Review* 29, no. 2 (May 1985): 151.
5. Webster, "On the Education of Youth in America," 5.
6. Thomas Jefferson, "79: A Bill for the More General Diffusion of Knowledge, 18 June 1779," Founders Online, National Archives, last modified June 13, 2018, https://founders.archives.gov. [Original source: Papers of Thomas Jefferson, vol. 2, 1777–18 (June 1779), ed. Julian P. Boyd, 526–35 (Princeton, NJ: Princeton University Press, 1950).]

7. Samuel Bowles and Herbert Gintis, "The Problem with Human Capital Theory: A Marxian Critique," *American Economic Review* 65, no. 2, Papers and Proceedings of the Eighty-Seventh Annual Meeting of the American Economic Association (May 1975): 74–82.
8. Michael B. Katz, "The Origins of Public Education: A Reassessment," *History of Education Quarterly* 16, no. 4 (1976): 381–407.
9. Boli, Ramirez, and Meyer, "Explaining the Origins."
10. "History," Harvard University, accessed December 2, 2018, https://www.harvard.edu; "History and Traditions," William & Mary, accessed December 2, 2018, https://www.wm.edu.
11. Judith Schiff, "A Brief History of Yale," Yale University Library, last modified July 2, 2018, https://guides.library.yale.edu.
12. Alexander Leitch, "The Founding of Princeton," in *A Princeton Companion* (Princeton, NJ: Princeton University Press, 1978), https://etcweb.princeton.edu.
13. Charles Loring Brace, *The Dangerous Classes of New York and Twenty Years' Work among Them* (New York: Wynkoop & Hallenbeck, 1872).
14. Katz, "Origins of Public Education."
15. Ibid.
16. David J. Rothman, *The Discovery of the Asylum: Social Order and Disorder in the New Republic* (Boston: Little, Brown, 1971); Gerald N. Grob, *Mental Institutions in America: Social Policy to 1875* (London: Collier-Macmillan, 1973).
17. John Ralph and Richard Rubinson, "Immigration and the Expansion of Education in the United States," *American Sociological Review* 45 (December 1980): 943–54.
18. Katz, "Origins of Public Education."
19. Donald K. Jones, *The Making of the Education System, 1851–81* (London: Routledge/Thoemms Press, 1977). It is worth noting that the concept of education as a mechanism for social control was not broadly accepted by all historic institutions. As we know from ancient Egypt and the early Americas, pure subjugation and physical repression were the tools used for social control and to delineate differentiation as well (Boli, Ramirez, and Meyer, "Explaining the Origins," 155).
20. Boli, Ramirez, and Meyer, "Explaining the Origins."
21. Robert Teranishi, Carola Suarez-Orozco, and Marcelo Suarez-Orozco, "Immigrants in Community Colleges," *Future of Children* 21, no. 1 (2011): 153–69.
22. Bureau of Labor Statistics, U.S. Department of Labor, "Foreign-Born Labor Force Nearly Half Hispanic and One-Quarter Asian in 2017," *Economics Daily*, accessed December 2, 2018, https://www.bls.gov.
23. Peter Michaelson, "The Invisible Wall of Psychological Resistance," WhyWeSuffer.com, accessed December 2, 2018, https://www.whywesuffer.com.
24. Knud Illeris, *How We Learn: Learning and Non-Learning in School and Beyond* (New York: Routledge, 2007).
25. David R. Shanks and Mark F. St. John, "Characteristics of Dissociable Human Learning Systems," *Behavioral and Brain Sciences* 17, no. 3 (1994): 367–95.
26. Neal J. Cohen and Larry R. Squire, "Preserved Learning and Retention of Pattern-Analyzing Skill in Amnesia: Dissociation of Knowing How and Knowing That," *Science* 210, no. 4466 (October 10, 1980): 207–10; Terry Winograd, "Frame Representations and the Declarative/Procedural Controversy," in *Representation and Understanding: Studies in Cognitive Science*, ed. Daniel G. Bobrow and Allan M. Collins, 185–210 (New York: Academic Press, 1975).
27. Jere Brophy, "Synthesis of Research on Strategies for Motivating Students to Learn," *Educational Leadership* 45 (1987): 40–48; Hermine H. Marshall and Rhona S. Weinstein, "Classroom Factors Affecting Students' Self-Evaluations: An Interactional Model," *Review of Educational Research* 54, no. 3 (1984): 301–25; Deborah Stipek and Denise H. Daniels, "Declining Perceptions of Competence: A Consequence of Changes in the Child or in the Educational Environment?" *Journal of Educational Psychology* 80 (1988): 352–56.
28. Carole Ames, "Classrooms: Goals, Structures, and Student Motivation," *Journal of Educational Psychology* 84, no. 3 (1992): 261–71.
29. Thomas W. Malone and Mark Lepper, "Making Learning Fun: A Taxonomy of Intrinsic Motivations for Learning," in *Aptitude, Learning, and Instruction*, vol. 3, *Conative and Affec-*

tive Process Analyses, ed. Richard E. Snow and Marshall J. Farr, 223–53 (Hillsdale, NJ: Lawrence Erlbaum, 1987).

30. Scott Paris and Peter Winograd, "Promoting Metacognition and Motivation of Exceptional Children," *Remedial and Special Education* 6, no. 11 (1990): 7–15; Brophy, "Synthesis of Research."

31. Roger Azevedo and Vincent Aleven, "Metacognition and Learning Technologies: An Overview of Current Interdisciplinary Research," in *International Handbook of Metacognition and Learning Technologies*, ed. Roger Azevedo and Vincent Aleven, 1–16 (New York: Springer, 2013); Lisa Delpit, *Other People's Children: Cultural Conflict in the Curriculum* (New York: Springer, 1995).

32. Nick Lee, *Childhood and Society: Growing Up in an Age of Uncertainty* (Oxford, UK: McGraw-Hill Education, 2001).

33. Robert Serpell and A. Wade Boykin, "Cultural Dimensions of Cognition: A Multiplex, Dynamic System of Constraints and Possibilities," in *Thinking and Problem Solving*, ed. Robert J. Sternberg, 369–408 (New York: Academic Press, 1994); Barbara Rogoff, *The Cultural Nature of Human Development* (New York: Oxford University Press, 2003).

34. Janet Bryan, Saskia Osendarp, Donna Hughes, Eva Calvaresi, Katrine Baghurst, and Jan-Willem van Klinken, "Nutrients for Cognitive Development in School-Aged Children," *Nutrition Reviews* 62, no. 8 (2004): 295–306; Virginia A. Rauh and Amy E. Margolis, "Research Review: Environmental Exposures, Neurodevelopment, and Child Mental Health: New Paradigms for the Study of Brain and Behavioral Effects," *Journal of Child Psychology and Psychiatry* 57, no. 7 (2016): 775–93.

35. Jaak Panksepp and Lucy Biven, *The Archaeology of Mind: Neuroevolutionary Origins of Human Emotions* (New York: Norton, 2012).

36. Toni Schamer and Michael Johns, "Converging Evidence that Stereotype Threat Reduces Working Memory Capacity," *Journal of Personality and Social Psychology* 85, no. 3 (2003): 440–52.

37. Mary Catherine O'Connor and Sarah Michaels, "Aligning Academic Task and Participation Status through Revoicing: Analysis of a Classroom Discourse Strategy," *Anthropology and Education Quarterly* 24, no. 4 (1993): 318–35.

38. Paul Saettler, *A History of Instructional Technology* (New York: McGraw-Hill, 1968).

39. Arthur S. Flemming, "The Philosophy and Objectives of the National Defense Education Act," *Annals of the American Academy of Political and Social Science* 327, no. 1 (1960): 132–38.

40. Robert A. Reiser, "Instructional Technology: A History," in *Instructional Technology: Foundations*, ed. Robert Gagne, 11–48 (New York: Routledge, 1987); Rodney S. Earle, "The Integration of Instructional Technology into Public Education: Promises and Challenges," *Educational Technology* 42, no. 1 (2002): 5–13.

41. Elementary and Secondary Education Act of 1965, Public Law 89-10, H. R. 2362, 89th Cong., 1st Sess., April 11, 1965, accessed December 3, 2018, https://www.gpo.gov; Reiser, "Instructional Technology."

42. Gary D. Borich, "A Needs Assessment Model for Conducting Follow-Up Studies," *Journal of Teacher Education* 31, no. 3 (1980): 39–42; Michael Scriven, "The Methodology of Evaluation," in *Perspectives of Curriculum Evaluation*, ed. Ralph W. Tyler, Robert M. Gagné, and Michael Scriven, 39–83 (Chicago: Rand McNally, 1967).

43. Richard E. Mayer, "Multimedia Learning," *Psychology of Learning and Motivation* 41 (2002): 85–139.

44. Ibid.

45. Richard E. Mayer and Roxana Moreno, "Nine Ways to Reduce Cognitive Load in Multimedia Learning," *Educational Psychologist* 38, no. 1 (2003): 43–52.

46. Ibid.

47. National Academies of Sciences, Engineering, and Medicine, *How People Learn II: Learners, Contexts, and Cultures* (Washington, DC: National Academies Press, 2018).

48. Margaret Wilson, "Six Views of Embodied Cognition," *Psychonomic Bulletin and Review* 9, no. 4 (2002): 625–36.

49. James J. Gibson, *The Senses Considered as Perceptual Systems* (Boston: Houghton Mifflin, 1966).
50. Wilson, "Six Views of Embodied Cognition."

Chapter Two

Innovation (Online Learning)

Christopher Jennings

> By 2030 the largest company on the internet is going to be an education-based company that we haven't heard of yet.
>
> —Thomas Frey, DaVinci Institute[1]

In the last two decades, online learning has grown into a $165-billion-a-year industry[2] and is estimated to hit $331 billion by 2025.[3] Looking back over how technology has influenced higher education, it is notable how much has changed and, simultaneously, how little has changed. Throughout the (relatively recent) history of online learning, there were scores of early adopters who used technology to teach in radical new ways and increase access to underserved populations.

Yet despite the fact that technology has changed how we consume information and remapped our social interactions, community colleges and universities still often rely on an entrenched model of lecture-based instruction and the prestige of accredited degree programs. But innovators along the way have challenged that historical learning model, taking risks and dreaming big, using technology to help evolve the process of teaching and learning.

This chapter looks at three phases in the evolution of online learning. The first took place in the late 1990s and early 2000s as more and more schools created online courses and programs amid an emerging industry of internet technology companies and social media platforms. Schools tried different business models that ranged from for-profit education to free and open education, supported by a growing demand for online learning that produced a number of educational hardware and software technologies such as the learning management system (LMS).

The second phase occurred with the creation of smart devices and apps that vastly increased internet access and engagement, and shifted media consumption to video, supported by cloud-based software that generated big data sets for analysis. This was accompanied by a strong, open learning movement that popularized massive open online courses (MOOCs) and spawned variations of the LMS for more specialized training and education needs.

The third phase of online learning has just begun. This includes the long-talked-about realization of technologies such as virtual and augmented realities, artificial intelligence, and machine learning with predictive models and personalization, and new connected devices that constitute the "internet of things." The chapter then speculates how community colleges and universities must evolve their teaching practices if they wish to stay relevant to the next generation of learners.

PHASE 1: LEARNING ONLINE

The biggest advance in educational technology since the printing press occurred with the broader adoption of the internet in the late 1990s. Born of the Department of Defense's Advanced Research Projects Agency Network (ARPANET) in the 1960s, the modern internet emerged in the early 1990s with the World Wide Web, a system of websites and hyperlinks invented by Tim Berners-Lee.[4] Internet service providers (ISPs) drove growth in the late 1980s with improved network services, which transitioned from dial-up modems using fiber-optic telephone lines to dedicated cable and Wi-Fi.

Computers in the late nineties became faster and more compact, creating smaller, more portable laptop computers with CD-ROM drives that could run software and web cameras that could be used for two-way communication. Web-browsing software enabled people to view the web in a consumable format, starting with Marc Andreessen's Mosaic in 1993 (which later became Netscape, then Firefox) and Microsoft's Internet Explorer in 1995. By 1997, seventy million people were online, which was approximately 1.7 percent of the global population, compared to 4,157 million users or 54.4 percent today.[5]

The early internet resembled a hodgepodge of different content creators, behaviors, and subculture communities, reminiscent of unregulated ham radio operators in the early 1900s who made "tremendous distances disappear into the ether."[6] Online communities were one of the earliest popular online mediums of communication with 84 percent of U.S. internet users in 2001 indicating they had contacted an online community and 79 percent in regular contact with one or more groups.[7] These online communities[8] varied across email discussion board lists, chat rooms, bulletin board services, and Usenet groups.[9]

"Communities of practice,"[10] such as the Whole Earth 'Lectronic Link (The WELL), represented some of the earliest organic forms of collaborative online learning, as users exchanged information and shared interests. Common internet vernacular such as "flame," "spam," and "LOL" grew out of these conversations, as well as typed "emoticons" designed to communicate more nuanced intentions or feelings.[11] Conversations in virtual communities fostered a network of programmers and would later promote movements such as open-source software to flourish.[12] Many early ISPs that launched dial-up services such as AOL, CompuServe, GEnie, and Prodigy included online communities as part of their offerings. It's telling that early popular search engines like *Yahoo!* and *Infoseek* organized their home pages similarly by topics of interest.

Different online formats for disseminating information also emerged as the web grew in the late 1990s and early 2000s. Web logs or "blogs" were serialized web pages that reflected information and opinions users conveyed online about various topics. Platforms like Blogger and LiveJournal brought blogging into the mainstream.[13] Additionally, audio and video encoding protocols, streaming media protocols, and file-sharing services enabled users to consume audio and video online, and distribute media more easily through networks of users. Businesses and schools began streaming, allowing users to broadcast themselves online and collect data and feedback in real time. Macromedia's Flash software in 1996 let developers create more interactive websites and online applications with a wide variety of uses, including animations, simulations, audio and video players, and video games.

Video games for education had existed almost since video games were commercially available. *Lemonade Stand* in 1979, *Reader Rabbit* and *Math Rabbit* in the early 1980s, and *Where in the World Is Carmen San Diego?* in 1985 were all successful games that sold millions of copies.[14] More commercial games such as *The Legend of Zelda* in 1986 included elements of puzzle-solving, and *Sim City* games taught city planning and management based on a number of lifelike conditions.

Video game platforms in the nineties offered networked gaming. Rich, online communities grew around sophisticated gaming worlds such as *Doom*, *Civilization*, *Quake*, and *Everquest*, connecting tens of millions of gamers and spawning global gaming competitions. Online virtual worlds such as *Active Worlds* in 1995 and *Second Life* in 2003 let users exist as representative avatars in three-dimensional worlds that could be built and customized with structures made out of digital abstractions like water or static. Users could even create and monetize their own user experience content such as clothing or accessories.

Some colleges and universities built communities and even taught classes in these virtual worlds using representative student avatars. Oakland University's Honors College launched the course "Second Life: Research and Creative Activities in a Virtual Environment";[15] the University of San Martin de Porres of Peru developed Second Life prototypes of archaeological buildings in Peru with training on how to teach in such virtual worlds;[16] and other schools such as North Carolina State University, the University of South Florida College of Medicine, and SUNY Empire State College have experimented with or have active Second Life worlds.[17]

Massively multiplayer online role-playing games (MMORPGs) combined role-playing games with globally networked games such as the massively successful *World of Warcraft* that launched in 2004. MMORPGs spread with the launch of networked home computers and video game consoles, and by 2016 there were 1.8 billion gamers worldwide.[18] The U.S. Army even created a recruitment video game in 2004 called *America's Army* that let prospective recruits learn about different jobs available in the army and offered one of the first successful first-person shooter (FPS) game perspectives.[19]

A 2018 survey found that an impressive 64 percent of U.S. households play video games on at least one device.[20] As video games infiltrated more households, educators recognized the potential for games to motivate students and explored the incorporation of gaming incentives such as points, levels, achievements, extra or infinite lives, bonuses, and other rewards.[21]

In 2002, a "serious games" movement emerged that strived to connect the electronic gaming industry with training, health, and public policy.[22] Educators began to explore in earnest the application of games in contexts beyond entertainment with educational technologists like Chris Dede at Harvard, who declared video game systems "learning environments of the future."[23] Henry Jenkins, the leader of MIT's Games to Teach Project, explored how to immerse children in computer-simulated educational microworlds.[24]

As teachers experimented with educational games, two camps emerged: educators and researchers that wanted to leverage existing games and gaming culture to educate learners, and those who wanted to reinforce traditional classroom education with games to supplement learning.[25] These two approaches fostered ongoing tension as educators, curriculum designers, and educational psychologists experimented with new digital spaces for learning (to radically subvert historical practices), while traditional educators sought to supplement the entrenched classroom model with more game-related elements. Chapter 5 explores applications of these new virtual learning spaces, new immersive hardware systems, and their limits and opportunities in the practice of teaching and learning.

The rise of online education in the late 1990s and early 2000s came from different institutions and partnerships that included traditional community colleges and universities, education companies partnered with schools, and for-profit schools. It's a testament to forward-thinking instructional designers, educational researchers, and teachers that some form of online learning emerged almost as soon as the technology was available. While universities had been experimenting with primitive versions of online education since the 1960s,[26] internet browsers in the 1990s made it easier to take entire courses online, and scholastic online programs and courses soon followed.[27] The adoption of online learning at community colleges and universities varied widely, however, as schools struggled to find the right business model and positioning of this new learning format among their traditional offerings.[28]

Some universities plunged in with purely online accredited programs that observed rigorous standards and guidelines, while others took a for-profit approach, leveraging their existing schools of continuing education. Many schools felt the competitive pressure of their peer institutions and rushed to launch unaccredited programs whose audience was ill defined.[29] Some schools created hybrid courses with limited online participation, while other universities leveraged existing distance education or extension programs to launch online ventures. Some universities waited in the wings to see if online learning would be taken seriously or if it would end up as another in a long fad of learning formats. Others partnered with for-profit education companies that allowed them to cautiously explore without significant risk. So while online learning had begun to entrench itself at some universities and colleges, the future remained unclear as both teachers and students took stock of its benefits and challenges.

For-profit colleges have a long history of providing vocational training and filling educational gaps that were underserved by nonprofit academic institutions.[30] For years, these colleges offered mailbox correspondence courses or local classroom-based courses that generally weren't seen as a viable substitute to a university education.

The University of Phoenix, founded in 1976, changed that, popularizing for-profit education by launching an asynchronous online-only MBA program in 1989 targeting the growing number of Prodigy ISP customers. By the year 2000, the University of Phoenix had more than one hundred thousand students and was growing by over 25 percent a year.[31] After going public as the Apollo Education Group in 1994, the University of Phoenix was the nation's largest and fastest-growing private university.[32] Other for-profit universities such as Jones University also grew substantially with the move to online education, helping to disseminate online learning and, in turn, putting pressure on community colleges and universities to build their own online programs.

Online courses offered at both for-profit and not-for-profit colleges and universities experimented with a variety of learning formats. There were courses conducted purely online and hybrid courses, which combined face-to-face classroom with online learning experiences. Some online courses were paced, moving students progressively through lessons concurrently, while others were self-paced, allowing students to move through course content at their leisure. Other online courses were synchronous, meaning students all logged in at the same time, and others were asynchronous, letting students log in at times of their own choosing. Some courses offered a software platform with preloaded course content and no dedicated instructor, while others included online content supplemented with discussion board communities, forums, online exams or projects, and office hours conducted over chat rooms or webcam.

This certainly represented a "wild west" of online learning and experimentation where researchers, instructional designers, and educators sometimes threw new online learning formats against the wall to see what stuck. Some instructors were naturally suspicious of online learning, questioning its rigor, requiring such a different teaching and learning dynamic than traditional face-to-face classrooms. Others immediately saw the possibilities of offering rich, on-demand, multimedia resources to enhance their teaching, and the potential of online networks to disseminate learning to people who previously had limited access. Toward the end of the twentieth century, as more college and university administrators, teachers, and learners became comfortable with the concept of online learning, the *Los Angeles Times* noted a distinct shift in attitude: "Indeed, the few online classes offered three years ago were widely dismissed as the high-tech version of the correspondence courses of notorious diploma mills. Now they are being embraced by virtually all colleges and universities."[33]

This rapid growth of online education inspired a gold rush of technology companies that designed and developed tools to support digital education. The learning management system (LMS) was the most common software platform that enabled teachers to deliver, monitor, and track online learning. An LMS typically included, and still includes, online registration, some degree of content authoring, permissions and publishing, a gradebook, an assessment engine, potentially synchronous or asynchronous communication tools, and some basic measurement tracking. By the turn of the century, Blackboard (founded by a Cornell undergrad) and WebCT (founded by a computer science professor at the University of British Columbia) emerged as two of the most successful learning management systems among a host of contenders that included eCollege, Desire2Learn, and open-source LMS Moodle.

The "dot-com" crash of the early 2000s brought into stark relief some of the major risks and assumptions of the online learning market and created a vast consolidation of education technology companies. A number of high-profile universities and colleges, as well as online for-profit schools, failed. The list included Virtual Temple (Temple University); UMBCOnline (the University of Maryland University College);[34] Harcourt Higher Education; U.S. Open University; for-profit Fathom.com from Columbia University; nonprofit venture AllLearn (Alliance for Lifelong Learning) sponsored by Oxford, Yale, and Stanford; the University of Illinois; and NYU Online. Many of these universities had burned through millions of dollars to create programs of varying quality, and some programs had thousands of students who would never matriculate through their online degree programs.

Common reasons cited for online program failure included lack of institutional support, such as advising and counseling, academic inconsistencies with established curriculum, marketing challenges, lack of accreditation (in some cases, brand-name recognition), and business planning issues.[35] But just as many programs failed, a new crop of companies and institutions offering online programs were launched, learning from the mistakes from their legacy forebears. These new online programs tended to align more closely with existing nonprofit continuing education and professional extension programs. New learners expanded to include established student population, as well as corporate and business customers.[36] UMassOnline, launched in 2001, generated $36.9 million in revenue in 2008, growing two and a half times faster than the national average for online enrollments.[37] Cornell University launched a successful venture called eCornell in 2002. As Judith V. Boettcher observed in 2006,

> The recent announcements about distance learning ventures suggest that we have, as a profession, passed the point of unbridled enthusiasm and possibility about the Web and the Internet. Our early enthusiasm caused many of us to believe that not only could learning and degrees be offered anywhere at any time, but that any institution could offer any programming to any student and be successful and productive at it. We are wiser and more discriminating now. The distance learning principle that we are being forcefully reminded of is that we are in the knowledge services business, and basic business principles must be applied if a program is to succeed.[38]

In the wake of the dot-com crash also came a consolidation of LMS and other educational technology companies. Blackboard purchased a number of competitors and finally devoured its largest competitor WebCT in 2005, increasing Blackboard's market share by an estimated 65 to 75 percent.[39] Blackboard would continue acquisitions through the next decade (along with some rather litigious patent claims for learning management systems),[40] thereby cementing its status as the higher education leader of online course delivery. In 2014, Blackboard software and services were used by approximately seventeen thousand schools and organizations across one hundred countries.[41] Seventy-five percent of U.S. universities and colleges, and more than half of K–12 schools, are estimated to use its products and services,[42] as well as 80 percent of academic institutions worldwide.[43]

Despite its ubiquitousness among schools and businesses, a persistent dissatisfaction would linger for the LMS. Its tendency toward one-size-fits-all content delivery, as well as its exorbitant cost and dependency on third-party providers, made "the dreaded LMS" a horrible necessity. Surveys found that the LMS was uniformly underutilized at schools and often used for learning administration, rather than as a tool to facilitate learning.[44]

A 2015 EDUCAUSE survey found only 41 percent of instructors used more advanced features to promote online interactions, and that 15 percent of schools planned to replace the LMS within the next three years.[45] In the world of corporate training, the reputation of learning management systems was even more dismal. A 2015 Brandon Hall Group survey found that 58 percent of companies that had an LMS older than five years were planning a replacement.[46] A rash of articles would eventually pronounce the LMS "dead,"[47] while others diagnosed the patient as alive but heavily sedated.[48] This dissatisfaction would later lead to a search for more specialized alternatives.

Despite the dot.com crash, educational software and hardware continued to grow in the early 2000s. Software launched to assist with classroom management and teaching, plagiarism detection, mind mapping, and note-taking. Courseware was created for interactive geometry, language learning, simulations of biology or chemistry experiments, reading instruction, and medical and health-care training. Innovative hardware produced "smart" classrooms that boasted lecture-streaming and recording systems, touch-screen podium control systems for lighting and screen control, interactive hand-controlled polling systems, interactive and learner-sharing whiteboards, downloadable textbooks (or e-books), digital highlighters and pens that scanned and uploaded what was written, and attendance tracking systems.

In 2001, Apple released its iPod digital portable music player with a downloadable audio service called iTunes. By 2004, serialized digital audio recordings could be subscribed to and downloaded—a process known as "podcasting." Apple's iTunes included the education-targeted iTunesU, and the platform would eventually offer more than two hundred thousand podcasts, including lectures and videos from thousands of esteemed faculty members from colleges and universities worldwide.[49]

By the early 2000s, online learning had established itself as a credible educational format. In 2003, 100 percent of public schools had internet access and 90 percent offered asynchronous online courses. College enrollments in credit-granting distance-learning courses increased 123 percent to 2.9 million.[50] A 2005 Babson research survey sponsored by the Sloan Consortium found that 3.2 million students were taking at least one online course (almost a million more than the previous year) and that 96 percent of the largest institutions had at least some kind of online course offering.[51] The *New York Times* reported that e-learning was predicted to grow 33 percent per year through 2004—a $12-billion-a-year business.[52]

The corporate market for e-learning was similarly exploding with estimates indicating it would double in size every year to an estimated $11.5 billion by 2003.[53] In 2006, the "50-percent rule" was repealed, allowing U.S.

students to receive financial aid if they were enrolled in an eligible online degree program at an accredited Title IV-eligible institution. It was clear that online learning was not only growing but also increasingly thought of as a legitimate educational option.

But many faculty members, still concerned about the lack of academic rigor, limited real-time interactivity with learners, and the potential for cheating, remained skeptical of online education. The Babson research survey reported that only one in four academic leaders thought that faculty members "accept the value and legitimacy of online education," with nonprofit colleges conveying the highest levels of skepticism.[54] So while the online learning sector grew at a tremendous pace and students actively adopted online curriculum as part of their educational practice, there was still friction from faculty members who struggled with the abstract idea of teaching in virtual environments compared to face-to-face classrooms. However, online learning was well received in the corporate world, where corporate training required much shorter learning segments and goals, overall less rigor, and limited cheating concerns. Eighty-three percent of CEOs and U.S. business owners supported online corporate training in 2010, and also considered online degrees credible. Fifty-seven percent of corporate trainers rated online learning outcomes equal or superior to traditional classroom education.[55]

PHASE 2: MOBILE AND OPEN LEARNING

When Steve Jobs launched the Apple iPhone and iOS in 2007, it forever changed the ease and frequency with which people interacted online. The iPhone put powerful connected computers in people's pockets and offered a veritable Swiss Army knife of software and hardware tools that have become embedded in the fabric of everyday life. Touch screens dramatically increased interactivity with software using motion and gestures, creating a physical relationship with media that transcended the screen. Apps not only offered easy ways to download and install new functionality but also empowered users to build their own apps and market them online.

In the years to follow, public spaces would be punctuated with people staring into the glow of their screen, seemingly oblivious to everything around them. To stay competitive, as every business felt the need to build a website or blog, now every business needed an app to express their brand and better deliver their services and support. Google's open-source Android operating system (OS) soon followed, offering a lower-cost alternative for mobile carriers. By 2017, Android was installed on 321 million units worldwide and Apple was selling 216 million—an unbelievable pace of adoption.[56]

Consumers quickly became dependent on their phones for communicating directly with others, finding directions, shopping, reading news, receiving social network updates, and playing games. In less than ten years, mobile smart devices have become a ubiquitous technology that is never very far out of reach.

Smart devices have also had a tremendous impact on teaching and learning, creating a continuous learning model where the curious and industrious user can access a variety of content on any subject instantaneously. This could be as simple as using a Google search to answer a basic question, watching an online instructional video, using a language-learning app, or taking an online course on any subject.

Learners in elementary and secondary school (as well as their parents) can access grades and receive teacher comments on their phones in real time. Learning apps offer learning-assisted tools to create class schedules, stay on top of assignments and important deadlines, collaborate in social learning groups, speed read, and take and organize class notes. Other apps offer content libraries with millions of free (or loanable) e-books, audiobooks, and podcasts. The empowering (and eerily addictive) nature of accessing such an overwhelming wealth of information with such ease has remapped our relationship with software and digital information, and created a permanent audience of learners hungry to consume new information.

The dissemination of smart devices has also augmented the growth of online video consumption. Popular video-hosting platforms like YouTube (purchased by Google in 2005) and Vevo let instructors upload instructional videos about virtually any subject and any level of complexity. By 2015, there was more than four hundred hours of content uploaded to YouTube every minute and the website was ranked second most popular in the world, second only to Google.[57] YouTube's astounding popularity created a continuous demand for different kinds of streaming content. Children who once grew up watching scheduled shows on television now browsed videos on YouTube. They watch instructional videos that teach new crafts, how to repair things, and how to improve video-game-playing skills, not to mention help with the sciences and humanities. One recent university graduate recounted how YouTube helped her through college:

> YouTube was my go to while doing homework, prepping for exams or just when I needed to refresh what a term meant. It's also the first place I go when I want to learn about a subject I don't know a lot about. Time and again, YouTube has helped me understand concepts, offering numerous different explanations till I found one that clicked. In my experience, YouTube's biggest benefit is that it offers something to students with many different learning styles. Many students learn much better with visual aids, and animation can add significantly to that. Many students also prefer to learn at their own pace, and YouTube allows them to pause and return to the same video a number of times. I have had professors who I loved and who spent many hours

> helping me over email and office hours, but their in-class explanations just did not suit my learning style. Here, YouTube was able to bridge the gap.[58]

The availability of a video library where students can discover different explanations of a concept until they find one that matches their learning style and preferred teaching method is incredibly powerful. It puts students in the driver's seat of their own educational experience and provides a wealth of open resources beyond the traditional classroom. With the YouTube comment feature and ratings tool, instructional videos can also be collectively and publicly critiqued, helping students find and access the best and most accurate videos on almost any topic and academic subject.

Shortly after the launch of YouTube, TedTalks, a media organization that had featured expert speakers on a variety of topics since the 1980s, offered all of their video lectures gratis online. Thanks in part to YouTube, TedTalks combined views in 2011 numbered over five hundred million, with over a billion TedTalks watched globally.[59] In 2009, YouTube devoted a section of its website to education and branded it YouTube/EDU. This included videos broken out by grade level such as primary and secondary, university, and lifelong learning.

As tech companies like Google and Facebook generated a jaw-dropping amount of data from users of their consumer and business products and services online, they began to use this data to glean insights about user behavior, activities, and interests. These new patterns were often used to understand user needs and quantify business model success. As Google and Facebook, and other companies like Doubleclick and Microstrategy, started similarly harvested and analyzing more of these new data sets, they noticed the results of their analysis could be used to drive future business decision-making, sometimes referred to as "data-driven decision-making" (DDD).

The *Harvard Business Review* found that DDD in U.S. manufacturing, for instance, nearly tripled between 2005 and 2010.[60] In 2005, Google released Google Analytics, a free product that enabled anyone to collect online behavior data, perform analysis, and visualize the results in shareable reports. This would become the most popular web analytics software in the world used on more than 50 percent of websites.[61]

The No Child Left Behind Act also mandated that elementary and secondary schools needed to provide more data about the quality of education being offered, which included accountability measures and annual assessments to demonstrate effectiveness and efficacy. The relative ease with which online data could be parsed and harvested began inspiring college's and university's education researchers and instructional designers to rely more heavily on data when making strategic decisions and designing online courses. Standards for interoperability and reporting such as SCORM and

AICC were created to help learning management systems and other software platforms and applications interconnect and work in conjunction together.

With more and more behaviors such as entertainment consumption, shopping, and learning from smart devices moving online, the results have generated massive data sets that could be mined for insights. "Big data" was the term for massive, voluminous data sets that could be analyzed for predictive or behavioral analytics, which couldn't be obtained by human or traditional data-processing software. Learning analytics companies emerged that could tie data together from in-classroom attendance systems, student registration systems, and online activity in LMSs or other education content like discussion forums to look for patterns that could help improve students' educational experience.

Chapter 3 explores how teaching and learning "big data" can be harvested and analyzed to identify detailed learning insights, from individuals and groups of learners. Chapter 4 provides examples of how these newly discovered data sets can be used to provide personalized interventions and guidance to help a learner reclaim a pathway to academic success. Just as many of the most successful technology companies like Google and Facebook have become more data driven, the most successful schools of the future will continue to be guided by data, using it as a compass to advance and improve upon the practice of teaching and learning, rather than as an afterthought of assessment.

In 2004, an unknown hedge fund analyst by the name of Salman Khan started tutoring one of his cousins in math remotely using a telephone and a drawing application called Yahoo! Doodle.[62] Other cousins needed Khan's excellent tutoring, so in 2006, Khan started posting his lessons on YouTube's educational channel for all of his family, and family friends could access the same lectures. Soon other learners started watching, and over the next few years, the lessons made Khan a star in the education and tech worlds—inspiring his "Khan Academy."

Shortly after, with financial support from Google and the Bill and Melinda Gates Foundation, the Kahn Academy contracted with other teachers and scholars offering lectures on other subject matters.[63] In 2014, Khan even opened a physical school called Khan Lab School in Mountain View, California. By 2015, Khan Academy was one of the top digital education platforms producing 440 million free "microlectures" to 2.2 million subscribers with more than 500 million views.[64]

Although his tutorials scaled to millions of users, there was something decidedly low tech about Khan's approach of just posting his videos online. It was a reminder that, amid all of the technology designed to aid instruction, teaching at its core remains an art and a science, an ability that some gifted individuals uniquely possess to explain complex subject matter in accessible ways.

The same year that Salman Khan started posting his tutorial videos, high school chemistry teachers Jonathan Bergmann and Aaron Sams started offering recorded lectures online to students who had missed their class. Eventually, they stopped in-class lectures altogether, videotaping their lectures in advance for students to review, so that class time could be used more productively for specific questions and in-depth problem solving. This type of "flipped classroom" model had been attempted before and reflected Alison King's proposed shift from "sage on the stage, to guide on the side."[65] In this teaching model, students became active participants in their own learning and instructors took a more "hands-off" approach, serving more as guides and mentors to better empower learners.

A number of schools have experimented with the flipped classroom approach, including the University of California at Santa Barbara for physics, Boston University for engineering, and Harvard University for physics.[66] Adapting to the use of technology, the flipped classroom represents a major shift in the way that classroom instruction is thought about and may represent an important evolution of teaching with technology. The ability to easily stream lectures on free platforms for dissemination presaged the notion of free, open courses available to mass audiences online.

For years, there had been a strong movement toward "open-source" learning offered by colleges, universities, and individual educators that self-publish to promote and strengthen their brands and to scale their courseware to more learners. The open-source education movement was also fomented by years of exorbitant LMS prices and a one-size-fits-all software platform.

In 2007, MIT created an OpenCourseWare (OCW) project that included almost its entire curriculum of more than 1,800 courses across thirty-three academic disciplines online.[67] Other universities launched similar efforts including the Open Learning Initiative at Carnegie Mellon University, and other universities like Yale, Utah State University, the University of Michigan, and the University of California, Berkeley, soon followed. Other movements to create open, free, more accessible educational content and tools were reflected in projects like One Laptop per Child in 2005, with the ambitious goal of providing computers to children in low-income countries, as well as free access to learning content, media, and programming environments (Child, 2009).[68]

The first massive open online course (or MOOC) was launched in 2007 from for-profit, social enterprise Alison, to provide basic online education and workplace skills.[69] In mid-2011, Sebastian Thrun, who had a storied career as a Google vice president and fellow, professor of computer science at Stanford, and cofounder of ride-sharing service Uber, taught an "Introduction to Artificial Intelligence" MOOC, which allowed anyone to take the course for free in tandem with Stanford students without any specific prerequisites. After 160,000 students enrolled, Thrun launched the for-profit educational company Udacity, which offered free courses across a range of skill levels and subject matter.[70] In 2014, the company created the concept of "nanodegrees" at a cost of $200 to learn programming skills and become prequalified for entry-level IT jobs.[71]

In late 2011, MIT responded by launching a MOOC platform called MITx. This was spun off the following year into EdX, a nonprofit co-owned by MIT and Harvard that would offer a "Micromasters" credentials that was equivalent to a semester's worth of coursework in multiple disciplines. The following year, Stanford launched Coursera, which included academic courses offered by Princeton, Stanford, the University of Michigan, and the University of Pennsylvania. Soon there were different variants of MOOCs including synchronous MOOCs (or SMOCs), which allowed for unlimited presentations but required all course registrants to be present at the same time;[72] small private online courses (SPOCs) that required a formal enrollment for limited number of spaces; and SSOCs, which required a formal enrollment for a limited number of spaces but required all course registrants to be present at the same time. Soon, many more colleges and universities were offering free, open access to their courses, and several large businesses followed, such as Google's Analytics Academy, YouTube's Creator Academy, and Goldman Sachs's 10,000 Women.[73]

As Stanford sociologist Mitchell Waldrop observed, "In 25 years of observing higher education, I've never seen anything move this fast."[74] Even the LMS company Blackboard launched a MOOC platform.[75] There were so many MOOCs available that apps like GroupMOOC were created to manage the various courses taken across different MOOC platforms![76] Disenchantment with MOOCs soon set in, however, as the realities of offering courses to hundreds of thousands of users with unchecked prerequisites and limited student-teacher or student-student interactivity produced high attrition rates and dismal academic performance outcomes.[77] But there were counterarguments that MOOCs represented a new learning paradigm whose engagement shouldn't be measured by traditional classroom standards.[78]

Responding to the market, LMS vendors have adapted over the years to become more customizable and opened their architecture to other learning-related technologies. Learning Tools Interoperability (LTI) standards created by the IMS Global Learning Consortium were adopted by many LMS vendors, extending features and functionality by interfacing with third-party technology tools and software plug-ins. This option provided more flexibility in learning management systems, allowing colleges and companies to better customize their platforms as needed.

In addition to the traditional LMS (both proprietary and open source), there also emerged next-generation digital learning environments and modular open platforms that depended on the LTI protocol to integrate different third-party systems. These platforms tended to focus more on teaching, rather than administration tasks, supporting features such as content personalization, universal design standards, and more formative learning assessments.[79] Other technology providers such as Google Classroom offered free basic learning management tools for elementary and secondary schools that accomplished the basic tasks of a traditional LMS, such as creating, distributing, and grading digital assignments online, but also offered an easy method to customize their platform through LTI integration with other specialized applications.

Learning content management systems specialized more in the creation, management, hosting, and tracking of digital learning content without the excess and many times superfluous bells and whistles of an LMS. Learning experience platforms offered easier ways to deliver learning videos and other content produced, managed, and delivered in a TV-like user interface. Microlearning platforms delivered bite-sized content optimized for mobile devices to learn on the go. Content libraries helped manage the explosion of free and paid learning content, while Learning Records Stores offered data collection and tracking without the other cluttering features offered by an LMS.

A new standard protocol for online learning outcome measurements and tracking of goals called Experience API (or xAPI) was also proposed. The protocol xAPI was designed to address limitations in SCORM tracking and allowed for the flexible tracking of learning activities and experiences, in both traditional LMSs and learning content that existed outside of a desktop internet browser.[80] The protocol was platform agnostic, allowing a teacher not to be trapped by a particular platform provider's data analytics architecture or dashboard.

Additionally, a host of assessment, development, and delivery tools emerged to assist with video authoring, intelligent assessment, spaced learning, gaming, collaboration, and simulations. The amount of new specialized learning software was overwhelming, and many aimed to chip away at the LMSs traditional market share. As Josh Bersin pointedly remarked, "With these new products becoming more useful and engaging, the LMS has generally been relegated to the role of a back-office training management application."[81]

Online learning continues to expand enrollments in colleges and universities, especially Western Governors, Arizona State, and Southern New Hampshire University, institutions that had adapted well to market demand,[82] while overall residential university enrollments have remained flat or fallen.[83] However, some of the largest for-profit schools such as University of Phoenix, American Public University System, and Kaplan University also saw drops in enrollments, perhaps due to negative press surrounding bad business practices[84] and the increasing availability of competitive free or inexpensive online learning content that offers credentials or certificates for some programs and tracks.

In 2010, the University of Phoenix enrolled more than 470,000 students but had dropped to 130,000 by 2016, forcing the school to close twenty campus locations and lay off hundreds of employees.[85] However, some smaller for-profit programs such as Grand Canyon University, Walden, Capella, and Ashford Universities did post modest gains in enrollments the past few years.[86] MOOCs democratized many subjects by offering gratis or inexpensive online classes to anyone with internet access. However, without prerequisite knowledge, improved interactivity, better proctoring systems to ensure trustworthiness, and advising and counseling services available to the online learner, their usefulness will remain little more than a fad.

With the transformation of education to mobile and massively open courseware supported by online streaming video and big data, educators continue to push the boundaries of traditional instruction, creating some minor revolutions along the way. Many dreamers imagined the day when learning systems would truly become personalized, intuitively adapting to learner needs, and mixed reality would be available in every classroom and home to situate learners in artificial immersive learning spaces designed specifically to match the requirements of any subject, which could permit teachers to convey knowledge in truly unprecedented ways.

Despite much hype and rhetoric of educational disruption over the years, many of the truly exciting fantasies of high-tech learning still have not taken root. But due to recent advances in artificial intelligence and machine learning, virtual assistants, internet-enabled appliances, and portable virtual reality (VR) systems, online learning is poised to make another leap in evolution.

PHASE 3: DIGITAL REALITIES

The promise of an educational future where students learn in virtual reality using educational tools and curriculum that adapt intuitively to individual learners has been made by educational technology vendors, researchers, and prognosticators for decades. In this next phase of digital learning, some of these ambitions finally seem within the grasp of teachers and learners. Synthetic realities have long been touted as a pathway to educate through virtual experiences. This dates back to predigital technologies that include panoramas and moving panoramas, dioramas, stereoscopes, world's fairs that built mock villages (using actual imported native peoples from around the world), staged historical battles and natural disasters, and early silent films.[87] Many of these technologies were marketed as educational experiences where consumers could be magically transported to different places and times to learn experientially. Digital simulation technologies that emerged in the 1990s very much exist within the continuum of that tradition.

The fantastic learning possibilities of virtual and mixed reality have only become available in the last few years with advances in technology, creating smaller, more portable headsets with better fidelity. Oculus Rift was funded from a grassroots Kickstarter campaign in 2012 and purchased by Facebook two years later. When Oculus Rift launched in 2016, it was the most sophisticated consumer VR available with an affordable price point and improved tracking designed to avoid motion sickness, which frequently occurred in early systems. Facebook is developing an entire platform for educational VR, partnering with schools like Yale University's play4REAL lab, MIT's Education Arcade, Cornell's Virtual Embodiment Lab, and NYU's Future Reality lab.[88]

Other consumer VR headsets soon followed, such as Samsung's Gear VR and Google's Daydream. The marketing for Google's VR app Expedition teases the possibilities: "Explore historical landmarks, go down to the atomic level, get up close with sharks, even visit outer space!"[89] Google released Cardboard, an extraordinarily low-budget version of VR (dubbed "Oculus Thrift"), made quite literally out of cardboard and cheap optical lenses. Cardboard is designed to be used with applications running on smartphones that create an immersive world. "Augmented reality" (AR) overlays digital information on a physical, real-world view (such as a smartphone screen), altering one's perspective of an actual environment. Chapter 5 provides a thorough description of VR and the Oculus Rift, as well as augmented and mixed realities used in training and education.

Another technology poised to revolutionize the internet, as well as education technology, is machine learning (ML). ML grew out of the study of artificial intelligence modeled on early research of biological intelligence that focused on human pattern-recognition and computational learning theory. With the availability of big data sets generated through cloud computing, machine-learning algorithmic models can use specific inputs to extract patterns out of vast amounts of data that would otherwise be impossible for humans to parse. Over time, with more and more data, these algorithms can learn based on trial and error, and adapt their models to improve accuracy and predict future outcomes.

With machine learning, colleges and universities may one day be able to customize curricula for individual learners; better understand group dynamics and create collaborative learning opportunities that have higher rates of success; intervene at the right time to increase student retention rates; grade complex answers on assessments; create adaptive educational games and virtual tutors; and offer innumerable other insights based on different data modeling that has yet to be excavated. The use of artificial intelligence in K–12 and higher education is predicted to grow 47.5 percent by 2021.[90] Chapters 4 and 5 explain in depth the theories behind modern machine-learning algorithmic design approaches and their applications to advising and counseling, personalized learning, and even teaching.

It's worth remembering the future learners who will someday take this innovative technology for granted. Current learners grew up embedded with the internet and engaging and dynamic smart devices. Many started using these devices as soon as they could swipe—indeed, before they could even talk or walk.

These learners are plugged in almost constantly and expect information to be open and accessible and content to adapt to their needs and personal preferences, curating and suggesting relevant content, much like their media services and shopping platforms. These always-plugged-in learners are extremely comfortable in globalized social networks and digital communities, and many have their baseline of interest and engagement set by short, targeted videos, social networks, interactive apps, and highly motivating digital games, all with built-in reward systems.[91] They are largely visual, rather than textual, learners, having spent more time learning from YouTube videos, web pages, and apps than traditional paper-based textbooks.

These students want learning that's immersive and experiential. They want learning that's targeted to their interests and learning preferences. They take their digital lives with them in their backpack and pocket and expect to be able to learn on demand from anywhere. They move at their own pace. Many will view education as a means to enhance their careers or provide the skills to round out their personal and professional interests.

Some will be motivated and self-directed, while many more may not have the motivation levels to be self-directed learners. They will increasingly expect digital systems to guide and mentor them based on their needs and goals, using insights from their expansive and extensive data footprint that every other app and application uses. These learners will be far more comfortable with, and in many cases dependent on, technology than any previous generation.

Colleges and universities must also confront the reality that learner social structures have been transformed by technology. Robotics and artificial intelligence will automate whole sectors of the job market, such as construction, driving and ride services, and service industries like food, bartending, hospitality, and the retail industry. Amazon has opened retail stores in Chicago and Seattle without any cashiers and plans to open three thousand more.[92]

There's a coffee shop called Cafe X in San Francisco with no employees, just a robotic arm dispensing lattes and cappuccinos. The cafe has 4.5 stars on Yelp. Examples like this will become more and more common, as jobs that once required a small subset of educational skills yield to learners who will design and build these new machines that never tire, never take time off, and maintain consistent quality of service. This displacement of workers is coming, and it will be incumbent on those who can make highly targeted, relevant education broadly available to retrain these workers and connect them with industries in new growing sectors. As Tim Burton's *Willy Wonka* illustrated when a machine replaced Mr. Bucket's job of screwing caps on tubes of toothpaste, Mr. Bucket was later rehired to repair the very machine that had made his job obsolete.

Community colleges and universities must anticipate this coming disruption and redesign curricula to better align learning outcomes with the knowledge and skills that these automated industries need. In addition, the traditional classroom lecture is not the most innovative method to convey knowledge for a larger and growing diverse population owning different learning styles, personality traits, motivation levels, and interests. Copying down everything that comes out the mouth of an instructor is no longer the best way to digest and learn new information.

Moreover, do instructors need an LMS if only a subset of features, such as an in-box and gradebook are being used? We also need to question the value of a diploma.

I love the disciplines of English and history, and earned an undergraduate degree in creative writing and a graduate degree in American studies. However, what would this knowledge base truly convey to an employer like Google? Given the data footprint we produce online, why can't colleges and school do a more nuanced job of explicating my knowledge and experience and help me discover what job roles would be available for any given industry? Having a career services office on campus does not provide the advice and counsel that matches the requirements of the twenty-first-century marketplace. Google's Grow with Google program is already partnered with more than twenty-five community colleges in the United States that uses the Coursera learning platform to place two-year graduates in IT jobs.[93]

In the near future, college and universities will no longer depend on the on-site classrooms to offer the majority of their curricula. Instead, there may be virtual learning spaces where learners join cohorts of other learners who have been dynamically grouped and regrouped to complement their learning styles, interests, hobbies, and activities to work together. Schools may provide physical study spaces for learners to meet in the real world that will be flexible and comfortable to also meet the social needs of learners. In the real world, think whiteboard wallpaper, top Wi-Fi, snacks, and maker spaces that also connect to their virtual spaces to allow learners to connect and collaborate wherever they reside.

The virtual learning space has a game-type knowledge-acquisition system whereby learning earns reward *and* grades that can promote students' academic progress and knowledge to others in both world. These virtual learning spaces may look very similar to game environments, maps, and levels that learners grew up with, offering a world where they can self-discover knowledge based on their personalized curriculum and teacher.

With so much dynamic information to be learned and organized to succeed in the twenty-first century, all learning will be stored in a "digital brain," or personalized artificial cognitive memory map. This is a software system that stores all of the knowledge experiences learners have mastered and helps them organize the knowledge that can demonstrate proficiency to anyone they may share the keys of the map. This map may also provide a record of progress that can be assessed by a third party or another teacher who could suggest supplementary content material or provide different insights into a student learning process. Learners' learning maps will be not just a record of the knowledge experiences that they built throughout their scholastic experience but also a map they will continue to build upon when they start their professional career. And they may use their cognitive learning map collaboratively with others to share, learn, and even recall and teach new information.

While the future is obviously difficult to accurately predict, some variation of this digital learning future may arrive soon. The traditional classroom transmission model of one-to-many may finally shift to a more distributed model where students can learn from anywhere, in different ways, at their own pace (or in concert in a cohort group), using a myriad of technologies driven by AI-assisted personal bots tied to academic achievement and career goals. The instructor's future role will be to develop the next generation of curriculum for this world of data-driven learning, and act as mentor and guide to empower learners to combine traditional learning and their social learning worlds together. Instructors will also need to manage a learners' relationship with technology. Students will always need to learn how to properly research online, avoiding disinformation, and how to properly cite and source digital and physical sources. They will also need to fundamentally teach critical and creative thinking skills that will help learners articulate, debate, and argue points of view.

Because of chronic underfunding in K–12 public schools, community college instructors in particular will need to accept the mantle of not just identifying and filling critical knowledge and skill gaps but also providing a framework that defines meaningful social and nation-state citizenship.

NOTES

1. As quoted by Chris Weller in "A Top Futurist Predicts the Largest Internet Company of 2030 Will Be an Online School," *Business Insider*, December 27, 2016, https://www.businessinsider.com.

2. Docebo, "Elearning Market Trends and Forecast 2017–2021," accessed December 2, 2018, https://eclass.teicrete.gr.

3. Accuray Research, "Global E-Learning Market Analysis and Trends: Industry Forecast to 2025," Research and Markets, September 2017, accessed December 2, 2018, https://www.researchandmarkets.com.

4. Tim Berners-Lee and Mark Fischetti, *Weaving the Web: The Original Design and Ultimate Destiny of the World Wide Web by Its Inventor* (London: Orion Business, 1999).

5. Internet World Stats, "Internet Growth Statistics," accessed December 2, 2018, https://www.internetworldstats.com.

6. Daniel Morat, *Sounds of Modern History: Auditory Cultures in 19th- and 20th-Century Europe* (Oxford, UK: Berghahn Books, 2014), 113.

7. John B. Horrigan, "Online Communities," Pew Research Center, October 31, 2001, http://www.pewinternet.org.

8. A variety of sources are included in the bibliography about online communities. For early online communities and their impact on education, see Hiltz's *Online Communities* (1985). For networked communities, see Rheingold's *Virtual Community* (1993) and Schuler's *New Community Networks* (1996). For office communities, see Sproull and Kiesler's *Connections* (1991).

9. Usenet groups were similar to bulletin boards, organized into topical hierarchies with open areas for discussion.

10. The concept of "communities of practice" in which engagement in informal social practice is the fundamental process by which people learn was first proposed in the book *Situated Learning*, by Jean Lave and Etienne Wenger (published in 1991). Wenger went further with the concept in *Communities of Practice* (published in 1998).

11. For how emoticons could be used to enhance online learning, see Rosemary Lehman's 2006 article "The Role of Emotion in Creating Instructor and Learner Presence in the Distance Education Experience," *Journal of Cognitive Affective Learning* 2, no. 2 (Spring 2006): 12–26.

12. Jae Yun Moon and Lee Sproull, "Essence of Distributed Work: The Case of the Linux Kernel," *First Monday* 5 (2000), https://firstmonday.org.

13. For a 2006 discussion of using blogs to bolster e-learning, see Keith Burnett, "Using Blogger to Get Teachers Started with e-Learning," Seb Schmoller, May 25, 2006, http://fm.schmoller.net.

14. Brett Atwood, "That's Edutainment: Software Developers Provide Education and Entertainment for Young Minds," *Billboard Magazine*, May 13, 1995.

15. Catheryn Cheal, "Student Perceptions of a Course Taught in Second Life," *Innovate: Journal of Online Education* 5, no. 5 (July 1, 2009).

16. See "Education and Nonprofits," Linden Research, accessed June 3, 2018, https://secondlife.com.

17. Ibid.

18. "Global Unit Sales of Current Generation Video Game Consoles from 2008 to 2017 (in Million Units)," Statista, accessed June 3, 2018, https://www.statista.com.

19. For more information, see Jaimie Holguin, "Army Recruits Video Gamers," CBS Evening News, March 30, 2004, https://www.cbsnews.com. As of June 2018, this game is still available to play online at https://www.americasarmy.com/.

20. Entertainment Software Association, "2018 Essential Facts about the Computer and Video Game Industry," accessed June 3, 2018, http://www.theesa.com.

21. Sebastian Deterding, Dan Dixon, Rilla Khaled, and Lennart Nacke, "From Game Design Elements to Gamefulness: Defining 'Gamification,'" in *Proceedings of the 15th International Academic MindTrek Conference: Envisioning Future Media Environments*, 9–15 (New York: ACM, 2011), https://doi.org/10.1145/2181037.2181040.

22. Damien Djaouti, Julian Alvarez, Jean-Pierre Jessel, and Olivier Rampnou, "Origins of Serious Games," in *Serious Games Edutainment Application*, ed. Minhua Ma, Andreas Oikonomou, and Lakhmi C. Jain, 25–43 (New York: Springer, 2011).

23. As quoted by Campus Technology in 2002. For full interview, see "Interactive Media in Education: An Interview with Chris Dede," accessed June 3, 2018, https://campustechnology.com.

24. Henry Jenkins, "Game Theory," *MIT Technology Review*, March 29, 2002.

25. Eric Klopfer, Scot Osterweil, and Katie Salen, *Moving Learning Games Forward: Obstacles, Opportunities and Openness* (Cambridge, MA: Education Arcade, 2009).

26. Joseph Rene Corbeil and Maria Elena Corbeil, "E-Learning: Past Present and Future," in *International Handbook of e-Learning*, vol. 1, ed. Badrul H. Khan and Mohamed Ally, 51–64 (Abingdon, UK: Routledge, 2015).

27. For more information, see "Historical Overview," Researching Virtual Initiatives in Education, accessed June 3, 2018, http://www.virtualschoolsandcolleges.eu.

28. Judith V. Boettcher, "The Changing Landscape of Distance Education: What Micro-Market Segment Is Right for You?" *Syllabus* 15, no. 12 (July 2002): 22–24, 26–27.

29. Dennis Carter, "eSchool News: How to Create a Successful Virtual Campus," UMass Online, last modified January 6, 2009, http://www.umassonline.net.

30. Daniel L. Bennett, Adam R. Lucchesi, and Richard K. Vedder, *For-Profit Higher Education: Growth, Innovation and Regulation* (Washington, DC: Center for College Affordability and Productivity [NJ1], 2010).

31. Emily Hanford, "The Story of the University of Phoenix," American Public Media, accessed June 3, 2018, http://americanradioworks.publicradio.org.

32. "About," Apollo Education Group, accessed June 3, 2018, https://www.apollo.edu.

33. Kenneth R. Weiss, "California Virtual University Has a Collision with Reality," *Los Angeles Times*, April 8, 1999, http://articles.latimes.com.

34. "What Went Wrong with AllLearn?" *University Business*, last modified on June 1, 2006, https://www.universitybusiness.com.

35. Katrina Meyer, "The Closing of the U.S. Open University," *Educause Review*, January 1, 2006.

36. Boettcher, "Changing Landscape."

37. Carter, "eSchool News."

38. Boettcher, "Changing Landscape."

39. Dan Carnevale, "Justice Department Sees No Antitrust Concerns in Blackboard's Plan to Take Over WebCT," *Chronicle of Higher Education* 52, no. 24 (February 7, 2006): 37.

40. For an example, see "Blackboard Patents the LMS," accessed June 3, 2018, https://mfeldstein.com/blackboard_patents_the_lms.

41. Betsy Corcoran, "Blackboard's Jay Bhatt Strikes Up the Brass Band," *EdSurge*, July 23, 2014.

42. Rip Empson, "Education Giant Blackboard Buys MyEdu to Help Refresh Its Brand and Reanimate Its User Experience," *TechCrunch*, January 16, 2014.

43. "US-Based Blackboard Inc Enters Indian Educational Market," *Webindia123*, September 10, 2017, https://career.webindia123.com.

44. Leah Lang and Judith A. Pirani, "The Learning Management System Evolution: CDS Spotlight Report," EDUCAUSE Research Bulletin, May 20, 2014, https://library.educause.edu.

45. Malcolm Brown, Joanne Dehoney, and Nancy Millichap, "The Next Generation Digital Learning Environment: A Report on Research," EDUCAUSE Learning Initiative (ELI), April 27, 2015, https://library.educause.edu.

46. Stacey Harris, "Should You Break Up with Your LMS?" Chief Learning Officer, April 12, 2013, http://www.clomedia.com.

47. For example, see Andrew Chaifetz, "The Learning Management System Is Dead," *Notebowl* (blog), October 18, 2016, https://blog.notebowl.com/the-learning-management-system-is-dead-5bfd966a8154; and Halden Ingwersen, "NGDLE and Why It Won't Replace LMS," *Capterra* (blog), March 29, 2017, https://blog.capterra.com/ngdle-and-why-it-wont-replace-lms/.

48. Mike Rustici, "Opinion: The LMS Isn't Dead . . . Yet." Chief Learning Officer, July 21, 2017, http://www.clomedia.com.

49. Josh Morgan, "How Podcasts Have Changed in Ten Years: By the Numbers," *Medium*, September 2, 2015, https://medium.com.

50. Anita Lee-Post, "e-Learning Success Model: An Information Systems Perspective," *Electronic Journal of e-Learning* 7, no. 1 (2009): 61–70.

51. Elaine Allen and Jeff Seaman, *Making the Grade: Online Education in the United States* (Needham, MA: Sloan Consortium, 2007), https://immagic.com.

52. Glenn C. Altschuler, "College Prep; The E-Learning Curve," *New York Times*, August 5, 2001.

53. Trace Urdan and Cornelia C. Weggen, *Corporate E-Learning: Exploring a New Frontier* (Berwyn, PA: Hambrecht, 2000).
54. Allen and Seaman, *Making the Grade.*
55. "A Brief History of Online Learning," StraighterLine.com, accessed June 3, 2018, https://www.straighterline.com.
56. "Android: Statistics and Facts," Statista, accessed June 3, 2018, https://www.statista.com; "Global Apple iPhone Sales from 3rd Quarter 2007 to 4th Quarter 2018 (in Million Units)," Statista, accessed June 3, 2018, https://www.statista.com.
57. "Hours of Video Uploaded to YouTube Every Minute as of July 2015," Statista, accessed June 3, 2018, https://www.statista.com; "YouTube.com Traffic Statistics," Alexa, accessed June 3, 2018, https://www.alexa.com.
58. Freia Lobo, "My Favorite College Professor Was YouTube," Mashable, May 12, 2017, https://mashable.com.
59. "TED Reaches Its Billionth Video View!" *TEDBlog*, November 13, 2012, https://blog.ted.com/ted-reaches-its-billionth-video-view.
60. Kristina McElheran and Erik Brynjolfsson, "The Rise of Data-Driven Decision Making Is Real but Uneven," *Harvard Business Review*, February 3, 2016, https://hbr.org.
61. "Usage of Traffic Analysis Tools for Websites," W3Techs.com, accessed June 3, 2018, https://w3techs.com.
62. "What Is the History of Khan Academy?" Khan Academy, accessed June 3, 2018, https://khanacademy.zendesk.com.
63. Ibid.
64. Karen Hua, "Education as Entertainment: YouTube Sensations Teaching the Future," *Forbes*, June 23, 2015, https://www.forbes.com.
65. Alison King, "From Sage on the Stage to Guide on the Side," *College Teaching* 41, no. 1 (Winter 1993): 30–35, http://www.jstor.org/stable/27558571.
66. Daniel Shumski, "6 Colleges that Flipped STEM Classrooms," EducationDive, February 20, 2014, https://www.educationdive.com.
67. "Our History," MIT OpenCourseWare, accessed June 3, 2018, https://ocw.mit.edu.
68. Child, One Laptop. "One laptop per child." *Recuperado de http://one.laptop.org* (2009).
69. Anjuli Bhargava, "Our Main Interest Is to Ensure Education Is Available Free to All: Mike Feerick," *Business Standard*, June 11, 2016, http://www.business-standard.com.
70. Steven Leckart, "The Stanford Education Experiment Could Change Higher Learning Forever," *Wired*, March 20, 2012, https://www.wired.com.
71. Eduardo Porter, "A Smart Way to Skip College in Pursuit of a Job," *New York Times*, June 17, 2014, https://www.nytimes.com.
72. Rebecca A. Clay, "SMOCs: The Next 'Great Adventure,'" *American Psychological Association* 46, no. 7 (July/August 2015), http://www.apa.org.
73. Henry Kronk, "Goldman Sachs Launches Their 10,000 Women Entrepreneurial Course as a Coursera MOOC," *Elearning Inside*, May 22, 2018, https://news.elearninginside.com.
74. M. Mitchell Waldrop, "Massive Open Online Courses, aka MOOCs, Transform Higher Education and Science," *Scientific American*, March 13, 2013, https://www.scientificamerican.com.
75. Jeffery R. Young, "Blackboard Announces New MOOC Platform," *Chronicle of Higher Education*, July 10, 2013, https://www.chronicle.com.
76. For more information, visit http://www.groupmooc.com.
77. Will Oremus, "University Suspends Online Classes after More than Half the Students Fail," *Slate : Future Tense*, July 19, 2013, https://slate.com.
78. René F. Kizilcec and Emily Schneider, "Motivation as a Lens to Understand Online Learners: Toward Data-Driven Design with the OLEI Scale," *ACM Transactions on Computer-Human Interaction* (*TOCHI*) 22, no. 2 (April 2015).
79. Brown, Dehoney, and Millichap, "Next Generation."
80. "xAPI Background and History," Advanced Distributed Learning Initiative, accessed June 3, 2018, https://www.adlnet.gov.
81. Josh Bersin, *HR Technology Disruptions for 2018: Productivity, Design, and Intelligence Reign*, Deloitte Development, 2017, accessed June 3, 2018, http://marketing.bersin.com.

82. Lindsay McKenzie, "The 100K Club," *Inside Higher Ed*, April 23, 2018, https://www.insidehighered.com.
83. Doug Lederman, "Who Is Studying Online (and Where)," *Inside Higher Ed*, January 5, 2018, https://www.insidehighered.com.
84. McKenzie, "The 100K Club."
85. Ibid.
86. Lederman, "Who Is Studying Online."
87. Christopher P. Jennings, "SimCity 1900: Virtuality and Spectatorship at the Turn of the Twentieth Century," master's thesis, University of Texas, 2000.
88. "Oculus Education Partners with Research Institutions to Explore VR's Impact on Learning Outcomes," *Oculus Blog*, November 15, 2017, https://www.oculus.com/blog/oculus-education-partners-with-research-institutions-to-explore-vrs-impact-on-learning-outcomes.
89. "Expeditions," App Store Preview, accessed June 3, 2018, https://itunes.apple.com.
90. Jim Goodell, Liz Glowa, and Brandt Redd, "The Implications of Gartner's Top 10 Tech Trends of 2018 for Education," Getting Smart, February 2, 2018, http://www.gettingsmart.com.
91. Goldie Blumenstyk, "Should the Future of Education Include a 'Personalized Prescription' of Video Games?" *Chronicle of Higher Education*, July 5, 2017, https://www.chronicle.com.
92. Matt McFarland, "I Spent 53 Minutes in Amazon Go and Saw the Future of Retail," *CNN Business*, October 3, 2018, https://www.cnn.com.
93. Melissa Locker, "Google Is Working with Community Colleges to Train Future IT Professionals," Fast Company, June 25, 2018, https://www.fastcompany.com.

Chapter Three

Big Data

Big data is going to transform how we live, how we work and how we think. It is going to help us manage our careers and lead lives of satisfaction and hope and happiness and health. So, we're going to need to be careful and take big data and adjust it for our needs, our very human needs. We have to be the master of this technology, not its servant.

—Kenneth Cukier, data editor for the *Economist*, in a 2014 TED Talk[1]

On April 5, 2017, an unknown young adult named Carter Wilkerson tweeted a question to the Twitter account of the Wendy's restaurant chain. He asked, "How many retweets for a free year of chicken nuggets?" Wendy's replied, "18 million," and Carter responded, "Consider it done." He retweeted the exchange to his then 517 followers with "HELP ME PLEASE. A MAN NEEDS HIS NUGGS."

On May 2, 2017, Wilkerson's plea was retweeted 3.6 million times, bolstered by social media support from Google, Amazon, Microsoft, newspaper articles, and blog postings. The stunt landed him television show appearances and even an Oscar invitation.[2] Typing in the Google search engine "Carter Wilkerson" points to 2.7 million matches, which includes all types of media, cross-referenced and indexed files from supporters, and critics alike. Besides being a case study in waiting about the potency of social media as a medium to engage users about banal personal subject matter (perhaps the strength to attract participation lies in the topic's banality), this example is also a treatise in the complex generation of big data.

According to IBM, every day consumers and machines generate 2.5 quintillion bytes of data, and the number will have risen by the time you read this.[3] Most of this big data is stored by the world's largest marketing firms, Google and Facebook, and the e-commerce giant Amazon. It is estimated that Google alone now stores more than ten to fifteen exabytes of data (one exabyte = one million terabytes). This data includes all our search queries, emails (Google Mail), drawings (Google Draw), prose and poetry (Google Docs), videos (YouTube), and travel habits and destinations (Google Maps).[4]

However, for Google to make any sense of all this big data and monetize their products, they developed new artificial intelligence algorithms to mine these large data sets for patterns and anomalies that may produce beneficial business information. In Google's case, they use this information to display targeted links from paid advertisers to high-potential customers and lease demographic profiles to third-party retailers. Hence the foundational issue with big data: how do we make sense of and use the vast amounts of data sets available for a useful purpose?

Just one example to consider is how we might be able to analyze videos and pictures of a natural disaster from Twitter feeds, texts, and emails from someone actually experiencing the disaster so we can also determine their location, their condition, and if they are in need of rescue. Perhaps if first responders could access and analyze the live Twitter feeds, texts, and mobile call content from witnesses of an active terrorist attack, police could respond faster, and emergency medical personnel could respond to injuries more quickly.

The HACE Theorem states that big data starts with large-volume heterogeneous, autonomous sources with distributed and decentralized control, and seeks to explore complex and evolving relationships among data.[5] In other words, big data is extremely complex, and the nature of the sheer number of structured and unstructured data points makes it difficult, but not impossible, to discover patterns, configurations, and connections *among* data sets that hold the true power within and that may reveal truly useful information.

This chapter outlines the definition and uses of big data in terms of how they can be applied to teaching and learning. It also discusses ways in which big data collation and analytics can uncover new insights into the learning process. The new field of learning engineering is also briefly discussed. Learning engineering is an applied-research discipline that constructs new software innovations (based on the research results from data scientists and learning scientists) to improve the learning process. This chapter concludes by examining my aggregate student learning (ASL) methodology that incorporates learners' social and personal experiences with their academic performance in order to build a conglomerate personal learning matrix that may be leveraged to provide personalized learning solutions in the future.

Although first appearing in a Silicon Graphics (SGI) slide deck presented by John Mashey in 1998,[6] the term "big data" was applied liberally in the late 1990s primarily due to the unprecedented amount of computer-generated data being produced by the ambitious international human-genome-sequencing and mapping project led by the National Institutes of Health's (NIH) National Human Genome Research Institute (NHGRI). Since a single human genome has between twenty and twenty-five thousand genes made up of more than three million based pairs, sequencing and mapping just a few human genomes produced thousands of petabytes of data, requiring thousands of servers to store the genetic codes.[7] Analysis of the genome code exponentially multiplied the required data storage sizes, and it required the creation of new pattern-recognition software and database algorithmic models to provide researchers with the data they needed to gain insights into our individual genetic predisposition.

Big data, sometimes referred to as *giant data*, is distinct not just because of its size but also because it draws its size from potential relationships between multiple, distinct structured *and* unstructured sets of data. Historically, the field of statistics has been employed to study data trends and patterns from small and structured domain-specific data sets. As data sets became larger, but still domain related and structured, the design and implementation of mathematical computer algorithms were designed to comb and sift large data sets to discover useful information. Big data incorporates both structured and unstructured data sets from multiple and disparate knowledge domains. Connecting nonrelational data sets from multiple domains poses quite a challenge to determine relevant relationships and useful information.

Using the big data introduction example at the beginning of this chapter, Google may mine a Gmail account, a Google Doc account, and a Google Draw document around the same time-stamped period and discover relationships between all three data sets. Patterns between the three may disclose that a user is working on a home landscaping project. The primary user sketches a layout where ornamentals and bushes may be planted by using Google Draw and then uses Google Doc to type out multiple lists of specific plants, bushes, and flowers for her friends to add their comments, suggestions, and critiques. The next time the user searches for "nurseries," Google may recommend at the top of the search results local and national nurseries and landscaping companies that match the criteria compiled from mining the data of the three data sets as one.

Another way to understand big data can also be summarized by the following characteristics:[8]

- *Volume.* Big data refers to the overall sheer number of data sets being created every day, from research labs, governments, think tanks, entertainment, traditional media, the web, and social media platforms.
- *Variety.* Big data involves different types of data, that is, text (in all languages), numbers, symbols, graphs, images, video, and sounds.
- *Velocity.* The dynamic nature and quickness by which big data is generated is unprecedented and involves the challenge of parsing and processing instantaneously generated data.

- *Variability*. Sometimes referred to as veracity, big data is known for the inconsistent nature of the quality, inconsistency, or incompleteness of the data.
- *Complexity*. Another characteristic of big data is the vast amounts of structured, unstructured, and incomplete data sets that must be parsed, processed, linked, analyzed, and mined for value and usefulness.

In the biosciences, big data allowed us to map our individual genetic predisposition to certain diseases, so we can now adjust our lifestyle decisions for a healthier life. Similarly, new education-focused software platforms now generate big data sets of student learning styles, tendencies, and characteristics that may expose the predisposition of a learner's cognitive abilities and aptitude. These data sets may also allow researchers to predict student intervention methodologies, predict individual academic support mechanisms, and tailor counseling services to help guide the educator and researcher together to sequence and "map" the road to academic success for every learner.

DATA EQUITY

Although we touch on some of the systemic bias found in the management and use of data in academic research and the commercial education technology vendor market at the conclusion of this chapter, we'll discuss the topic of data equity in this section. Data equity, defined as the unbiased and impartial use of data in low-impact and high-impact studies, is of major concern in teaching and learning research. Biased selection, inclusion, exclusion, and interpretation of data that may taint and tilt major research studies concerning the efficacy of this or that learning platform, pedagogical approaches, or adaptive learning solutions are not uncommon.

One powerful case study that disclosed how data bias and prejudiced data interpretation occurs in a school system was conducted by Vicki Park, Alan Daly, and Alison Guerra in a 2012 case study titled "Strategic Framing: How Leaders Craft the Meaning of Data Use for Equity and Learning."[9] In this study, the researchers discovered how the divide among a school district superintendent's office, a high school's administration, and a school's faculty sensemaking (shared collective experience) but separate framework influenced the interpretation of the same research data, and failed to resolve the inequity of academic resources available to advance low-income Hispanic learners in a California public school. Although everyone's heart was in the right place, and everyone agreed the data demonstrated that the school needed to increase academic opportunities for the Hispanic population, the different frames of reference influenced and motivated by additional beholden constituencies distorted data-driven decision-making and ultimately didn't provide the resources to rectify the inequitable environment. So even though everyone in the system chain had access to the same data that showed an inequitable situation, the superintendent feared the school board and the press, the principal feared the parents and the superintendent, and the teachers feared the principal, resulting in decision-making stasis.

Another recent publication that looks at the equitable use of data is offered by Cathy O'Neil's *Weapons of Math Destruction*. Although there are many broad assumptions made and leaps of faith required in her text, she does outline several crucial examples of how the inequitable use of personal data negatively affects our daily lives, and especially the lives of low-income populations. She outlines the example of how a college student on leave with a medical issue struggled to secure a part-time retail job based on one taking of the Big Five personality test, a test that he scored in a predetermined range that the retailer predetermined was unfit for employment. All the other retailers in his region he applied to for a job used the same test, resulting in not one part-time job offer—for a Vanderbilt college student with almost perfect SAT scores.[10]

Another power example that O'Neil offers is of the misuse of data to train the new machine-learning models that derive e-scores: algorithms used to determine insurance rates, credit card interest offers, and even how long a call center person operation will put you on hold. E-scores now encompass not just Earl Isaac and Bill Fair (FICO) credit scores, listing your payments history and debt to determine credit worthiness, but also shopping habits, health status, transportation destinations, residential home value, and quality of nearby schools and neighborhood crime statistics—all to infer a wealth and risk factor.[11] That she also provides examples of employers that force their employees to provide scheduled personal health data to feed a machine-learning algorithm in order to qualify for lower health-care premiums is beyond disturbing.[12]

Although chapters 4 and 5 provide an explanation and overview of artificial intelligence (AI) and its potential application to advance and improve upon the practice of teaching and learning, we need to address the importance of unbiased, impartial, and "pure" data use in training AI models in this section. Data is the blood of the AI body, required to train AI algorithms about what is a baseline, preferable outcome, wrong outcome, or just an acceptable outcome when programmed to accomplish a certain task. A machine-learning model is just a decision network, in which the decision logic is obtained by algorithms fed or ingested by data. Although a programmer may have explicitly designed the logic of the algorithms in a machine-learning model, the model implicitly makes decisions after its creation.

The output of a machine-learning model is a task prediction, and the prediction can be altered based on input decisions made from the programmer, or it can learn by itself from successes and failures originally identified in its logic structure. In essence, it can reprogram itself to find the best solution to an assigned task. Its unsupervised learning speed and adaptation may surpass human learning, depending on the hardware and network architecture.

The success or failure of this process, or the precision or the accuracy of the predictive output, depends on the quality or "purity" of the data that feeds the model. Once the unsupervised model begins the training process, one cannot actually examine how the input and output data is internally being labeled and reprogramming the initial layers and nodes. So even if the original machine-learning model architecture was pure and unbiased, external training data sets with nefarious purposes could distort and alter the model's original intent.

This is the vulnerable soft spot for AI. For what standards and laws do we hold a machine-learning model accountable when it recommends a particular bank credit card and associated interest rate to a particular demographic? What about a model that may diagnose a disease and treatment plan for an impoverished single mother of five with no insurance? How do we ensure transparency when a machine-learning model recommends admission to an elite school for one student over another more deserving student with higher test scores and greater accomplishments? Or how do we ensure the unbiased output from a machine-learning model that recommends to judges the likelihood of recidivism from an inmate up for parole? What were the criteria that originally trained the model?

In addition, as outlined toward the end of chapter 4, new machine-learning tools will soon be able to store human semantic and episodic memory experiences in an artificial cognitive memory map, mimicking a user's biological cognitive memory model. Here the sights, ambient sounds, and eventually smells may be captured alongside actual learning experiences. A learner could be lured with episodic memory triggers to recall long ago long-term-memory-stored information and experiences. The algorithms that generate these cohort data sets, and the stowage of such in a convoluted architecture, may represent the next generation of big data trepidation. Not just the concern about the use of pure data at the front end to train these models, but also the ability to securitize these personal and intimate experiences at the back end may be of equal concern.

Logic confirms since humans are biased, and humans code and train the machine-learning algorithms, the output from the models will be biased. Therefore, with this logic, we must find ways to counter inherent bias.

We can start with the development of a data-equity framework, an augmented and expanded version of the Family Educational Rights and Privacy Act (FERPA) for data equity. In this way students would have the right to inspect and review their machine-learning data sets and request corrections, similarly to their current school records. Maya Gupta, a lead researcher at

GoogleAI, is working on a project named Glassbox (as opposed to black box) that seeks to build new types of machine-learning algorithms that are more opaque and that can smooth out and disregard the data outliers that may represent human bias in the training process.[13]

David Gunning, at the Defense Advanced Research Projects Agency, is working on a project called Explainable Artificial Intelligence that allows one to peer into the machine-learning model black box through an explainable user interface to observe a translation of the labels, nodes, and layers to detect potential bias, and even to make incremental changes, that would be open and transparent, to the training process.[14] These examples represent a few of the methods being explored to combat potential data inequity, but the introduction of a new data-equity framework, initiated either federally or at the state level for education, should still be mandated prior to any large-scale adoption of AI in teaching and learning.

DATA SCIENCE

Commonly understood as an expansion of the fields of mathematical statistics and data analytics, data science is the application of scientific study that employs historical and new quantitative and qualitative methodologies to solve specific problems and anticipate outcomes from very large and mostly unstructured data sets. An unstructured data set is defined as data that is not easily structured, such as unnatural language, slang, and even audio and video files. These data sets are critical to decipher and classify today within big data schemas, being common formats encountered in social media, entertainment, business, and education platforms and communication channels.

John Tukey, a pioneer of data analytics, predicted the role of the data scientist in his seminal 1962 publication "The Future of Data Analysis":

> Special Growth Areas. Can we identify *some* of the areas of data analysis which today offer unusual challenges, unusual possibilities of growth? [Unstructured data sets] . . . the development of organized techniques of dealing with (these) "outliers," . . . or "large deviations" (from our current models such as unnatural language and slang) has lagged far behind both the needs, and the possibilities presently open to us for meeting these needs.[15]

Tukey already foresaw the limitations of traditional statistics to manage and produce useful outcomes from large and unstructured data sets, calling for a new expanded process and discipline (data mining) to overcome the shortfalls. In 1996, Usama Fayyad, Gregory Piatetsky-Shapiro, and Padhraic Smyth wrote in "From Data Mining to Knowledge Discovery in Databases,"

> Historically, the notion of finding useful patterns in data has been given a variety of names, including data mining, knowledge extraction, information discovery, information harvesting, data archeology, and data pattern processing. . . . In our view, KDD [Knowledge Discovery in Databases] refers to the overall process of discovering useful knowledge from data, and data mining refers to a particular step in this process.[16]

In the above quote, Fayyad and colleagues infer their KDD methodology may presage the new field of data science, and that the process of mining data for usefulness is just one step within the overall evolution.

Finally, Bill Cleveland's 2007 "Data Science: An Action Plan for Expanding the Technical Areas of the Field of Statistics" quantifies the field and proposes that its place resides not within the business school or mathematics department but in the academy alongside computer science and other sciences, where "departments of data science should contain faculty members who devote their careers to advances in computing with data and who form partnerships with computer scientists."[17]

However, in order for the application of the scientific study of data to produce value, usefulness, or any relevance, scholarly domain knowledge is also crucial. An example of this is an engineer employing scientific methods to three year's worth of data comprising quiz and test grades from a high school U.S. Civil War course, in an effort to discover learner-type patterns of academic success. A Civil War history professor employing the same scientific methods to the data will not just see outcomes as numbers but also may determine patterns of success or failure related to the actual quiz and test content, perhaps inconsistencies between the test questions and the historical period described in the course textbook.

Shelly Farnham, a research team leader at Microsoft's Fuse Lab, was quoted in the 2013 paper "Educating the Next Generation of Data Scientists": "One of the challenges is that data science is not agnostic of domain. For example, when we are looking for people, interns or full-time people on our team, we definitely look for people who have experience analyzing data, but they also should be deeply engaged with the topic. . . . I think that the domain knowledge is a very important aspect of what we are looking for."[18]

In addition to domain knowledge, a data scientist requires analytical skills and diagnostic expertise in order to correctly and accurately decipher, quantify, and then mine big data sets for relevant and useful patterns of information to be employed to accomplish a task. In education, someone that possesses both the domain knowledge of disciplines, such as educational psychology, instructional or curriculum design, learning technology, and the new field of learning science, and statistical and analytical skills would be an ideal educational data scientist.

Within the practice of teaching and learning, a one semester undergraduate course alone produces massive data sets, including the syllabus, assigned books and articles, learning outcomes, evaluation matrix, assessment instruments, assessment and evaluation results, student evaluations, attendance records, course forum chat data, office hour meetings transcripts and notes, SIS system information, and student and teacher email exchanges. Even the best educator doesn't possess the skills or time to collate, qualify, and quantify all these data points in order to provide detailed answers as to why Mateo's academic scores increased 78 percent from quiz 1 to quiz 5, and why Elizabeth's academic performance dropped 47 percent during the same time frame. We as educators may determine the increases or decreases were the result of absences, limited forum participation, or limited participation or engagement during class time.

An education data scientist may discover within the same data points that Mateo's scholarship finally came through and that he shared in the forum that his father's cancer is in remission. We might find that Elizabeth shared with other students in her forum chats that she is the first in her family to go to college, and to pay tuition she must work overtime and therefore keeps missing classes.

As third-generation online and in-class learning platforms are being deployed to offer greater educational opportunities to a more diverse student body, more and more data points are available for data scientists to exploit to help us better understand the teaching and learning process. The educational data scientists will be crucial to help us not just better understand the context of these data points but also provide the science to help us make corrective changes to improve upon the future practice of teaching and learning.

LEARNING SCIENCE

Humans acquire knowledge (semantic memory), retain the knowledge-acquisition experience (episodic memory), and can retrieve the stored knowledge to a greater degree and depth than any other species. Humans also have the ability to contrast and compare acquired knowledge, possessing the ability of abstract and nonlinear thought that may manifest as creativity or originality of thought. Humans are also the only species that has developed sophisticated frameworks and structures to improve and enrich the knowledge-acquisition process, the learning process.

Humans have also solely created the discipline of education, the profession of teaching, and the concept of learning spaces of schools and colleges. Although only theories exist that can definitively explain human learning, and indeed the origin of human intelligence, insights resulting from the study of infant cerebral cortex and prefrontal cortex development have provided many clues.[19]

During the first year of life, new neural pathways are created within the cerebral cortical areas of the human brain generated from external sensory stimuli, such as sounds, smells, tactile experiences, and social interactivity, all essential for what we later refer to in chapter 4 as declarative memory experiences. This sensory processing first occurs very early in life, and the cortical modules continue to develop and forge more and more circuits and pathways, as it grows in size and connectivity to adult size during puberty. The prefrontal cortex continues to develop and mature well into adulthood and beyond.[20]

The study of early human brain development, approached slightly differently from various research fields such as psychology, psychiatry, neuroscience, education, and data science, has greatly informed the field of computational artificial intelligence. Babies and young children use pattern recognition and discrimination, both aurally and visually early on from external stimuli, to learn language rules and the concept of cause and effect.[21] From parental training, babies also use frequency and amplitude filters and distribution to learn phonemes, syllables, words, and meaning.[22] In fact, one could trace early and current breakthrough studies of child language and social learning: early human intelligence and social understanding that parallel breakthroughs and advancements of machine-learning artificial intelligence algorithmic designs and applications.

Learning science is a relatively new interdisciplinary subset of the data science rubric and is focused specifically on the analysis of multidisciplinary data sets than can shed light and understanding of how we learn. Learning science is a most difficult area of research because it includes research data produced by traditional science disciplines, such as neuroscience and neurobiology, but also includes many areas of social science research such as sociology, psychology, and education. Through all of these collaborating disciplines, learning science also strives to provide new and improved methodologies of teaching, and influence and improve the overall practice of education. Figure 3.1 depicts all the knowledge domains that influence and compose the new learning science discipline.

The new science of learning is focused on using scientific methodologies to better discover how humans learn and acquire knowledge, and how the art and craft of teaching transfers knowledge.

Sometimes these discoveries are gathered from running controlled, randomized, or blind studies, as one would see in both medical and social scholarly studies.

Other times, discoveries emerge from testing assumptions. Learning science draws on general research conclusions about the human biological knowledge-acquisition process, and then draws on specific demographic

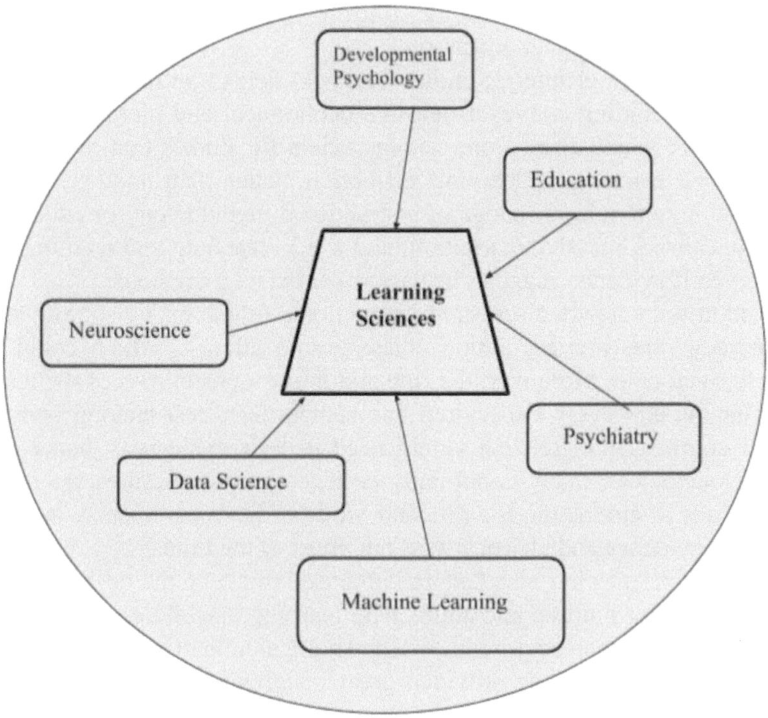

Figure 3.1. Knowledge domains of learning science

studies so that the correct pedagogical method can be tailored for each discipline taught to each unique learner. Understanding the general process of biological knowledge acquisition and then the uniqueness of each learner's acquisition *style* also allows for customized academic intervention processes and methods: better known as personalized learning.

The challenge of course in reexamining figure 3.1 is that the learning science discipline combines both the traditional sciences and the social sciences, a most messy research assignment. Historically, the two sciences divide in scientific study approach and methodology, as the social sciences are notoriously imprecise as they primarily focus on the sociological dimensions of human activity.

One of the most important outcomes of learning science research is not just customized strategies and tools for learning but also the efficacy of such strategies and tools. Regardless of the features and tools a learning solution may offer with claims to improve the learning process, learning scientists are charged with determining whether the claims are sincere and accurate with evidence-based outcomes. The learning scientist must conduct evidence-based research to prove the efficacy of such claims. However, in some cases, the learning sciences have had to confront resistance to conducting such studies in K–12 and higher education.

As discussed in chapter 1, unlike scientific fields, the field of education, with its longstanding conveyer-belt-like economical and hierarchical structures in place, shies away from running scientific studies that may demonstrate if one teaching or learning method is better than another. For that revelation may require a change of instructional methodology or educational practice, causing massive disruption, and a new teaching and learning paradigm, even if evidence suggests its value over existing methods.

In addition, a newly discovered instructional model may also pose standing privacy rules and regulation challenges to address, which could take years to overcome. Moreover, the role and the responsibilities of the teacher may change, and every curriculum and standardized test-making body and teacher compensation scheme would need to be reevaluated—hence resistance. Nonetheless, many community colleges and universities are making great strides in embracing the role and value of learning science, as slowly but surely evidence and efficacy wins out, most of the time.

Learning science has also had an immense impact on the design of learning strategies for children and adults with learning disabilities. Better understanding how children acquire knowledge alongside their social, empathetic, and emotional growth has provided great insights into designing effective techniques to foster successful learning strategies and intervention methodologies for learners that fall within the autism spectrum. For example, children with high-spectrum autism have difficulty with loud and unpredictable social learning environments. Controlling the dynamic range and sound/noise predictability is one example of a personalized learning strategy a learning scientist may recommend.

Another personalized learning strategy for both traditional and special learners that learning science has advocated is adaptive learning. Adaptive learning is generally understood to be a quasi-personalized learning strategy that adapts the content being studied to a learner's knowledge level and learning style. Although some type of adaptive learning strategies has existed in an educational setting since the early twentieth century, only recently, with the advent of learning science to help prove its efficacy in some environments, has adaptive learning become widespread as a recognized personal learning methodology.[23]

In the twenty-first century, adaptive learning is primarily offered through scalable education cloud-based platforms and is designed for specific courses and learner types within pre- or postsecondary schools. In addition, artificial intelligence (AI) is now commonly deployed as the engine of many adaptive learning platforms, used to finely detect and track a student's academic success rate from an initial base assessment, and either suggest or provide more challenging content along the learning pathway. If a student is struggling, the engine can back up, determine the knowledge gaps within the content, and reinforce the same content within an overall academic experience.

One example of an AI-driven adaptive platform in wide use is McGraw-Hill's ALEKS, offering extensive mathematics courses for K–12 and higher education, as well as business and science courses.[24] At log-in, ALEKS presents a student with twenty to thirty initial assessment questions, each one based on the results of the previous. Through the assessment process, ALEKS determines base knowledge and potential aptitude to learn the desired course content. ALEKS then "adapts" the course content and assessment instruments tailored to each learner's acquisition speed and knowledge level comprehension rate.

Per the ALEKS website, "To ensure that topics learned are retained in long term memory, ALEKS periodically reassesses the student, using results to adjust the student's knowledge of the course. Because students are forced to show mastery through mixed-question assessments that cannot be predicted, mastery of the ALEKS course means true mastery of the course."[25] Another example is D2L's Brightspace Core, offering intelligent adaptive courses and course tracks for K–12, higher education, and even customizable corporate training content.[26] Brightspace Core offers the same customizable content engine for individualized learners but adds awards and certificates to recognize learning milestones, a combination of adaptive and gamification learning strategies.

Although adaptive learning as a personalized learning methodology has not been embraced as a panacea by all educators, the advent of AI combined with more granular-level subject-matter content offers greater potential for its success, both as a teaching system and as a learner diagnostic tool to measure competence and aptitude.

Another semi-personalized learning strategy that is common in corporate training is competency-based education (CBE). CBE is generally understood as an approach to learning and teaching that clearly defines subject-matter competencies that a learner must acquire and achieve mastery in before moving on to a new set of competencies or to receive a credential. CBE models focus on the student acquiring, and demonstrating mastery of, specific knowledge skills and abilities, rather than on the traditional model's focus on "seat time," that is, how many classes in a term a student must attend to receive credit regardless of his or her mastery level.

Within an ideal CBE framework, curriculum content and matching competencies are clearly defined and transparent. Learners acquire and demonstrate knowledge and skills with proactive support and guidance from teachers, advisors, and learning coaches by engaging in learning activities, exercises, and experiences that align with specific programmatic competencies.[27] If a learner struggles with competency acquisition, an additional activity or experience is assigned that repeats or reemphasizes that same content but perhaps in a different context. CBE models appear most frequently in trade-focused schools and corporate training companies that are purely job focused. This strategy does offer a personalized learning approach but is also designed to lower costs *and* accelerate the time-to-graduate generally to meet workforce demands.

Figure 3.2 provides an example of a competency-based educational framework that demonstrates examples of subject-matter competency goals and content learning reinforcement through additional exercises.

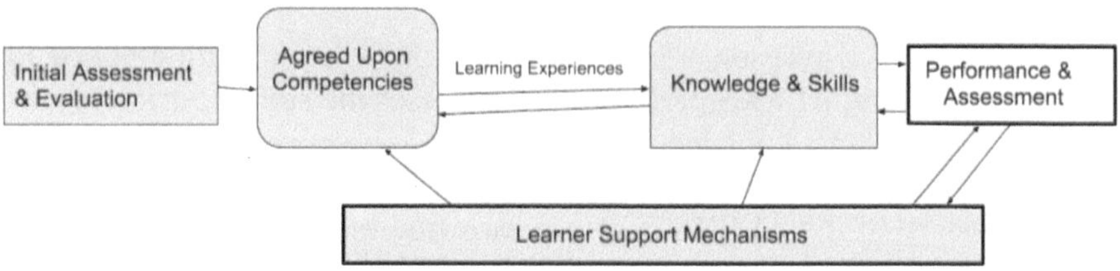

Figure 3.2. Example of a competency-based educational framework

Within a CBE framework, a learner is guided by a competency rubric with clearly defined assessment methodologies, learning goals, objectives, support mechanisms, and continuing assessment. Figure 3.3 outlines a typical CBE rubric devised by Jackie Krause, Laura Portolese Dias, and Chris Schedler.[28] This rubric aligns the student and teacher from the outset of a training or learning experience ensuring that the expectations of both are clearly understood and agreed upon.

Assessment & Evaluation

Assessments measure mastery of competencies with specific evaluation criteria.

IM = Improvement Needed EF = Effective, EX = Exemplary	IM	EF	EX	Notes/Recommendations
1. Assessments are rigorous and valid measures of learners' mastery of competencies				
2. Requirements are clearly stated for achieving mastery-level on competencies				
3. Assessment rubrics provide detailed and specific guidelines and criteria for evaluation				
4. Learners have opportunities for ongoing assessment and practice with mentor feedback				
5. Expectations for evaluator's response time and feedback on assessments are clearly stated				

Competencies & Learning Activities

Competencies and learning objectives are measurable and aligned with learning activities.

IM = Improvement Needed EF = Effective, EX = Exemplary	IM	EF	EX	Notes/Recommendations
6. Competencies and learning objectives identify measurable knowledge, skills, and abilities to be demonstrated by learners				
7. Learning activities support achievement of competencies and learning objectives				
8. Instructions on how to complete learning activities and meet competencies are clear				
9. Learning activities provide opportunities for interaction with content for active learning				

Learner Support

Course facilitates access to support services essential to student success.

IM = Improvement Needed EF = Effective, EX = Exemplary	IM	EF	EX	Notes/Recommendations

Figure 3.3.

10. Instructions are provided on how to access technical support services			
11. Instructions are provided on how to obtain accessibility support services			
12. Instructions are provided on how to access academic support services (e.g., Library, Writing Center, Tutoring)			
13. Instructions are provided on how and when to contact mentor for instructional support			

Figure 3.4.

These two learning-science-supported examples above represent just a few successful learning strategies deployed in the past decade. Learning science helps refine, fine-tune, and improve many learning strategies through research outcomes and efficacy studies; although not successful for every learner, it's just enough to prove these strategies work sometimes under certain circumstances, and for certain populations, in certain environments. Remember, learning science is a combination of the traditional sciences and the social sciences—the art and sciences of learning, and the art and craft of teaching.

It was only in 2002, when the Bush administration established the Institute for Education Sciences within the Department of Education, that learning science was legitimately accepted as a formal member of the academy's data science and social sciences evolving domain tree. Since then, data derived from the study of the practice of teaching and learning has been considered on equal par to the data collected for any other social science investigation. The field of learning science as an academic discipline to pursue and study within schools of education in higher education was launched, and the quality and quantity of learning science scholarly research since produced is respected and occasionally replicated equally to the other social science research findings around the globe.

LEARNING ENGINEERING

Also at the crux of the future of teaching and learning is learning engineering. In the last section, we reviewed the concept of learning science. What's the difference between learning science and learning engineering? Let's go back in time for insights into the answer.

Considered the first engineer, Imhotep was the chief builder of Pharaoh Djoser and designed and supervised the first Egyptian pyramid in 2600 BC. Although little is known about his techniques, it is believed he applied rudimentary mathematics to available materials to build a long-lasting structure to house the remains of his pharaoh upon his death, and hopefully provide a pathway from him to the afterlife. Having no models to copy, his building method was undoubtedly trial and error until he was able to discover the perfect balance of three equal sides of stones and molded bricks, layered and displaced slightly inward, that would lean upon each other when reaching the top—a perfect geometric shape that could withstand the stresses of time.

The first scientist, however, is recognized not for his discoveries per se but for his formation of the earliest scientific method used for discovery. The tenth-century Mesopotamian Ibn al-Haytham was indeed recognized as the originator of the study of modern optics, astronomy, and mathematical science, but it was his advocacy for using a process of experiments—a scientific method leading to a conclusion—that gave rise to modern science that he is recognized for today.[29]

Although the roles of engineers and scientists are different, they are intrinsically connected. To build a safe and efficient airliner, an aerospace engineer needs to work hand in hand with a materials scientist. To build the next battery to safely and successfully power the next mobile device, electrical engineers must collaborate with chemists. Indeed, to solve problems in education, and design, build, and test the next generation of teaching and learning solutions, learning scientists and learning engineers must work together too.

Just as the sciences and engineering disciplines tend to be housed in different buildings on traditional higher education campuses due to their different approaches to invention and discovery, so too are the differences between learning science and learning engineering.[30] Although many fields in both buildings are merging ever so slowly, with emerging majors such as chemical engineering, biological statistics, and genetic engineering, the fact remains that the "act of engineering" doesn't necessarily require the use of scientific method to build a new solution.

The act of engineering is the process of applying test results from scientific experiments (math, physics, or chemistry) to build a new solution to solve an existing problem; an engineer solves problems. "A learning engineer is someone who draws from evidence-based information about human development, including learning, and seeks to apply these results at scale, within contexts, to create affordable, reliable, data-rich learning environments," says Bror Saxberg, one of the leading flag carriers for the need of learning engineers, and vice president of learning science at the Chan Zuckerberg Initiative.[31]

Learning engineers apply learning science outputs, results, and conclusions to build new teaching and learning solutions to solve known teaching and learning problems. The solutions may manifest themselves as a new classroom arrangement of tables and chairs; a "flipped" classroom where learning is done at home but applied in the classroom; or a new digital learning platform that offers artificial intelligence tutoring or advising intervention for online learners.

In December 2017, the (international) Institute of Electrical and Electronics Engineers (IEEE), the standards-bearer and sanctioning body of all things engineering since 1963, approved the IEEE IC Industry Consortium on Learning Engineering (IEEE ICICLE) with the following mission:

> The past 20 years have seen the emergence of many new tools, products, media formats, and technologies meant to support learning, education, and training. In recent years, the use of technology to support the way people learn in school, on the job, and on their own has accelerated dramatically. These technologies include learning management systems, MOOCS, authoring tools, mobile learning environments, serious games, simulations, applications of virtual and augmented reality, learning record stores, open badges and micro-credentials, pedagogical agents enabled by artificial intelligence, online laboratories, and much more. There is a significant engineering aspect to the development and deployment of these learning technologies that is supported by a portfolio of existing and planned standards, but that has yet to coalesce as an identified field of endeavor. Learning Science research has generated many of these new technologies and explored their potential benefits. . . . Motivated by the need to provide this guidance, ICICLE was established by leading organizations across the world.[32]

As of mid-2018, fifty-six international companies, colleges, universities, and organizations have joined the ICICLE initiative, including my Virginia Serious Game Institute and Cognitive Technologies and Deep Learning Lab for Teaching and Learning. As the value and significance of learning engineering starts to take shape, both as a recognized discipline and as a profession, expect impactful scholarship and inventions to begin to permeate and transform teaching and learning, fed by the increasing knowledge breakthroughs and discoveries from the learning sciences. There is a great need for community colleges and universities to establish learning science and learning engineering tracks, minors, and degrees to fill an acute void in educational practice.

Most teaching and learning platforms are offered by tech vendors with little in-house learning science or learning engineering expertise. Most colleges and universities employ or recruit historic instructional designers, IT faculty or staff, learning technologists, or chief learning officers (who mostly hold degrees in one of these disciplines) to advise their administration about what new learning products and solutions to buy. Hence, the platforms are sold, and the colleges and universities stumble through trial-and-error improvements working with the vendors to not just fix the bugs and tailor the platform to their specific needs but also prove the efficacy of the platform to justify its cost.

This common dance could be avoided if there were more learning scientists and learning engineers in both the product design and the development side, and in client evaluation and testing phase prior to signing a contract.

Most importantly, however, learning scientists and engineers could help advise college and university decision-makers about whether this platform or that platform truly matches and integrates with their learning strategies by exploring questions such as whether the solution will scale, allow real learner engagement, allow teacher interactivity, measure academic performance, provide adaptive learning, and so forth. Only learning scientists and engineers, both working for the vendor and engaged at the institution, can best answer these questions and provide the efficacy both parties require.

SO, WHAT DATA DO WE USE?

Everything we use that contains a microprocessor generates data. Historically, that data was stored on random access memory (RAM) chips located on a computer mother board, along with the central processing unit (CPU), graphics card(s), I/O chips, power supply, and the electronic components required to supply the correct electricity to all of these devices. As RAM chips were historically volatile, meaning when the power goes away, so does the data, internal and external memory storage devices were created to semi-permanently store the data. As CPUs followed Moore's Law, and larger, faster, and multiple interconnected CPUs produced greater volumes of data, the creation of larger memory storage devices followed suit.

Today, in addition to solid state memory devices, such as USBs and larger SSL drives that can store data persistently, much of the data produced by CPUs and graphical processing units (GPUs) are stored in the cloud. Cloud storage is essentially multiple memory server farms (logic pools) housed in various physical locations that allow users to access their data regardless of device, operating system, or their device's physical location.

Cloud servers also allow the storage of immense amount of data, in the 110 exabyte range, as mentioned earlier in this chapter. In fact, when connected to most software applications and devices, these cloud storage farms store *all* of the data we generate: the blurry picture, years-old email drafts, out-of-date contact information, and files from applications that no longer exist. Vast amount of data is everywhere, and the amount of data is growing with every click, upload, download, like, and share.

The same issues occur with digital learning platforms today that sweep up every slang word, punctuation mistake, smiley face, meme, or emoji. The challenge for the education researcher, learning scientist, and learning engineer is this: with so much data available to study, what learner data is relevant and useful to help understand a learner population's determination, motivation, or persistence? Do freshman-year high school transcripts from a particular population really provide insight into higher education success? Does a junior high school year grade of C in biology truly predict struggles in college biology and forestall a similar major? With so much data to choose from, the questions will be what digitally captured data sets, data points, or data structures we should use to provide the greatest understanding and insights about teaching and learning to help us build the next experience and help all learners.

For traditional schools, undergraduate colleges, and universities, conventional data points for an instructor or learning scientist to measure and assess a learner's academic performance are summarized as follows:

- Attendance/absences
- Grades (quizzes, tests, assignments, papers, group projects, e-portfolios—all weighted differently)
- Participation (usually subjectively applied by an instructor)

Graduate school offers a few more (and somewhat ambiguous) data points to use to measure academic performance, such as thesis or dissertation quality, originality, and scholarly impact, but generally we're not talking about unstructured "big" data sets to parse and mine. However, the ambiguousness of some academic scoring matrixes demonstrates the social science "art" of the academic experience, and may be acceptable to the instructor, but will make the learning scientist mad with frustration.

For online academic offerings, school, colleges, and universities are primarily dependent on legacy and legacy-plus learning management systems (LMS). Developed more than twenty years ago (hence "legacy"), the LMS was originally designed as a classroom management tool, metaphorically speaking, to replace the wicker basket on the teacher's desk. Originally, the assessment data points offered by legacy LMS platforms changed little from the data points available from an on-site classroom, besides offering an actual time stamp of sign-ins, mouse clicks, video play, pause and stop time stamps, and upload and download time frames. The newer legacy-plus systems not only offer learning management core functions such as uploading/downloading of syllabi, course content, and grade posting but also provide additional features such as chat functions, forums, pop-up questionnaires, live-streaming, group and teaming capabilities, and quiz-building tools.

These additional features may produce invaluable additional digital learning data sets that the learning scientist and researcher can exploit for insights into student learning experiences, but in many cases, these additional feature toolkits must be superimposed over the core digital learning LMS databases due to their inorganic origin. In essence, the additional data points offered by these interactive tools are not organically interconnected to the core legacy LMS functions, and it is therefore difficult for the learning scientists to correlate and associate data points in order to measure the impact and relevance that these exciting tools could be making on the teaching and learning process.

In the past several years, most of the large LMS vendors released software application programming interfaces (APIs—essentially a set of defined methods to connect different software applications) and toolkits designed to add additional features such as digital content libraries, parent messaging services, interactive forums, collaboration tools, expanded reporting dashboards, and mobile app versions of their legacy LMS. The additional functionality of all these services could be a boon for data and learning scientists, but the mostly lack of full integration, or inorganic origin from the learning management platform core, again inhibits and many times taints the data's value, frustrating learners and instructors alike.

How valuable is the addition of a digital content library to a learning scientist if you can't measure the frequency learners have used it for course x and track if the learners' academic performance has improved after they used those resources y number of times, as opposed to z number of times? How valuable is the addition of video chat dialogue between four students if you can't parse the discussion and measure the relevance against the course module learning goals?

Employed as designed, these new features also chew up instructors' time, as they need to learn themselves how to assimilate which ones they want to incorporate within their pedagogical framework. In addition, multiple learner communication channels, mostly in asynchronous learning environments, do not necessarily facilitate increased student and instructor engagement but may increase faculty office hour meetings with individual students, copious student email questions, and phone voice-mail messages to answer. It's as if LMS vendors simply said to learning scientists, instructors, and learners, *here are all these pieces we've stitched together. It's up to you to figure out how best to use them.*

As Julia Freeland and Alex Hernandez write in their revelatory 2014 publication, "Schools and Software: What's Now and What's Next,"[33] because of this lack of seamless integration, most of this learning data is now derived and collated piecemeal, and in many cases, manually by learning scientists and educational researchers. In some cases, instructors and students give up trying to use all these new disparate features.

Recently, with new multifunctionality added to their legacy platform, Blackboard published on their company blog that 96 percent of client use consisted of simple uploading and downloading of content, and checking and posting grades.[34] Digital learning management systems, course management systems, and other types of asynchronous and synchronous software platforms and tools deployed for teaching and learning do allow for improved collection, measurement, and analysis of learning data sets compared to a traditional on-site classroom setting. However, few are designed to capture and incorporate informal and incidental learning—a type of learning that may occur within a formal learning experience but is not typically classroom based or structured, and the control of learning rests primarily with the learner.[35] Few LMSs are designed to encourage and facilitate peer-to-peer learning and social learning—learning by observing the actions of others.[36]

It would be wholly unwieldy for a learning management system as currently designed and deployed to even consider integrating additional data points from informal learning networks to help the learning scientist or instructor better understand the whole learning experience. Theoretically, digital learning platforms could parse online interactions and compare and contrast academic performance to assigned dynamic personality theory grids, determine learning types and styles, gauge motivation, and measure and compare the cognitive processing aptitude of learners, on a daily or hourly basis.

Could all of these additional informal data points, together with formal learning data sets, generate the biggest of big data collections of learning and teaching experiences? Could this finally allow learning engineers together with learning scientists and educational researchers to fashion a platform to offer true personalized learning for every learner? As Chris Dede and Andrew Ho wrote, "Big data can include detailed traces of student-to-student interactions. By integrating these and other sources of data, we may be able to measure more complex problem-solving and collaborative skills."[37]

AGGREGATE STUDENT LEARNING SUMMARY

So now that we have discussed the value and potential importance of different types of informal, formal, and perhaps social learning data that can be theoretically captured, measured, and assessed from digital learning platforms, let us now explore a new learning data framework that organically accounts for these data sets. This new framework is specifically designed to allow learning scientists and engineers to measure the impact or influence these additional data sets have on the teaching and learning experience, regardless of type, population, or demographic group of the learner. This framework is one of many theoretical models that sheds additional light into the nucleus between the art and science of learning.

Aggregate student learning (ASL) can be considered an online transposition of whole student learning (WSL), which is generally summarized in postsecondary education to be an expansion of the classroom and lab educational experiences to include integrated social activities and formal support from the offices of student affairs, student counseling, and student life in the overall learning plan of a student. However, ASL doesn't necessarily just integrate meta and micro data sets that are generated from within the overall formal framework, such as defined and informal learning metrics to help measure and assess academic impact and outcomes.

ASL is defined as a unified consideration, analysis, and assessment of both formal academic subject data points *combined* and *assessed equally* with subject-matter-related informal, and non-subject-matter informal/social learning data points, all compiled to measure and assess scholarly achievement within a student's overall learning experience or plan. Informal and incidental learning is a type of learning that occurs within a formal learning experience but is not typically classroom based or structured, and the control rests primarily with the learner. Valerie Crane and colleagues, in their *Informal Science Learning*, defined informal learning as follows: "Informal learning refers to activities that occur outside the school setting, are not developed primarily for school use, are not developed to be part of an ongoing school curriculum, and are characterized by voluntary as opposed to mandatory participation as part of a credited school experience."[38] ASL, for the purpose of this chapter, implies the consideration of formal and informal learning data, including social data points freely shared by students within a digital learning platform with one another. Informal data points may include learner-to-learner and learner-to-instructor subject-matter-related chats and video discussions (VoIP). Social data points include learner-to-learner non-subject-matter-related chat and voice discussions, and also include additional data points derived from online learner support services such as academic advising, counseling, and even professional mentoring, all parsed, tagged, and labeled as such, and all included to evaluate and assess academic status.

Traditional formal learning can be defined by the following characteristics:

- Instructor led and directed
- Instructor focused and regulated
- Classroom focused
- Curriculum focused
- Highly structured
- Compulsory
- Evaluated and assessed
    - Attendance/absences
    - Grades (quizzes, tests, assignments, papers, group projects, e-portfolios—all weighted differently)
    - Participation (usually subjectively applied by an instructor)[39]

Informal learning in an ASL framework can take two forms. The first form is informal subject-based-related learning, which is academically related but less structured than classroom formal learning; examples include field trips, museum visits, and travel abroad excursions. The second form is informal banter with other learners and instructors, about topics and issues semi-related to the function and purpose of these activities and visits. Although informal in nature, and generally student led and directed, discussion topics may venture off course but would still be included as valuable to the measurement of informal, academic, subject-based learning metrics.

Informal subject-based-related learning can be summarized by the following characteristics:

- Learner led and directed
- Learner focused and self-regulated
- Non-classroom focused
- Semi-curriculum focused
- Semi-structured
- Semi-compulsory or voluntary
- Semi-evaluated and assessed but generally weighted lower than classroom assessment
    - Attendance/absences
    - Grades (quizzes, tests, assignments, papers, group projects, e-portfolios)
    - Participation[40]

Lastly, informal non-subject-based learning would include discussions or exchanges solely between learners about topics and issues completely separate from academic subject matter. Informal subject-based discussions that venture off course are many time bridges to the generation of academic/learning data points. Figure 3.4 provides an example of two learners engaged in informal subject-based discussion, and informal non-subject-based discussion.

Examples of informal non-subject-based learning would include two or more learners participating in a calculus course discussing personal and romantic relationships, music, food, politics, health, or financial status. In the ASL construct, these exchanges would hopefully occur within a digital learning platform, via instance text channels, or on integrated social media platforms, so they can be parsed, measured, and indexed within the context of the calculus learning experience, and measured to identify if and how much impact or influence the content of the discussions may or may not have on the learner's calculus achievement outcomes.

Informal non-subject-based learning characteristics can be summarized as follows:

- Non- or multilearner led

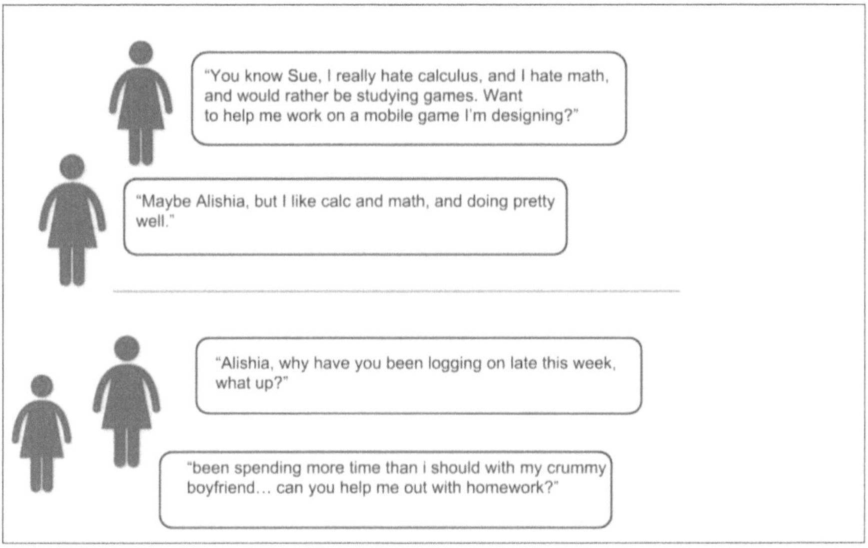

Figure 3.5. Examples of ASL informal subject-based and informal non-subject-based discussion

- Multilearner-focused nonregulated
- Nonclassroom focused
- Noncurriculum focused
- Unstructured
- Spontaneous
- Voluntary
- Not evaluated or assessed[41]

For the purposes of this chapter, social media platforms can be understood as a multiuser chat or voice communication channel within a commercial software platform designed to facilitate discussion and the sharing of images, sounds, videos, memes, and emojis. Although social media commercial platforms are designed to facilitate topic discussions of a nonacademic nature (just like some successful digital learning [media] platforms) to better engage and connect users, they can also offer insight into the phenomena of social learning. Social *learning* platforms borrow from commercial social media platforms, and from a sociological, psychological, and communication theory standpoint, and should also facilitate personal and information sharing. But they should also allow the ability to manage to whom disclosure is made and the frequency of disclosure, and help foster relationship discovery.

First described by Irwin Altman and Dalmas Taylor as the Social Penetration Theory, when people discover some initial common interests and activities, a desire to develop closer relationships emerges. This in turn requires an even more gradual disclosure of private and sensitive personal information in order to form stronger social connections to further deepen the relationship.[42] Jan Schmidt in "Social Software: Facilitating Information-, Identity- and Relationship Management" has broken these social and learning media traits into three categories.

The first category is information management, or the self-regulated ability to choose where and what to publicly or semipublicly share with other users. Another category is identity management, the voluntary decision, sometimes spontaneous, to offer personal and professional aspects of one's life, such as interests, activities, skills, and knowledge. The third category is relationship management, managed through the disclosure of additional or less professional and personal information that, in turn, strengthens or weakens relationships.[43]

Because informal nonregulated social learning requires the management of self, sometime a change of self-representation is required to maintain social bonds. This entails competence (perceived self-efficacy and value), relatedness (sense of being part of a learning activity and that contributions are recognized), and acceptance (the psychological need for social/personal approval and acceptance).[44]

Although these attributes may be occasionally observed from formal learning group project assignments in any physical classroom, they are a prerequisite for academic success within online self-regulated social learning environments.[45] The consideration, capture, and mining of traditional formal, informal, and social data sets to help assess and evaluate academic performance holds great promise for the advent of truly personalized learning solutions. Although there are certainly privacy and security issues to address, an ASL framework may provide new ubiquitous insights into the cognitive knowledge-acquisition process, and may provide new big data resources for learning scientists and learning engineers together to build the next truly personalized learning platform.

WHY THIS MATTERS

Although I consider myself a learning engineer, I've had the privilege of helping my children with high school science research projects using well-established scientific methods and supervising several student group scientific studies in higher education. Inevitably, in both cases, the difficult decision of what to do with outliers arises. When we encounter a variable or data point that doesn't truly fit entirely within the scope of the project, but might still have some relevance, how should it be handled? Including the outlier may swing the study results in a direction that might be unfair, or completely the opposite of the hypothesis, ruining the entire study. Not including the outlier raises the ethical red flag. In one case, students wanted to vote whether to keep or delete the outlier data altogether, or what they perceived to be the outlier in their study so the conclusion could support their original hypothesis.[46]

Recognizing that human bias influences all scientific study is critically important to discovering real answers to the challenges of understanding human learning. The ethics of data use, inclusion, exclusion, and the selective editing is a severe problem in the sciences, and indeed in engineering as well. We have seen when clinical trials of the next promising cancer drug fails and even kills patients after FDA approval. Or when the next new certified bridge design, when built, fails and collapses. In the academy, forget just excluding outliers to support a funded research study's hypothesis; the "publish or perish" culture and grant-generating pressure has created a fraud epidemic.

To prove this point, John Bohannon outlines in his 2013 *Science* article "Who's Afraid of Peer Review" how 157 open-source journals, some backed by major international publishers, accepted a made-up research paper, by a made-up scientist, from a made-up university, with made-up data, and finally, a completely made-up conclusion.[47] Which data to include or exclude in a scientific teaching and learning study available from an engineered learning platform is not equal to the severity of a deleted stress-test data set that resulted in a bridge collapse, but the accurate and ethical outcomes of the study may be no less important to the administrator, educator, and learner alike.

Outside of the academy, education technology vendors' claims of potential learning success for all learners on their digital learning platform are many times rampant with fallacies. Although I am a firm believer that teaching and learning technological innovation will primarily originate from the private sector—because of the limiting higher education budget cycles, risk-taking aversion, and common political gridlock—ed-tech vendors are notorious for inflating and exaggerating their efficacy claims.

To be fair, it's not just that vendors lie to sell product. Sometimes the environment in which the vendors tested their products and the application of the same product in an actual learning environment, with all the legacy technical architecture and traditional pedagogical methods and approaches in place, are incompatible. In many cases, the lack of success of new technology integration in higher education has been synthesized by Sarah Guri-Rosenblit in her paper, "Eight Paradoxes in the Implementation Process of e-Learning in Higher Education," as a number of paradoxes.[48] Although she identifies differential infrastructure, the inconsistent impact on various learner demographics, information acquisition versus knowledge-acquisition expectation, costs, learner adaptation progress, and cultural differences between industry and education, one interweaving string that ultimately explains the divide is the dissimilar uses, purpose, interpretation, and application of data to ascertain efficacy.

Are we back to asking ourselves, *so what data do we (all) use to measure the practice of teaching and learning?*

As Bohannon underlines, one solution to the issues outlined above is peer review, or better stated, peer study replication. Replicability of research findings is the core of any empirical science study. Common in the pharmaceutical and medical research communities, replication allows additional researchers to further validate or disprove a research study's findings using the same research design, data, and conditions. However, even though the practice and process of replicating research findings in the social sciences, such as psychology, has been deemed at a credibility crisis level according to some practitioners,[49] education research replication studies rarely even occur at all.

According to a 2015 study by Matthew Makel and Jonathan Plucker, only 0.13 percent of education articles published in the field's top hundred journals are replications.[50] In the psychology domain, they discovered in a 2012 study that only 1.07 percent of studies in the field's top hundred journals are replications.[51] Well, if replicability in science is critical to reinforce research findings and lend credence to efficacy, why isn't it conducted more often in the educational research community? What are the factors that might be contributing to the drop-off?

Although several studies have suggested a litany of disincentives for researchers to pursue replication studies, a 2012 article by sixteen different contributing authors in the *European Journal of Personality* titled "Recommendations for Increasing Replicability in Psychology" summarizes the disincentives well: "an underdeveloped culture of making data transparent to others, an over-developed culture of encouraging brief, eye-catching research publications that appeal to the media, and absence of incentives to publish high-quality null results, failures to replicate earlier research even when based on stronger data or methodology, and contradictory findings within studies."[52]

One can assume how the first factor informs and influences all the others. If researchers are not confident in the quality of the shared data used in their replication study; if data has been corrupted, altered, or excluded; or if the data is not pure or equitable, the study can't be replicated, hence a severe problem in scientific research, and most notably in the education research community specifically. So now we are aware it's not just "what data do we use," which will be further discussed in chapters 4 and 5 but also the additional unbiased, unprejudiced, equitable treatment of the data collected and used in any research study that is crucially important to accurate scientific discovery.

> Only when certain events recur in accordance with rules or regularities, as in the case of repeatable experiments, can our observations be tested—in principle—by anyone. . . . Only by such repetition can we convince ourselves that we are not dealing with a mere isolated "coincidence," but with events which, on account of their regularity and reproducibility, are in principle inter-subjectively testable.
>
> —Karl Popper (1959, 45)[53]

NOTES

1. Kenneth Cukier, "Big Data Is Better Data," filmed June 2014 at TEDSalon Berlin 2014, Berlin, Germany, video, 14:44, https://www.ted.com.
2. Harold Stark, "Carter Wilkerson: The Nuggets Guy Who Broke Twitter," *Forbes*, May 3, 2017, https://www.forbes.com.
3. "Big Data Analytics," IBM, accessed February 26, 2018, https://www.ibm.com.
4. Colin Carson, "How Much Data Does Google Store?" Cirrus Insight, last updated November 18, 2014, https://www.cirrusinsight.com.
5. Deepak S. Tamhane and Sultana N. Sayyad, "Big Data Analysis Using HACE Theorem," *International Journal of Advanced Research in Computer Engineering and Technology* (*IJARCET*) 4, no. 1 (January 2015): 18–23.
6. Karuppiah Kalaivani and K. AmuthaPrabaker, "Analysis of Big Data with Data Mining Using HACE Theorem," *Journal of Recent Research in Engineering and Technology* 2, no. 4 (Apr. 2015), https://docplayer.net.
7. Leroy E. Hood and Lee Rowen, "The Human Genome Project: Big Science Transforms Biology and Medicine," *Genome Medicine* 5, no. 9 (September 2013): 1–8, https://doi.org/10.1186/gm483.
8. Neha V. Deshmukh, Surbhi G. Atal, and Pushpanjali Chauragade, "Big Data Mining: An Overview," *International Journal for Engineering Applications and Technology* 7, no. 1 (January 2015): 76–79, http://www.ijfeat.org.
9. Vicki Park, Alan J. Daly, and Alison Wishard Guerra, "Strategic Framing: How Leaders Craft the Meaning of Data Use for Equity and Learning," *Educational Policy* 27, no. 4 (2012): 645–65.
10. Cathy O'Neil, *Weapons of Math Destruction: How Big Data Increases Inequality and Threatens Democracy* (New York: Broadway Books, 2016).
11. Ibid.
12. Ibid.
13. "Maya R. Gupta," accessed December 21, 2018, http://mayagupta.org.
14. David Gunning, "Explainable Artificial Intelligence (XAI)," DARPA, accessed December 21, 2018, https://www.darpa.mil.
15. John W. Tukey, "The Future of Data Analysis," *Annals of Mathematical Statistics* 33, no. 1 (March 1962): 1–67, JSTOR.
16. Usama Fayyad, Gregory Piatetsky-Shapiro, and Padhraic Smyth, "From Data Mining to Knowledge Discovery in Databases," *AI Magazine* 17, no. 3 (1996): 37–54.
17. William Cleveland, "Data Science: An Action Plan for Expanding the Technical Areas of the Field of Statistics," *International Statistical Review* 69, no. 1 (May 21, 2007): 21–26. https://doi.org/10.1111/j.1751-5823.2001.tb00477.x.
18. Edd Dumbill, Elizabeth D. Liddy, Jeffrey Stanton, Kate Mueller, and Shelly Farnham, "Educating the Next Generation of Data Scientists," *Big Data* 1, no. 1 (March 2013): 21–27, https://doi.org/10.1089/big.2013.1510.

19. Steven R. Quartz and Terrence J. Sejnowski, "The Neural Basis of Cognitive Development: A Constructivist Manifesto," *Behavioral and Brain Sciences* 20, no. 4 (December 1997): 537–56, https:doi.org/10.1017/S0140525X97001581.

20. Ibid.

21. Alison Gopnik, Clark Glymour, David M. Sobel, Laura E. Schulz, Tamar Kushnir, and David Danks, "A Theory of Causal Learning in Children: Causal Maps and Bayes Nets," *Psychological Review* 111, no. 1 (January 2004): 3–32, https://doi.org/10.1037/0033-295X.111.1.3.

22. Janet F. Werker and Richard C. Tees, "Speech Perception as a Window for Understanding Plasticity and Commitment in Language Systems of the Brain," *Developmental Psychobiology* 46, no. 3 (April 2005): 233–51, https://doi.org/10.1002/dev.20060.

23. Susan Talley and D. Hollinger Martinez, eds., "Tools for Schools: School Reform Models Supported by the National Institute on the Education of At-Risk Students," U.S. Department of Education, last updated April 1998, https://www2.ed.gov.

24. "ALEKS," McGraw-Hill Education, accessed December 21, 2018, https://www.aleks.com.

25. Ibid.

26. "Brightspace Core," D2L, accessed December 21, 2018, https://www.d2l.com.

27. "Frequently Asked Questions," Competency-Based Education Network, accessed December 21, 2018, https://www.cbenetwork.org.

28. Jackie Krause, Laura Portolese Dias, and Chris Schedler, "Competency-Based Education: A Framework for Measuring Quality Courses," *Online Journal of Distance Learning Administration* 18, no. 1 (Spring 2015), https://www.westga.edu.

29. Roshdi Rashed, "A Polymath for the 10th Century," *Science* 297, no. 5582 (August 2, 2002): 773, http://d2ufo47lrtsv5s.cloudfront.net/content/sci/297/5582/773.full.pdf.

30. Computer science being the exception, although arguably not really a science in any case.

31. Shelly Blake-Plock, "Learning Engineering: Merging Science and Data to Design Powerful Learning Experiences," Getting Smart, last updated January 29, 2018, http://www.gettingsmart.com.

32. "Mission," IEEE ICICLE, accessed December 21, 2018, https://www.ieeeicicle.org.

33. Julia Freeland and Alex Hernandez, "Schools and Software: What's Now and What's Next," Clayton Christensen Institute, accessed April 28, 2017, https://www.christenseninstitute.org.

34. John Whitmer, "How Successful Students use LMS Tools—Confirming Our Hunches," *Blackboard Blog*, September 7, 2016, http://blog.blackboard.com.

35. Victoria J. Marsick and Karen E. Watkins, *Informal and Incidental Learning in the Workplace* (New York: Routledge, 1990).

36. Albert Bandura and Richard H. Walters, *Social Learning and Personality Development* (New York: Holt, Rinehart, and Winston, 1963); Etienne Wenger, *Communities of Practice: Learning, Meaning, and Identity (Learning in Doing: Social, Cognitive and Computational Perspectives)* (Cambridge: Cambridge University Press, 1998).

37. Chris Dede and Andrew Ho, "Big Data Analysis in High Education: Promises and Pitfalls," *EDUCAUSE*, last updated August 5, 2016, http://er.educause.edu.

38. Valerie Crane et al., *Informal Science Learning: What the Research Says about Television, Science Museums and Community-Based Projects* (Epharata, PA: Science Press, 1994).

39. Avi Hofstein and Sherman Rosenfeld, "Bridging the Gap between Formal and Informal Science Learning," *Studies in Science Education* 28, no. 1 (1996): 87–112, https://doi.org/10.1080/03057269608560085.

40. Ibid.

41. Ibid.

42. Irwin Altman and Dalmas A. Taylor, *Social Penetration: The Development of Interpersonal Relationships* (New York: Holt, Rinehart, and Winston, 1973).

43. Jan Schmidt, "Social Software: Facilitating Information-, Identity- and Relationship Management," in *BlogTalks Reloaded: Social Software; Research and Cases*, ed. Thomas N. Burg and Jan Schmidt, 31–49 (Norderstedt, Germany: Books on Demand, 2006).

44. Mustafa Ali Türker and Stefan Zingel, "Formative Interfaces for Scaffolding Self-Regulated Learning in PLEs" Slideshare, last updated July 2008, https://www.slideshare.net.
45. Patrick R. Lowenthal, "The Evolution and Influence of Social Presence Theory on Online Learning" (PhD diss., University of Colorado Denver, 2009), 1–30.
46. And no, I didn't let my students exclude the perceived outlier in their study, and I'm not going to disclose the result of their vote.
47. John Bohannon, "Who's Afraid of Peer Review?" *Science* 342, no. 6154 (October 4, 2013): 60–65, https://doi.org/10.1126/science.342.6154.60.
48. Sarah Guri-Rosenblit, "Eight Paradoxes in the Implementation Process of e-Learning in Higher Education," *Distances et saviors* 4, no. 2 (2006): 155–79.
49. Brian D. Earp and David Trafimow, "Replication, Falsification, and the Crisis of Confidence in Social Psychology," Frontiers, last updated May 19, 2015, https://www.frontiersin.org.
50. Matthew C. Makel and Jonathan A. Plucker, "Facts Are More Important than Novelty: Replication in the Education Sciences," *Educational Researcher* 43, no. 6 (August 1, 2014): 304–16.
51. Matthew C. Makel, Jonathan A. Plucker, and Boyd Hegarty, "Replications in Psychology Research: How Often Do They Really Occur?" *Perspectives on Psychological Science* 7, no. 6 (November 7, 2012): 537–42.
52. Jens B. Asendorpf, "Recommendations for Increasing Replicability in Psychology," *European Journal of Personality* 27, no. 2 (April 18, 2013): 108–19, https://doi.org/10.1002/per.1919.
53. Karl Popper, *The Logic of Scientific Discovery* (London: Hutchison, 1959), 45.

Chapter Four

Invention

> We need technology in every classroom and in every student and teacher's hand, because it is the pen and paper of our time, and it is the lens through which we experience much of our world.
>
> —David Warlick[1]

According to Georgetown University's Center on Education and the Workforce, by 2020, 65 percent of all jobs in the U.S. economy will require postsecondary education and training beyond high school, and there will be fifty-five million job openings: twenty-four million new jobs, and thirty-one million openings created by baby boomer retirements.[2] Meanwhile, nearly thirty-seven million American adults currently have some college credits but no degree or certifications.[3] According to the National Center for Educational Statistics, 40 percent of these learners are nontraditional first-time learners and come from historically underserved populations, a number that is projected to rise and even surpass those of traditional learners by 2024.[4] What is higher education going to do to meet these urgent needs?

This chapter outlines emerging and future inventions and innovations designed to help universities, schools, and especially community colleges address both meeting these projected enrollment demands and providing the potential additional academic support the nontraditional learners require in order to meet their academic goals. It also brings to light new educational and social sciences research and technological achievements that may enhance and greatly improve the future of online learning models.

The first two sections of this chapter, "Scaling Teaching and Learning" and "Machine-Learning Artificial Intelligence," provide some historical and descriptive background, and then present emerging technologies in these spheres related to teaching and learning. One such invention includes my group learning algorithms, designed to both facilitate social learning and help successfully scale teaching and learning. These sections also lay the groundwork for the final two chapter sections: "Artificial Intelligent Advising, Counseling, Mentoring" (and Teaching) and "Personalized Learning, Finally!"

As colleges scale their courses and degrees online, academic and counseling support mechanisms need to also scale. The chapter concludes with a description of two learning solutions. My Deep Academic Learning Intelligence (DALI), an artificial intelligence academic and personal learner support engine, is described alongside an artificial cognitive learning map architecture designed to aid in constructing a future personalized learning solution. The challenges facing higher education are real and urgent, but the good news is that innovative solutions are in development that have the potential to support learners, both new and old.

SCALING TEACHING AND LEARNING

Although a few organizations have had the luxury of maintaining their size for great lengths of time, most organizations eventually try to scale their products and services. Some scale to grow revenue to just survive, some scale to meet growing customer demand for their product or service, and some scale to meet shareholders' or their board's demand for revenue growth to stave off competition, or to make themselves an attractive acquisition target. However, as many business school scholarly case studies have validated, to scale haphazardly without strategic planning and foresight can cause the overall demise of an organization.[5] With a pool of eligible traditional, nontraditional, and historically underserved learners growing in the next several decades, this section discusses how colleges and universities can successfully scale their academic content online; better captivate, challenge, and engage their learners; and therefore better improve academic retention and matriculation rates.

From the advent of the correspondence school, introduced by Isaac Pitman in the 1840s, to early municipal government-mandated public access and cable television channels dedicated to education and community interests in the early 1980s, distance education could be characterized as a promising and less expensive venue for colleges to scale their courses without hiring more faculty or building additional classrooms. Subsidized cable television courses seemed the most promising and cost effective, as colleges and universities could scale their on-site courses to a fifty-mile radius from their campuses without adding faculty or facilities.

However, they neglected to realize in order to accomplish this goal they needed to turn their distance education on-site classrooms into production studios. This transformation process required multiple cameras and microphones, switchers and mixing boards, the hiring of new staff to run all this equipment, and unveiled immense unexpected costs to reach these new distance education students. Moreover, these new students still required advising and counseling services as well, so when they did make it to campus for their advising session, long lines awaited their arrival. Most critically, however, was the unintended discovery that the one-way isolated learning experience produced dramatically lower academic achievement rates, lower retention statistics, and lower student satisfaction surveys compared to on-site in-classroom learning experiences.

Legacy online learning platforms, some now more than twenty years old, were originally designed as asynchronous tools so learners could check their grades and assignments outside of classroom hours. As colleges collectively began to employ the learning management systems (LMS) to actually teach courses to scale their academic offerings, a historic problem slowly re-merged: the online learners exhibited lower academic achievement rates, lower retention statistics, and lower student satisfaction surveys compared to their on-site in-classroom peers.

Although these learning platforms could scale course content to a much higher degree (and initially less expensive) than other alternatives, they were still a one-way isolated learning experience for the student.[6] However flawed, it appeared these new online learning platforms finally allowed cost-effective scaling of curricula to a greater number of the traditional learner demographics *and* held promise to finally serve historically underserved populations.[7]

As advances in telecommunication allowed for greater bandwidth at lower cost connecting colleges and consumers to the multigigabyte internet, one approach that select colleges and universities adopted to scale courses to a greater number of diverse learners was the creation of the massive open online course (MOOC) design. Popularized by learning platforms consortia Coursera and edX, MOOCs provided a pathway for a massive number of participants to attend the same archived or live-streamed course taught by consortia faculty.[8] Popular MOOCs offered learning opportunities not only to a greater diversified U.S. student body, some with tens of thousands of enrollees but also for a truly globalized audience. Some studies suggested students who were enrolled in MOOCs came from 196 countries, an immensely diverse demographic.[9]

However popular, MOOCs still presented a primarily one-way noninteractive isolated learning experience, and therefore levels of motivation and engagement were low, resulting in large attrition rates and poor academic performance outcomes for the majority of learners.[10] Specifically, even though MOOCs seemed like the panacea for the academy to finally scale their course offerings *and* reach the socially diverse learner, the one-to-many model cannot consider modalities of motivation or learning style disparities, requiring a learner of MOOCs to be all self-directed autodidact.[11] Even adding course-associated live message boards to help engage learners, with so many culturally diverse learners from so many different age groups possessing numerous levels of subject-matter knowledge, the MOOC board and forum postings become confusing and incoherent. A successful student in a MOOC class must be a self-guided independent learner, similar to the correspondence school or cable TV learner of the past. So, MOOCs may be incompatible for the more common type of learner, those who require guidance and assistance to define their learning pathway.[12]

Within a traditional postsecondary educational environment, if a learner's academic standing begins to drop midway through a course, there are many remediation options available. Students may schedule office hours with their instructor, visit the tutoring center, or seek out advising or counseling center support. Or students may seek out their faculty mentor, if they are so fortunate to have established one, for guidance and wisdom about how to overcome their challenges. However, MOOC-like online education models offer minimal options for the struggling student.

As the numbers of students entering postsecondary education overall are projected to swell,[13] and slowly but more accurately reflect the demographics in the United States, the need for student support structures to expand and integrate more fully within an academic plan has risen as well. As nontraditional, first-generation learners and historically underserved populations are entering postsecondary colleges in greater numbers, and increasingly in online classes,[14] student support structures are needed to ease these new learners' transition into higher education, provide remedial attention some may require for success, and provide the important academic advising and counseling services as well.[15]

Moreover, the more closely integrated that student support services are within the academic curriculum—and the more they are proactive and offered earlier during the initial academic experience, sometimes *intrusively*—the greater the increase in the student retention rate and subsequent success rate.[16] Furthermore, the more aggressive student support initiatives are at implementing intervention and mitigation solutions within the onset of a students' academic struggles, the greater will be the recovery to academic success.[17]

Unfortunately, the primary student within an online education system has no true learner support mechanisms available outside of student-teacher question-and-answer sessions conducted via a chat channel or phone call, or from email exchanges with someone at a counseling or advising center if they even exist at their online college. Neither of these options can replace the role of a traditionally experienced academic advisor, counselor, or mentor who understands each individual student's needs and issues, and who can help facilitate the appropriate interventions required for each learner to achieve academic success. As outlined, there are two main issues resulting from scaling academic offerings online that need to be addressed: lack of real-time interactivity with peers and teachers resulting in learner isolation, and the absence of integrated learner support structures, such as advising and counseling.

Besides the ability to scale courses to a greater number of diverse learners at low cost, live-streaming of teacher-led educational content has also exhibited the concept of teacher social presence for the online student. If the stream is live and not archived, and a learner has the option to post real-time questions and answer in a course chat channel or forum, research studies have demonstrated students are more engaged and motivated, and therefore perform at a greater academic level.[18]

Although influenced by the teaching style and personality of the instructor, even live nonverbal gestures and cues, such as eye contact, body language, facial expressions, and tone of voice positively affect learner focus and concentration within a learning experience.[19] Though asynchronous online learning management platforms allow students to dictate when and where they learn, live-streaming synchronous platforms more closely mimic the bridging of transactional distance that occurs through verbal and nonverbal cues exchanges between a learner and teacher in an on-site classroom.[20] However, knowing the teacher is being live-streamed online is one-half of this successful equation; facilitating learner interactivity with this live teacher, seeing the nonverbal cues in response to a question, or from a team discussion, is the other. But how do we facilitate this live interactive learning that offers these affirmational transactional exchanges to better foster engagement and motivation, and scale this course taught by a single teacher to hundreds of learners and ensure that each can be heard?

Discussions that occur on a bidirectional audio and video (AV) live-streaming platform between twelve or more simultaneous participants tends to decompose in the first five to ten minutes—the amount of time it takes for everyone to trouble-shoot, log on, and adjust their camera angle and audio levels, and for the leader to begin the discussion. That's if everyone invited has a working video camera and microphone on their laptop and router port permission from their workplace to stream their visage.

Moreover, environmental and ambient sounds in each participant's location—such as crowd noise, traffic, fans, air conditioners, and dog barking—can also disrupt and delay a live AV discussion, forcing several outed offending participants to mute their microphone. Too often, those same participants unwillingly forget to unmute their microphone when they wish to add a salient point to the overall discussion. It's also not uncommon for a few participants traveling in a car, or perhaps not in proper attire, to block their camera, allowing just a disembodied voice to represent their contribution. Of course, not having a visual representation of participants, whether they are talking or just listening, offers no nonverbal feedback to the group and, therefore, their social presence likewise evaporates.

Lastly, bidirectional streaming AV platforms are not good candidates to track and collect learning data used to understand and determine potential academic challenges or patterns of success. Most AV platforms are originally designed as business conferencing software, and so generally do not parse clicks, time-on-task, and voice and chat window communications, nor tie any of this data to set learning outcomes. Bidirectional AV streaming platforms may be useful for small graduate seminar courses, or small team project collaborations, but are ill suited to conduct classes larger than fifteen enrollees and, therefore, are technically impractical to deploy for any large undergraduate courses at scale.

For successful online scaling of courses that also offers the learner both a live-streamed teacher's social presence and learner interactivity, perhaps a simple integrated student chat channel would be ideal. The chat channel should also be able to host all document and media file formats, so learners can share assignments and materials related to the class topics. During a live-streamed course, teachers could halt their lecture and solicit questions from the students, moderating the posted responses and answering the questions via the AV platform window, just as naturally as one would manage the information exchange in an on-site classroom.

The ideal learning platform would automatically archive every streamed course and linked associated chat data, so learners who miss a class can access the course later and see the questions and answers previously posted at exactly the same spot during the lecture. Moreover, if teachers wanted to provide a private answer to a learner's question, they could also have a chat window available that enables one-on-one private chat, keeping the exchange off the semipublic course chat channel. Figure 4.1 provides a screenshot of a live-streaming learning platform student-user interface (UI) with a linked interactive learner chat channel.

Corporate training platforms, many built from scratch, lead the way in seamless integration of most of these features, in addition to offering scalability across mobile devices. Corporate training vendors such as eLogic Learning, Litmos, Growth Engineering, Unicorn LMS, and Sum Total do not just provide live-streaming and "pass the broadcaster window" ability, interactive chat, private chat, and course archiving but also offer robust knowledge-acquisition analytics, albeit tied to corporate-related competencies.[21]

As affordable high bandwidth networks have been strung across colleges and schools, live-streaming learning platforms coupled with integrated chat communication channels have become more common. To modernize their legacy asynchronous platforms, vendors such as Blackboard (Collaborate), Canvas (Mediasite), and Desire2Learn (Brightspace) have added live-streaming capabilities, coupled chat channels, and course archiving.

Even most open-source learning platforms like Moodle can accommodate many types of live-streaming and chat channel features through third-party plug-ins to offer a semi-seamless interactive learning experience. Some even include pop-up surveys and lexicon-based or AI-driven chatbots that post subject-matter questions or comments during a class that seek to both solicit learner subject-matter comprehension and keep learners engaged and motivated. Moreover, these new modified interactive learning platforms all feature robust data analysis dashboards, allowing researchers and data scientists to parse and extract learner demographics, clicks, time-on-tasks, academic scores, and individual and student team performance metrics.

So, it appears we have solved the issue of learner isolation, but can we scale this solution? Hypothetically, our new learning platform can now scale an interactive learning experience to hundreds of learners in real time, but what happens when teachers halt their lecture and solicit questions from the hundreds of students at the same time?

When using a single chat communication channel for a large number of learners, chat confusion can occur and disrupt the learning process.[22] As anyone that has tried to contribute to a chat communication channel with a large number of participants on a website or social media app can attest, as the chat posts alternate from one topic to another, and scroll up faster and faster from more and more comments, complete confusion and incomprehensibility ensues. Chat confusion within a synchronous chat communication channel may occur in courses of more than thirty learners.[23] This statistic

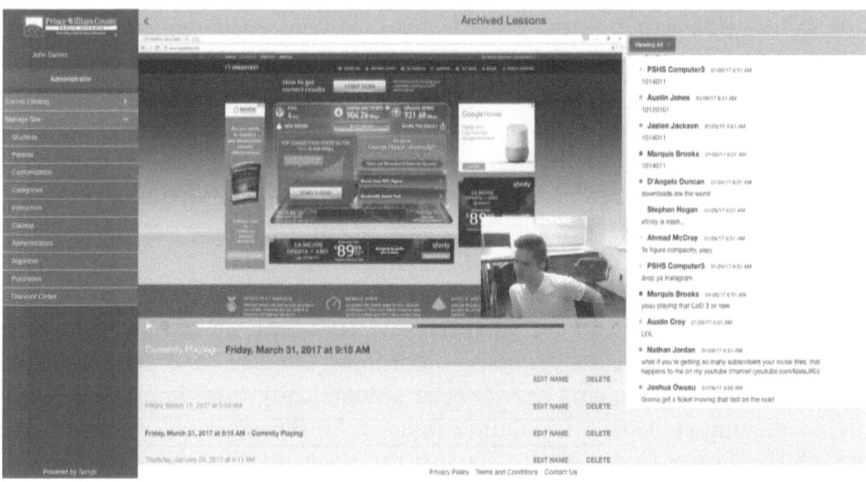

Figure 4.1. Screenshot of a live-streaming learning platform and linked interactive chat channel

assumes half the learners are observing the chat and not contributing to the chat discussion. If greater than 50 percent contribute to the dialog, total incomprehensibility ensues, as described above. But if we cap the number of learners in an online interactive course to increase chat coherence, wouldn't that also hinder the ability to scale the course to a greater number of students?

One solution to better scale a college's curricula online that can also avoid chat incoherence and maintain the important interactivity to foster student engagement and motivation can be found in a teaching and learning platform like Scriyb.com. Based on my invention, "System and Method for Providing Group Learning via Computerized Student Group Assignments Conducted Based on Student Attributes and Student-Variable-Related Criteria,"[24] this platform is designed to help facilitate peer-to-peer learning, foster social engagement between learners, and provide some remedies to several other online learning issues previously discussed.

Scriyb's goal is to segment a large number of learners into smaller groups of no more than thirty learners each, and then wall them off from the next group, and then next group, and so on, all taught by a single live-streamed teacher and streamed to all the groups simultaneously. In effect, learners in one small group of learners watching and interacting with their peers are not aware, unless the teacher wishes to disclose it, that they may be in a class of hundreds or thousands of students.

Each group of learners will have its own chat communication channel in which to post questions, answer questions, and socialize within the cohort. Forming groups of learners of thirty or fewer satisfies our chat confusion mandate. The secondary goal of the invention is to group learners in a way that fosters interactivity among themselves, to help encourage peer-to-peer and student-led social learning.[25] As we witness on social media platforms, and that demonstrates the Social Penetration Theory previously mentioned in chapter 3, when people in general discover some initial common interests and activities, a desire to develop closer relationships emerges. This in turn requires an even more gradual disclosure of private and sensitive personal information in order to form stronger bonds of similar interests and activities, further deepening the relationship.

Through self-reporting (or collected during an initial registration process), learner commonalities, interests, and activities are critical data sets used in the initial subclass grouping algorithms. Studies have demonstrated that low-achieving students may benefit academically from interacting with high-achieving students with similar interests in the same classroom.[26] Although the two students may differ greatly academically, one being an A student and one being a D student, with comparable nonacademic interests, say, in music, sports, or even clothes, the higher-achieving student is drawn to support the lower-achieving student within an equitable joint-learning environment.

In short, learners are segmented in each subclass by their social interests and by the range and scope of their academic standing. The Scriyb platform's algorithms merge high, mid-, and low achievers altogether in each group, but again, only as long as they all have a socially strong link. This model is designed to aid cohort and social learning, leveraging the nonacademic relationship to enhance the learning process. Moreover, if the grouping algorithms are successful in matching students correctly, the peer-to-peer learning and peer teaching, offered voluntarily from the high-achieving students to the mid- or low-achieving students, also greatly assist the teacher of a large-scaled class, taking pressure off to consistently accommodate every small inquiry during a lecture or demonstration. Figure 4.2 exhibits a screenshot of the Scriyb instructor's user interface (UI) with four grouped classes of twenty students each.

Learners in their online class group can chat with each other, but not with learners in other groups. They can pose questions and socialize with each other in their own small group and can pose questions directly to the instructor during the course as well. Preliminary evidence has suggested that the social engagement and peer-to-peer learning strategies that initially grouped learners have also fostered extracurricular relationships, such as individual and group friendships, business partnerships, romantic relationships, and overall social bonding outside of their academic experiences.

Lastly, the design of the student group academic achievement schemata was also inspired by the modern multiplayer entertainment game. In these games, through chat and sometimes voice and video communication channels, more experienced players on a team inevitably help to guide team members who are not as experienced to win a video game challenge together. This same phenomenon happens within Scriyb's learner groups. Students who may know more about a topic than others *help their whole group* better understand the topic content through chat, voice, or video communication. Ultimately, socially connected learner groups achieve greater understanding of course content and successfully complete an academic journey together at a greater level of understanding than they would if they had to attempt the journey on their own.

Social engagement, social learning, and peer-to-peer learning are recognized by learning scientists and LMS vendors alike as critically important factors in online learning success.[27] However, superimposing social engagement tools on top of a legacy LMS is not the same as incorporating learners' commonalities and interests at the forefront of an academic experience to foster organic connections between students. Moreover, algorithmic grouping of students using similar variables to foster social and peer learning could also be deployed asynchronously.

Figure 4.2. Scriyb instructor user interface

For example, traditional on-site colleges and residential universities could use these grouping algorithms to form ideal cohorts in residence halls, in dorm rooms, or for physical classrooms course learner composition. Admissions offices could even create ideal classes of entering freshmen that fosters greater social engagement, peer mentoring, and community collaboration.

Until the development of online learning platforms that allow the ability for learner performance and interactivity to be captured, measured, and analyzed, researchers and learning scientists never had a complete portrait of all the academic and nonacademic variables that can affect the learning process. Grades, quizzes, and other evaluation instruments were the primary sources of assessment data of a learner's academic status, always discovered after the knowledge exchange experience and offering limited insight into a complete learning rubric.

As Chris Dede and Andrew Ho wrote in their *EDUCAUSE Review* article, "We believe that what is happening with data-intensive research and analysis today is comparable to the inventions of the microscope and telescope. Both devices revealed new types of data that had always been present but never before accessible."[28] Aggregate student learning data have also always existed but have never before been accessible, quantified, or collated within an academic experience prior to the advent of online education coupled with digital data learning sciences and engineering. Incorporating and analyzing these data sets within the overall assessments of student learning is equivalent to the invention of the electron microscope or a geostationary space telescope; two inventions that allow us to glean both a granular and a more expansive observation of the overall practice of teaching and learning.

MACHINE-LEARNING ARTIFICIAL INTELLIGENCE

As was discussed in chapter 2, the combination of innovative algorithmic mathematical designs plus the switch by software engineers and programmers to assign computer graphics cards (GPUs) to compute AI software instructions, rather than primarily by the slower central processing unit (CPU), has advanced the field of artificial intelligence to a point that the associated mathematical algorithms can finally solve complex human problems and analytically predict tasks. Machine-learning artificial intelligence applied to teaching and learning holds great promise to disrupt and improve upon the higher education model that has been replicated over and over again—only slightly altered and modified since the eleventh century. This chapter section provides a brief description of the history of artificial intelligence, explains how it works, outlines different types of machine-learning algorithms, and provides examples of the application of new machine-learning models in online education.

Nestled in the crossroads of both the data sciences and the social sciences, teaching and learning is a complicated topic to research and quantify. So many factors influence a learner's academic achievement levels, positively or negatively, and the research literature is rich in theoretical studies that demonstrate that cognitive processes,[29] organizational ability,[30] and time managements skills can have as much impact on academic achievement as motivation[31] and personal characteristics.[32] Moreover, learner academic achievement can also be negatively affected if an instructor's teaching methodologies and pedagogical approach differ greatly from a student's learning style.[33]

There are many general theoretical categories of human cognitive learning, including procedural, declarative, and conditional knowledge acquisition. Artificial intelligence (AI) networks, algorithms, or models can be understood as the synthetic analogy of these biological categories. Biological neural network design (i.e., how dendrites communicate to a cell body, how the cell body passes the information through an axon to other brain neurons, and how neurons receive, process, and organize electrical signals) has been the inspiration for the design of artificial intelligence networks for more than seventy-five years.

A biological neuron receives one thousand multiple input signals a second and assigns each signal a level of importance. Artificial neural networks define this signal level of importance as mathematical weights. If the number of input signals are weighted high or strong versus other inputs, the biological neuron enters an excited state and produces a stronger collective network synaptic output, which then forms a stronger pattern in our long-term memory. The more engaging a human activity, the stronger and deeper the neural pathways are formed, providing greater multiple neural synaptic links in our cognitive memory. Figure 4.3 provides an example of a biological neural network compared to an artificial neural network.

Historically, when one wanted a computer system to complete a complex task, a computer programmer would have to design a matrix of rules and conditions of the task as an algorithm, and then arduously program the algorithm into computer software code for the computer to "compute" the algorithm and accomplish the desired task. If the original task needed to be altered, the programmer needed to reprogram the algorithm all over again. Machine-learning AI algorithms lessen the burden on the programmer by imitating aspects of human cognitive learning and allotting software algorithms to reprogram themselves, generating their own code to accomplish a new task.

Deep learning, compared to machine learning, generally refers to the greater number of hidden layers within an artificial intelligence algorithmic model, but both terms are commonly used interchangeably. Layers are made up of a number of interconnected nodes, like biological dendrites, which possess an "activation function," essentially what defines a node's output value given a set of input values. Nodes contain the "deep" decision trees, programmed based on complex statistical probability and correlation functions. You can have any number of nodes within each hidden layer.

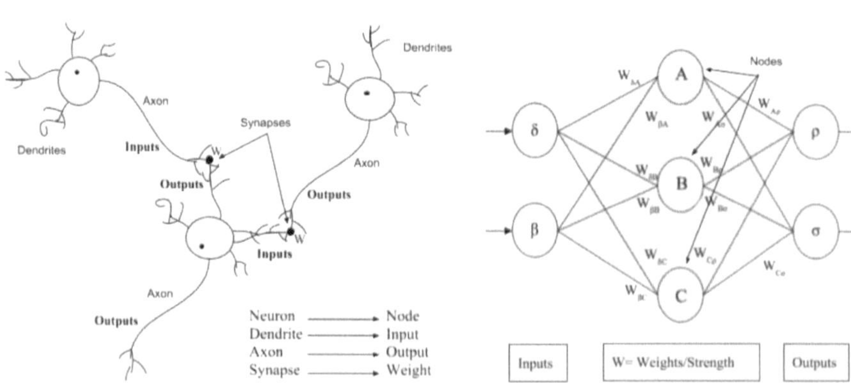

Figure 4.3. Comparison between a biological neural network and an artificial neural network

Deep neural networks "learn," or the weights in their hidden layers are trained, using trial and error, just as our cognitive memory learns. Data sets, whether text, sound, or image, are ingested into an artificial neural network through an observable input layer, which interconnects to thousands of middle, hidden layers, a type of random forest, which calculates and averages any number of decision trees within the forest. The hidden layers then link to an output layer, where the results of the computational processing are experienced. If the output is in error, a programmer corrects the mistake and feeds the data sets back into the network until the hidden layers are more precisely trained about the expected output.

The goal is to achieve a predictive output, which in essence means we train the network to visually recognize one object from many, to detect an acoustic anomaly from many waveforms, or to tag violent scenes in an entire movie. The greater the number of hidden layers, the better the error weight correction and the greater the precision of the desired output. Hidden layers are actually "hidden" in a deep-learning model, as even the original programmer has no idea what the functional status of "random forests" are at any given moment in time![34]

Just like human knowledge acquisition, machine-learning algorithms need multiple inputs of information, repeated and reinforced from multiple sources, to become accurately trained.

Humans compartmentalize these inputs as important, somewhat, or not very important, which is the same as a programmer assigning strong or weak weights (importance) to inputs of a machine-deep-learning algorithm. Within machine-learning algorithmic design, these multiple inputs are known as training data sets, and the importance of the data sets are assigned variable mathematical weights (strengths) within the hidden layer's network. These weights continually self-modify and reprogram until the output of the models is statistically near or matches the expected outcome.

Examples of such outputs and associated outcomes might include a story or review that is comprehensible and interesting, a car that drives itself without crashing, a digital picture style that is similar to a known artist, and so on. Machine-learning networks may contain thousands or millions of hidden layers, with shifting dynamically trained weights, based on output results, and the ever-changing error correction of these weights. The required continual training exposes one of the biggest issues with deep learning: time. Depending on the desired task, and the design and number of GPUs (graphics processing units) calculating the training, deep-learning models can take months or even years to accurately train to predict a robust task.

One type of machine-learning algorithmic training is procedural training. Popular examples of this type of training can be seen in autonomous driving vehicles, whereby a human spends thousands of miles manually driving multi-sensor-rigged vehicles interconnected to machine-deep-learning models, training the models via video, radar, lidar, sonar, and infrared cameras all interconnected to the driver's controls as data set inputs for all types of roads and traffic conditions. So, one day, the vehicle will know how to drive us from point A to point B, regardless of weather or traffic conditions.

Supervised machine-learning models are being trained in finance, logistics, medical diagnostics, and even agriculture, but rarely in learning engineering and learning sciences. Supervised training is human focused, in that it is human developers that select what data sets to use to ingest into a model and then are human corrected if the output of the model was in error, over and over again.

In unsupervised machine-learning training, the inputs are selected and ingested by the machine-learning model itself. An example of this is a Global Positioning System (GPS) app's deep-learning model that is trained from the decisions you make by driving a particular route from one location to another. The next time you type in "home" in the app, the model will provide the fastest route you've used in the past, based on time of day and external traffic patterns, and not the preprogrammed main highway route suggested when you first starting using the GPS app.

Another type of a machine-learning algorithm is image pattern-recognition training. Figure 4.4 outlines an example of how a deep-learning model learns to recognize an image of a bicycle within a collection of labeled images. The hidden layers identified in the figures have a progressively more complex function in the training process. The first pattern-recognition layer may learn about the visual edges that represent a section of the image of a bicycle. The deeper layers may learn that a bicycle always has two large circular shapes, one in the front and one in the back of the object. Eventually the model will recognize and detect a bicycle in a crowd of other objects and, if trained correctly, will be able to detect a bicycle from any angle and plane.

An additional type of machine-learning algorithm is a natural language-processing (NLP) neural network. NLPs are designed to mimic human neural language-processing abilities, specifically natural text processing. A well-trained NLP can decipher natural language text based on conditional and relevant structured and unstructured data set inputs. Structured inputs include formal and semi-informal language, and nonstructured inputs include features such as slang.

The training data for such a deep-learning model can be derived from text data sets such as books, hotel reviews, newspapers, chat logs, or social media postings. Predesigned training of an NLP model occurs by the parsing of a word or phrase into their syntactic components within a predescribed and programmed natural language rubric. A pretrained NLP is able to recognize several words or phrases among many subcategories of words or phrases within a particular data set that may be similar in structure but may still be encoded separately from each other.[35]

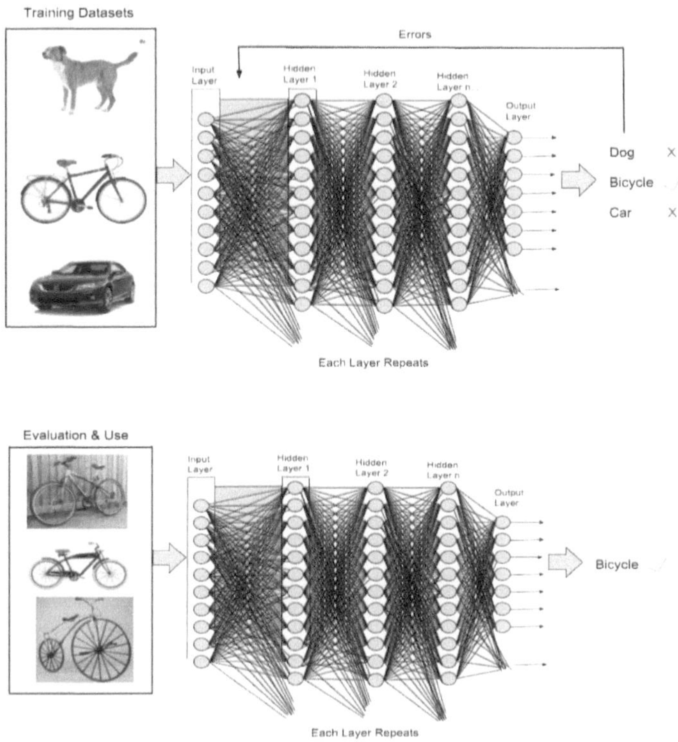

Figure 4.4. Simplified visual pattern-recognition deep-learning training process

Statistically, neural language models share strength between one word or phrase (or groups of words and phrases) and their context with other similar group of words or phrases and their structured context. The neural natural language model can be trained so that each word, or series of words or phrase representations, is embedded to treat words and phrases that have aspects, components, and meaning similarly in common. The results of these models can create a distributed ontological map. Words and phrases that may appear with similar features, and are thereby treated with similar meaning, are then considered "adjoining words," and can be semantically mapped accordingly. Figure 4.5 provides an example of a simplified distributed representation map.[36]

Let's turn our attention to how these kinds of machine-learning models can be applied across the world of higher education. One current example is how colleges have leveraged the power of NLP algorithmic models to deploy chatbots (or bots) to handle student inquiries related to student services functions. Such chatbots have been programmed to learn how to respond to

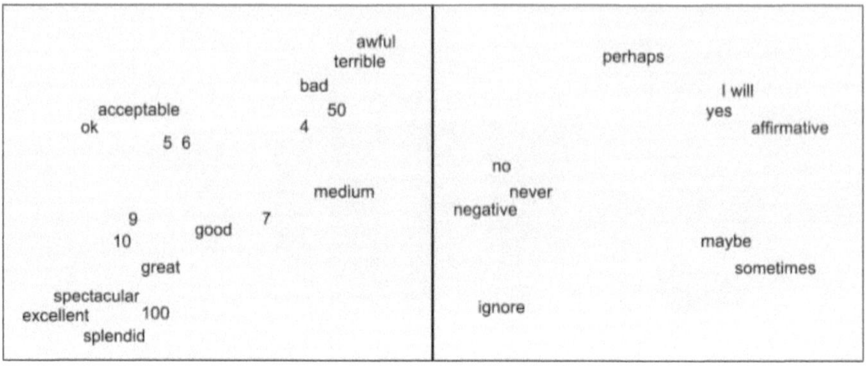

Figure 4.5. Simplified distributed word representation map

frequently asked questions about how to register for classes, how to pay tuition, and how to look up a student's financial aid status, and can even respond to student grade inquiries, if the pretrained NLP models are integrated within a college's Student Information System (SIS).

A machine-learning teaching assistant (TA) bot is another example, whereby learners can pose academic subject-matter-specific questions in a chat channel linked to an academic-subject-trained NLP model. A model used for this function would need to be pretrained about the subject-matter content prior to deployment, with ongoing learner questions and bot answers then functioning as unsupervised active training data sets during the term of an academic experience.

But how would the NLP model know if the answers given to student questions were correct? What if the answers provided to a student were factually incorrect? For an unsupervised machine-learning model to mature, second, third, or fourth corrective feedback training data sets related to the first chatbot answer are required to help the model learn if the answers it provided were correct. Providing a follow-up query such as, "Was this helpful?" and a related "Why or why not?" may function as this feedback retraining loop, so the positive feedback will be assigned higher weights than negative responses, retraining the model accuracy. These data sets can then help the AI TA bot learn, over time, to provide better and more useful recommendations and answers provided to a learner.

Over time, with increasing numbers of a learner academic and social chat exchanges being parsed and digested derived from an online education platform as training data sets, an NLP model may also "learn" more about an individual student's learning style, comprehension abilities, knowledge, or even aptitude: Did the learner provide a teacher or peer a correct answer, a wrong answer, or an inconclusive one? Is that because the same learner scored low on the past two subject-matter related quizzes? Or was it because this learner was absent or late for the past two weeks of classes because she shared in the chat communication channel she needs to work two jobs, or her car broke down and public transportation is unreliable, or she now needs to provide adult care for her mother?

Through the power of machine learning, a personalized NLP model could emerge that parses a learner's scholarly aptitude and academic talents *and* also learns about learners' personal issues, social likes, dislikes, and anything else they may have freely shared within a chat communication channel found on social media or within an online educational platform. Pretrained with enough structured and unstructured data sets, a robust NLP model can also be used to monitor course chat channels used by hundreds and thousands of students in real time. NLP models may even use overall chat discussions as active training data sets and can decipher and detect behavior issues and student-to-student conflicts, including identifying a learner's personality type or emotional status, in any given moment in time.

We started this chapter section acknowledging the ways in which the process of teaching and learning is very complicated and difficult, combining the social sciences and biological sciences, to research, measure, assess, and effectively scale. It may seem ironic, but one has to wonder, given the advances of machine learning in recent years and its trajectory to have an even bigger impact on society, will we find that machine-learning models begin to deeply understand and better support learners than other educated (trained) humans? We explore this question further in the next section of this chapter.

ARTIFICIAL INTELLIGENT ADVISING, COUNSELING, MENTORING: DEEP ACADEMIC LEARNING INTELLIGENCE (DALI)

Now that we understand artificial intelligence, machine learning, and deep learning, and what they can do, this chapter section discusses my direct application of machine learning, called Deep Academic Learning Intelligence (DALI), designed to detect academic issue patterns and provide learner support interventions. As research has demonstrated, for the nontraditional or historically underserved student populations, student support services, such as advising and counseling, may have an equal or greater impact on student success as to what transpires in the classroom. Online education is notorious for its lack of student support options, a passageway that many of these learner populations use to access primary educational opportunities. DALI is just one example, although robust, of deploying deep-learning models to improve upon the traditional means of providing accurate and timely intervention recommendations to help improve learner academic outcomes.

As was explained earlier in chapter 3, aggregate student learning (ASL) is a revision to the definition of the whole student learning (WSL) paradigm, which is understood to be the inclusion of the classroom and lab academic experience coupled with a support plan from the offices of student affairs, student counseling, and student life in the overall learning map of a postsecondary learner. ASL, however, also considers academic experiences and student support services, *and* combines them with semi-academic, social (nonacademic) experiences, and potentially even social media postings that may provide insights into a learner's academic milieu. So, if we can parse all these data sets, can we differentiate them, mine them, classify them, and label them into useful categories for analysis and assessment to gain better insight into the learning process, and use these data sets to train unique machine-learning models to aid a struggling student?

My Deep Academic Learning Intelligence (DALI) models consist of specifically designed and pretrained artificial cognitive NLP algorithms that parse, label, classify, and store learner academic subject and nonsubject communications, and compare this chat content and context against an academic matrix in order to detect patterns that may have a negative effect on academic performance.[37] If a learning anomaly is detected, DALI suggests an intervention method or a series of methods to hopefully ameliorate or resolve the issue. In order to understand the differences between academic and pure social-nonacademic chat within an academic learning experience, DALI models are pretrained about both.

In order to prepare DALI to assist learners in a course experience, the machine-learning models are first ingested with the course syllabus using a prestructured template that includes course overview, learning goals, grading schemata, meeting schedule, and required textbooks. An open-source textbook, or one with an open-source digital use license, is critically important, as the textbook's content, along with the course syllabus, is what a DALI academic subject-matter model would use as training data.

For instance, after being trained from a math textbook that covers Algebra I to Calculus I, and from a properly labeled course syllabus for Algebra II, the DALI model would recognize and weigh higher (i.e., the importance or relevance) all Algebra II–related content in the textbook (including text, formulas, and diagrams) and interconnect it to the learning goals and grading rubrics for the course. Secondarily, DALI would also be pretrained with general structured and unstructured syntactic English language data sets. To this end, DALI can decipher the differences among formal, informal, and slang, by digesting content in the publicly supported Urban Dictionary available online. So in essence, the DALI NLP algorithms consist of multiple integrated pretrained models in preparation for the launch of an academic course, including deep-learning models designed, programmed, and trained specifically to classify between learner subject and nonsubject communication chat.

Let's dive into what this looks like—and the power behind it—a little more. Figure 4.6 is an example of subject-matter and non-subject-matter parsed text exchange between two learners. Because DALI's indexed student communication and social data sets are weighted against each individual student's academic achievement performance, in some cases, DALI may provide unique insight into the effect that social engagement has on learning. Is the non-subject-matter interaction between students Sue and Alishia in student group C having a positive or negative impact on student Sue's academic performance? Does the data set trend line demonstrate that both Sue and Alishia have improved academically since they began helping each other two months ago?

As was previously discussed, besides an instructor's teaching style, pedagogical philosophy, or instructional methodology, peer interactivity may strongly influence a student's learning success or struggles. Subject-matter chat *coupled with* purely social chat could offer important clues into potential external or tangential issues and conflicts that may have an indirect but adverse effect on the learning process.

As we can see in figure 4.6, in the first exchange, Alishia may be an accounting degree student, but her true interests lie in a potential game de-

Figure 4.6. Example of DALI parsed sentences/exchanges between two students, Sue and Alishia

sign degree major. In the second exchange, Alishia's academic performance may be suffering because of car trouble, making her repeatedly late for her course start time. Both examples indicate some level of empathetic relationship, as semiprivate information has been shared from one learner with the other. Well-trained deep-learning models may also harvest parsed and labeled data about a learner's academic performance *and* insights into a learner's social tendencies, personality type, and even emotional state at a moment in time.

Alishia's final chat closure may also be detected by a pretrained sentiment machine-learning model with a gradient scale that can detect emotion and parse her "piece of garbage" as "anger" and "frustration" and compare this emotional state, alongside her tardiness and recently stored academic performance scores, to detect a potential adverse pattern that may negatively affect Alishia's future academic achievement. Machine-learning models provide a semiprivate window into personal and professional external events, conditions, and states that influence a student's learning process and adversely affect their learning environment. These conditions and states might warrant an intervention to remedy any potential negative outcomes.

With multiple NLP models that parse, label, and store subject-matter and non-subject-matter social exchanges that occur within chat communication channels, DALI provides pretrained academic advising; professional, personal counseling; and even mentoring intervention options for individual learners. DALI can *learn* about each student's evolving external environment, condition, state, and situation as it affects (or *could* affect) each student's "internal" academic performance.

Upon detecting a pretrained potential adverse issue or state, DALI makes recommendations to the learner to ameliorate potential negative academic outcomes. However, as was mentioned earlier, machine-learning models need to be constantly trained with feedback in order to adjust the weights, bias, and errors to conform to the programmers desired outcome. DALI is no different.

Individual learners train their DALI models by responding to an intervention recommendation with a simple click of either *Yes I will*, *No Thanks*, *Maybe*, or *Ignore*, and responding to a simple question such as, "Was this Helpful?" via a text box. Learners initial response options from the recommendation are limited to *Yes I will*, *No Thanks*, *Maybe*, or *Ignore*, but a follow-up "active training" *Helpful* solicitation allows DALI to receive a complete feedback loop to offer more accurate intervention recommendations in the near future.

Consider figure 4.6 again, but consider DALI's pretrained and active training capability. Alishia does not like her major degree program, and hates the coursework required, but does like game design. DALI parses the text, matrixes the text against her current grades in the two courses mentioned (accounting and finance), and if she scored poorly, suggests she may want to either study alternative texts, seek a tutor, or consider a change of major to game design. With proper pretraining, the recommendation is a simple ontological and syntactical process. Also, perhaps the college's catalog has been digested in the DALI models and stored into an integrated database. Then DALI could provide the link to the game design degree online catalog description. Or perhaps, during the second exchange, DALI can recommend to Alishia a link to her college's preapproved financial bank that can provide a microloan to repair her car. Figure 4.7 provides examples of the three learner support service recommendations from DALI.

All learners' DALI recommendation and corresponding responses are stored in their personal learning map as a cohort data set, along with their labeled overall communication and social chat matrix, and their current and past academic achievement performance scores, records, and transcripts. Although described in detail later in this chapter, the personal learning map is a unique approach to labeling, indexing/storing, and retrieving student learning data within an artificial cognitive declarative memory model.

DALI represents just one example of the application of machine-learning artificial intelligence that can be deployed to provide learners with important individual academic and personal support to help improve their academic journey. Over time, models like DALI may provide additional learner support by combining social learning pedagogy with traditional academic learning. DALI could tag some learners with certain behavioral attributes and personality traits alongside aptitude as "natural" tutors, and match them in learning groups with lower-level struggling learners. The models may even

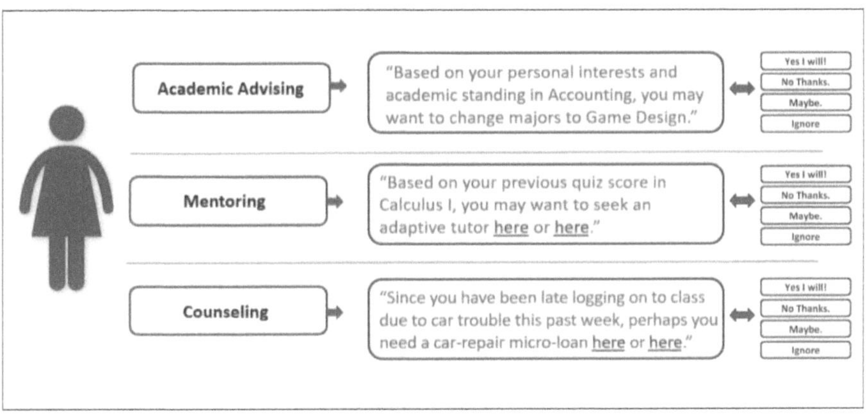

Figure 4.7. Example of initial DALI recommendations

connect upper-level learners with lower-level learners, asking them to check in with students who could use extra support.

A prompt might be "I see you are a little behind in accounting; need any help?" or "Everything okay with your studies? Need a tutoring session?" or "Congrats! You scored exceptionally high in this section! Would you be willing to help a classmate?" These DALI suggestions could help facilitate important peer-tutoring connections that benefit all learners, not just lower-performing ones. When ASL data sets are parsed, classified, labeled, indexed, and stored by a multitude of interconnected machine-learning models, the options to leverage these data sets to positively affect the teaching and learning process are only constrained by the limits of imagination.

Since its invention, I've been frequently asked, "Can DALI (or a differently modified deep-learning model) be trained to actually teach course content and supplant a human teacher? After all, if a well-trained DALI model can 'read' chat exchanges, decipher human conditions, and predict academic struggles, then certainly it's not a big leap to actually take over the instructor role."

My lawyerly answer: yes and no. A machine-learning model can be ingested and trained with all the textbook material ever written about accounting, in order to differentiate and classify subject matter and non-subject-matter chat discussion within an Accounting II course, but it's a long way from classifying these two domains to detect and predict academic issues to actually comprehensively convey Accounting II content to a new learner.

Open questions remain: Could we ever train a machine-learning model to offer a dynamic and engaging personality? To also possess the most recent research and have original thought? And have the ability to adjust and modify its teaching pedagogy to match every student's learning style? Can a teaching DALI model own the powers of deduction and reason? Lastly, in the absence of quantum computers, deep-learning models take much time to be accurately trained. New content and discoveries in a branch of scholarship must be constantly ingested, and that can take a lot of time.

But some might argue it's only a matter of time before Professor DALI will take over the instruction of academic foundational courses in the near future. Toward the end of chapter 5, I hint at such a revolutionary invention and provide an imaginary academic context where a department chair may very well order up two different versions of Professor DALI to teach two distinct courses, in the future.

PERSONALIZED LEARNING, FINALLY!

For some education researchers and learning scientists, the holy grail of superior academic instruction is the elusive personalized learning prefecture:

whereby every element of instruction is tailored specifically to how an individual learner acquires knowledge. Cognitive-based machine-learning models and cognitive storage memory maps, formed to match a learner's individual memory configuration, hold promise of offering this breakthrough pedagogy. This chapter section highlights an original knowledge-acquisition system modeled on human biological memory modules that offers one possible pathway to a future personalized learning solution.

Personalized learning ensures educational content is customized or adapted to a student's learning style, motivation level, and personal circumstances. This approach is counter to the traditional learning structure, where it is the learner's responsibility to adapt to the content type, delivery, and method.[38] Even as research has proven no two individuals learn the same, educational institutions still pack students into standardized lecture halls and classrooms, or in the case of historical online education, onto the same standardized LMS platform.

Although there are many theories of how we learn, one particular learning theory, based on forty years of psychological and developmental educational research, is the Intentional Learning Construct (ILC) model.[39] Besides human factors, such as desire, motivation, and intention, that influence individual learning outcomes, ILC considers conative, affective, physical, and behavioral attributes, alongside cognitive and social factors. Together, it accounts for a whole-person learning cognitive model.[40]

Simon Cassidy's "Learning Styles: An Overview of Theories, Models, and Measures" also provides an excellent survey of salient research into cognitive learning styles and models.[41] Another pedagogical model of note that strives to define and practice personalized learning on the web is the adaptive learning methodology. Various algorithms and solutions have been proposed, such as the Intelligent Tutoring System and Adaptive Hypermedia,[42] but in essence, adaptive learning is the dynamic adaptability to display and teach content to a learner, based on continual microassessments of the learner's knowledge level, comprehension speed, and learning style.

Many of these adaptive pedagogical systems and platforms overlook the magnitude that an ASL system offers for a comprehensive customized learning environment for an individual learner. Some online learning platforms do try to collate more detailed information about a learner, such as soliciting more extensive login information, personal evaluation instruments, and in-class surveys, or through different types of external web services, such as games and social media apps.[43] However, these data sets offer just a sliver of the information required to match the unique and complex cognitive style of a learner for true personalized learning.[44]

At issue, of course, is the question of how learning scientists, education psychologists, and researchers might attempt to apply their cognitive study findings to actually personalize learning in the real world. Since machine-learning models mimic human cognitive neural network functions, such as information processing and organization, they may also simulate human biological memory processing, storage, and retrieval methods. Perhaps then, artificial cognitive memory maps, which are machine-learning models with similar architecture to that of human knowledge acquisition may offer the best models for personalized learning.

As was discussed earlier in this chapter, machine-learning models can be actively trained to provide personalized learner-intervention recommendations (such as to seek out a tutor, or change a major area of study), *and* they can also provide deeper understanding of the learners themselves. Pretrained machine-learning models already exist that can detect a learner's personality type, behavioral traits, sentiment, persona, emotions, and even intent of chat or voice at any moment in time. Using these existing models, combined with DALI's interleaved machine-learning models, a learning engineer could match similar types of learners in a group and also reprogram DALI to recommend customized time-management advice to a learner, or adjust demeanor or attitude within a learning group, or even offer "Congratulations" on receiving a great quiz grade to boost self-esteem. However, for a conglomeration of machine-learning models to actual offer such interventions and support, they require a unique and complex map to store and retrieve all these coupled and interlocking data sets, a schemata and architecture that should probably resemble how we cognitively store and retrieve such information.

Enter the Omega Learning Map (ΩLM), an artificial cognitive memory learning map specifically developed to store and recall machine-learning data output sets in a structure that mimics human biological memory functions.[45] This declarative memory map also includes a unique Episodic Recall Promoter (ERP) apparatus that can assist a learner with recall of previously learned academic subject matter as it relates to knowledge recollection.

I, along with several student researchers, developed a unique memory information processing system called the Knowledge Acquisition System (KAS) that is the basis of these two inventions. The KAS performs the filtering, processing, recognition, assignation, and classification that mimics the various memory components of the human prefrontal cortex and hippocampus brain regions, and then passes the surviving categorized and classified data sets to the ΩLM long-term memory construct.

The KAS is divided into four prime component groups, each representative of a human prefrontal context and hippocampus memory model, including sensory memory (v), working memory (w), short-term memory (m), and long-term memory (l). Lastly, the KAS includes a Universal Memory Bank (j; UMB) that stores best practice results from the successful intervention recommendations made by DALI to learners. If DALI detects that a learner's academic or personal struggles or conflicts are similar to conditions and circumstances exhibited by a previous learner, the UMB address is triggered to search for a previously successful universal intervention and offer that method to remedy the conflict.

Within the KAS, sensory memory inputs are divided into two categories: semantic inputs and episodic inputs. Semantic inputs are comprised of all data sets representing general information about the learner, such as traditional achievement scores, nontraditional achievement assessments, foundational data, subject and nonsubject communication channel data sets, and historical data sets derived from an ASL rubric. Episodic inputs are comprised of all data regarding an individual's personal learning event experiences, such as adjoined ambient sounds, music, voice discussions, video feeds, timbre, and even odors.

These inputs are collected through various machine "senses," such as from computer microphones, external microphones, webcams (speech-to-text and facial recognition), and room cams, which can detect all the environmental and sensory variables a learner may engage with or experience during a cohort semantic learning experience.

The structure of the ΩLM simulates and mimics biological cognitive long-term declarative memory, which is comprised of both episodic and semantic memory information, and possesses the ability of conscious recollection. Episodic memory consists of sequences of events, and semantic memory consists of factual information.[46] The semantic inputs received directly from the working memory leap over the short-term memory (STM) module and are stored in the semantic memory component of the declarative memory module. The episodic inputs that survive the STM entropy filter are stored in the episodic memory component of the declarative memory module in the ΩLM.

Another component of long-term memory also found in the KAS is *procedural memory*, which in a biological model, acquires and stores acquired motor skills and habits formed over time.[47] The procedural memory module in the KAS also contains rules for processing and storage in the working memory and STM. Storing the rules, weights, errors, and corrections in a machine-learning simulation procedural memory component allows constant adaptation and modification.

Imagine we each possess our own personal and private cognitive memory map, propagated by our own personally trained machine-learning models that contain not just a timeline of our learning journeys, married to our social experiences, but also the entire context of that journey—the circumstances, surroundings, and settings in which they all occurred. Is it plausible then to postulate that memories consist of many interrelated components that represent experiences and information that are stored in tandem in our biological cognitive memories and that all of the related components of one thought or experience can be *recollected* when one or two associated memory experiences are somehow triggered?

The Episodic Recall Promoter (ERP), also invented by our student research team, is an artificial episodic memory apparatus that *tempts* and *attracts* a learner into recalling long-term memory information through multisensory associative exposure and conditions. Similar to a memory "lure," where different episodic memory components that are stored together as a cohort memory experience with the factual semantic information, such as background music that may have been playing, or smells of the food a learner was eating when studying, are offered to jog semantic memory recall.

The ERP doesn't actually provide the semantic memory answers to previously learned subject-matter material. Rather, it provides a related episodic cognitive sample of the context in which the learner experienced or previously acquired the semantic knowledge to help cure the "tip of the tongue" syndrome.

In summary, to purposely group learners with similar social interests and activities to facilitate and foster social engagement and social learning is not necessarily a novel idea. However, how one uses the resulting social exchanges, using machine-learning models to parse, classify, label, and assess these exchanges and compare them directly to an academic rubric, *is* novel. To recognize that a learner's social and private nonacademic life has a direct impact on their academic journey, being able to measure that impact, to detect the symptoms of a potential adverse issue, and to use artificial intelligence to proactively intervene to remedy a learner's academic journey *is* truly groundbreaking.

Furthermore, to deploy active training of machine-learning models to aid in deciphering the cognitive learning style of a student, to be able to store learners' acquired knowledge in a synthetic replica of their biological cognitive memory, whereby learners' artificial cognitive models begin to actually resemble their own biological one, also offers promising new pathways to personalized academic instruction. Whence constructed, these cognitive learning tools and maps open up a cornucopia of new learning insights, assessment possibilities, and academic support methodologies, such as the ERP, to further advance and improve upon our understanding of the art and craft of teaching and learning.

WHY THIS MATTERS

During my thirty-year academic career, I have often taught an entrepreneurship course at both the undergraduate and the graduate level. One of my favorite lectures is the discussion about "Barrier to Entry." In essence, if your business becomes successful selling your product or service, what is your enterprise going to do to erect a barrier to prevent a larger, more established competitor from just copying your business model, revenue model, or your whole organizational structure and put you out of business? This is a most difficult conundrum to solve for the most advanced student of entrepreneurship. I put forth a few options, such as first to market (grow as fast as you can) intellectual property (build a strong IP portfolio) and establish exclusive major partnerships (with established companies that compete with a potential competitor). However, there is never a foolproof solution.

As more and more "smart" online platforms begin to offer a greater and deeper learning experience and surpass the historical benefits of a physical classroom or campus, what happens to the traditional university or college that cannot adopt and adapt to match or surpass these experiences? Likewise, a question for the higher education administrator is, What is your "barrier to entry" if Apple, Google, Facebook, or Amazon, or the thousands of other well-capitalized companies with a broad technical social/media ecosystem, enters the higher education market?

Because there is a huge underserved market and because there is revenue to be made, they will and, in many ways, already have. Don't assume just because higher education is an unknown and untested market for these tech giants that they will struggle when they enter it. Apple was a computer company and now dominates the music industry. Google, the search engine company, is the front-runner in autonomous vehicle design. Amazon, the online retailer, dominates the smart home speaker market, a market that didn't even exist five years ago. These companies all use machine-learning algorithms to accomplish these goals.

Highly innovative and well-capitalized tech companies could offer higher education degrees and certificates to more learners, provide more engaging and interactive academic experiences online, produce more accurate and effective assessment instruments, and offer thorough student support services—all at a lower cost than anything available at an on-site university or college.

To potentially stave off this coming disruptive tsunami, higher education administrators must dedicate human and financial resources to restructure their largest and most popular degrees and certificates, and start piloting new cutting-edge online platforms to assess the most promising future solutions across the curricula to meet incoming enrollment demands. Second, administrations and faculties need to reach out to these potential competitors and seek new innovative partnerships to establish joint academic offerings, integrate their academic faculties and researchers with their tech partner's own researchers, and jointly adopt a roadmap to meet the academic, personal, and professional expectations, requirements, and desires of the learner, who in turn must meet the expectations of an ever-changing workforce. This is how universities and community colleges, regardless of whether they are publicly subsidized or private, must confront these very real threats and challenges in the years to come. Do not underestimate the speed and impact of this coming change. Investments in time and resources to support these kinds of innovations and collaborations are imperative—for colleges to not just flourish but also survive.

NOTES

1. David Warlick, "Curriculum Is Dead," *2¢ Worth Blog*, May 22, 2006, http://2cents.onlearning.us/?p=420.
2. Anthony P. Carnevale, Nicole Smith, and Jeff Strohl, *Recovery: Job Growth and Education Requirements through 2020* (Washington, DC: Georgetown University, Center on Education and the Workforce, June 2013), http://cew.georgetown.edu.
3. Ibid.
4. U.S. Department of Education, National Center for Education Statistics, Digest of Education Statistics, 2016 (NCES 2017-094), 2018, https://nces.ed.gov.
5. C. Chet Miller and Laura B. Cardinal, "Strategic Planning and Firm Performance: A Synthesis of More than Two Decades of Research," *Academy of Management Journal* 37, no. 6 (1994): 1649–65.
6. M'hammed Abdous and Cherng-Jyh Yen, "A Predictive Study of Learner Satisfaction and Outcomes in Face-to-Face, Satellite Broadcast, and Live Video-Streaming Learning Environments," *Internet and Higher Education* 13, no. 4 (2010): 248–57; Nicholas Croft, Alice Dalton, and Marcus Grant, "Overcoming Isolation in Distance Learning: Building a Learning Community through Time and Space," *Journal for Education in the Built Environment* 5, no. 1 (2010): 27–64.
7. Denise Green, "Historically Underserved Students: What We Know, What We Still Need to Know," *New Directions for Community Colleges*, no. 135 (2006): 21–28.
8. Franka Grünewald, Christoph Meinel, Michael Totschnig, and Christian Willems, "Designing MOOCs for the Support of Multiple Learning Styles," in *European Conference on Technology Enhanced Learning*, 371–82 (Berlin: Springer, 2013).
9. Lori Breslow, David E. Pritchard, Jennifer DeBoer, Glenda S. Stump, Andrew D. Ho, and Daniel T. Seaton, "Studying Learning in the Worldwide Classroom Research into edX's First MOOC," *Research and Practice in Assessment* 8 (2013): 13–25.
10. Daniel F. O. Onah, Jane Sinclair, and Russell Boyatt, "Dropout Rates of Massive Open Online Courses: Behavioural Patterns," *EDULEARN14 Proceedings* (2014): 5825–34.
11. René F. Kizilcec, "Collaborative Learning in Geographically Distributed and In-Person Groups," *AIED 2013 Workshops Proceedings* 67 (2013).
12. Catherine Elizabeth McLoughlin, "The Pedagogy of Personalised Learning: Exemplars, MOOCS and Related Learning Theories," in *EdMedia: World Conference on Educational Media and Technology*, 266–70 (Chesapeake, VA: Association for the Advancement of Computing in Education [AACE], 2013).
13. William J. Hussar and Tabitha M. Bailey, "Projections of Education Statistics to 2022: NCES 2014–051," National Center for Education Statistics, 2014, accessed April 5, 2017, https://nces.ed.gov.
14. Ibid.
15. Helene G. Abrams and Louise Podojil Jernigan, "Academic Support Services and the Success of High-Risk College Students," *American Educational Research Journal* 21, no. 2 (1984): 261–74.
16. Joseph B. Cuseo, Viki Sox Fecas, and Aaron Thompson. *Thriving in College and Beyond: Research-Based Strategies for Academic Success and Personal Development* (Dubuque, IA: Kendall Hunt, 2010).
17. Vincent Tinto, "Building Community," *Liberal Education* 79, no. 4 (1993): 16–21.

18. Terry Anderson, "Getting the Mix Right Again: An Updated and Theoretical Rationale for Interaction," *International Review of Research in Open and Distributed Learning* 4, no. 2 (2003), https://auspace.athabascau.ca.

19. Roger N. Conaway, Susan S. Easton, and Wallace V. Schmidt, "Strategies for Enhancing Student Interaction and Immediacy in Online Courses," *Business Communication Quarterly* 68, no. 1 (2005): 23–35.

20. Michael Grahame Moore, "The Theory of Transactional Distance," in *Handbook of Distance Education*, ed. Michael Grahame Moore, 84–103 (New York: Routledge, 2013).

21. Gireesh Sharma, "Top 10 Learning Management Systems (LMS) of 2018." eLearning Carnival, February 22, 2018, https://elearningcarnival.com.

22. Hugo Fuks, Mariano Pimentel, and Carlos José Pereira De Lucena, "RU-Typing-2-Me? Evolving a Chat Tool to Increase Understanding in Learning Activities," *International Journal of Computer-Supported Collaborative Learning* 1, no. 1 (2006): 117–42.

23. Vanessa Paz Dennen and Kristina Wieland, "From Interaction to Intersubjectivity: Facilitating Online Group Discourse Processes," *Distance Education* 28, no. 3 (2007): 281–97.

24. Scott McKay Martin, "System and Method for Providing Group Learning via Computerized Student Group Assignments Conducted Based on Student Attributes and Student-Variable-Related Criteria," U.S. Patent 9,691,291, issued June 27, 2017.

25. Elisha Babad, *The Social Psychology of the Classroom* (New York: Routledge, 2009).

26. Caroline M. Hoxby and Gretchen Weingarth. *Taking Race out of the Equation: School Reassignment and the Structure of Peer Effects*, working paper 7867 (Palo Alto, 2005), https://www.pausd.org; Susan L. Stockdale and Robert L. Williams, "Cooperative Learning Groups at the College Level: Differential Effects on High, Average, and Low Exam Performers," *Journal of Behavioral Education* 13, no. 1 (2004): 37–50.

27. Marcia D. Dixson, "Creating Effective Student Engagement in Online Courses: What Do Students Find Engaging?" *Journal of the Scholarship of Teaching and Learning* 10, no. 2 (2010): 1–13, https://www.iupui.edu.

28. Chris Dede and Andrew Ho, "Big Data Analysis in High Education: Promises and Pitfalls," *EDUCAUSE Review*, last updated August 5, 2016, http://er.educause.edu.

29. Mary J. Thompson and Terrance P. O'Brien, "Learning Styles and Achievement in Postsecondary Classrooms," Annual Conference of the American Educational Research Association, Chicago, 1991 (ERIC No. ED 331 554); Doris B. Matthews, "An Investigation of Learning Styles and Perceived Academic Achievement for High School Students," *Clearing House* 69, no. 4 (1996): 249–54.

30. J. Lawrence, S. Volet, A. Dodds, and B. McGaw, "Students' Representations of Problems," *Problem-Based Learning in Education for the Professions* (Sydney: Higher Education Research and Development Society of Australasia, 1985).

31. Markku Riipinen, "Extrinsic Occupational Needs and the Relationship between Need for Achievement and Locus of Control," *Journal of Psychology* 128, no. 5 (1994): 577–87.

32. Ulrich Schiefele and Mihaly Csikszentmihalyi, "Motivation and Ability as Factors in Mathematics Experience and Achievement," *Journal for Research in Mathematics Education* (1995): 163–81.

33. R. J. Charkins, Dennis M. O'Toole, and James N. Wetzel, "Linking Teacher and Student Learning Styles with Student Achievement and Attitudes," *Journal of Economic Education* 16, no. 2 (1985): 111–20.

34. A new area of research called explainable artificial intelligence (XAI) tries to better understand the rationale behind deep-learning model decisions to improve human trust in their outputs. For more information on this topic, see David Gunning, "Explainable Artificial Intelligence (XAI)," DARPA, accessed March 16, 2019, http://www.darpa.mil.

35. Yoshua Bengio, Réjean Ducharme, Pascal Vincent, and Christian Jauvin, "A Neural Probabilistic Language Model," *Journal of Machine Learning Research* 3 (February 2003): 1137–55.

36. Joseph Turian, Lev Ratinov, and Yoshua Bengio, "Word Representations: A Simple and General Method for Semi-Supervised Learning," in *Proceedings of the 48th Annual Meeting of the Association for Computational Linguistics*, 384–94 (Stroudsburg, PA: Association for Computational Linguistics, 2010).

37. Scott McKay Martin, James R. Casey, and Christopher Etesse, "Deep Academic Learning Intelligence and Deep Neural Language Network System and Interfaces," U.S. Patent Application 15/901,476, filed August 30, 2018.

38. K. K. Thyagharajan and Ratnamanjari Nayak, "Adaptive Content Creation for Personalized E-Learning Using Web Services," *Journal of Applied Sciences Research* 3, no. 9 (2007): 828–36.

39. Margaret A. Martinez, *An Investigation into Successful Learning: Measuring the Impact of Learning Orientation, a Primary Learner-Difference Variable, on Learning* (Provo, UT: Brigham Young University, 1999), http://www.trainingplace.com.

40. C. Victor Bunderson and Margaret Martinez, "Building Interactive World Wide Web (Web) Learning Environments to Match and Support Individual Learning Differences," *Journal of Interactive Learning Research* 11, no. 2 (2000): 163–95; Margaret A. Martinez, "Key Design Considerations for Personalized Learning on the Web," *Educational Technology and Society* 4, no. 1 (2001): 26–40.

41. Simon Cassidy, "Learning Styles: An Overview of Theories, Models, and Measures," *Educational Psychology* 24, no. 4 (2004): 419–44.

42. Declan Kelly and Brendan Tangney, "Predicting Learning Characteristics in a Multiple Intelligence Based Tutoring System," In *International Conference on Intelligent Tutoring Systems*, 678–88 (Berlin: Springer, 2004); Peter Dolog, Nicola Henze, Wolfgang Nejdl, and Michael Sintek, "Personalization in Distributed e-Learning Environments," in *Proceedings of the 13th International World Wide Web Conference on Alternate Track Papers and Posters*, 170–79 (New York: ACM, 2004).

43. Thyagharajan and Nayak, "Adaptive Content Creation."

44. David Hartley, *Education and the Culture of Consumption: Personalisation and the Social Order* (New York: Routledge, 2012).

45. Martin, Casey, and Etesse, "Deep Academic Learning Intelligence."

46. Howard Eichenbaum, "A Cortical-Hippocampal System for Declarative Memory," *Nature Reviews Neuroscience* 1, no. 1 (2000): 41–50.

47. Ibid.

Chapter Five

Invention II

> Virtual reality could open up a whole new form of learning. While some people can pick up everything from a lecture or reading, others are more visual learners. Virtual reality could allow students to put on headsets and be transported to another time and witness an important battle or historical moment first hand.
>
> —Nat Levy, *GeekWire*, September 2016[1]

In late February 2014, Mark Zuckerberg, cofounder and CEO of Facebook, and Brendan Iribe, cofounder and CEO of Oculus VR (i.e., virtual reality) began an unusual corporate dance together. Facebook is and was a publicly traded global social media company, or as we've mentioned before, an advertising platform, then with 1.3 billion and growing active users owning a market capitalization of $170 billion.[2] Oculus VR was a very small private company with an alpha version of unproven technology, created for an unproven untested market, with no proof of concept (no sales).

After a quick courting, in late March 2014, Facebook acquired Oculus VR, a twenty-month-old company, for $2 billion.[3] So why would an advertising company spend that kind of money to acquire a company making a gaming headset that didn't even work yet? Posting on Facebook on March 25, 2014, after the acquisition closed, Zuckerberg wrote,

> After games, we're going to make Oculus a platform for many other experiences. Imagine enjoying a courtside seat at a game, studying in a classroom of students and teachers all over the world or consulting with a doctor face-to-face—just by putting on goggles in your home. This is really a new communication platform. By feeling truly present, you can share unbounded spaces and experiences with the people in your life. Imagine sharing not just moments with your friends online, but entire experiences and adventures. These are just some of the potential uses.[4]

This bold 2014 declaration about what VR will allow users to experience turned out to be a little overly optimistic at the time. From an impressive semi-canned early Oculus Rift demo, Zuckerberg never anticipated the complex issues and technological hurdles that still needed to be overcome to offer a user a truly immersive and cost-effective VR experience.

Since the 1960s, artificial immersive environments have been deployed to train pilots and NASA astronauts, and enhance entertainment media, all with impressive proclamations, fanfare, and promise, but all with mixed results. In a December 2015 *Raconteur* article, Citibank analyst Kota Ezawa was quoted as saying, "We expect 2016 to be the year that VR takes off" across medicine, shopping, and theme parks.[5]

Well, we are still waiting for VR to take off.

As with most bleeding-edge technology concepts—from artificial intelligence to space travel and, yes, virtual and augmented reality—it may take decades after inception for supporting technological and scientific breakthroughs to catch up and allow what the technology futurists predict to eventually become reality. However, due to the realization of Moore's Law, science and technology *have* caught up with each other, allowing the mass production of affordable and miniaturized lightweight displays, cell phone chips, solid-state memory chips, and tiny gyroscopes, accelerometers, and power supplies.

These breakthroughs have allowed the shrinking of the massively heavy, tethered goggles offered by the original Oculus Rift to now become a lightweight tether-less and tracker-enabled virtual reality headset that can be simultaneously shared by multiple users from around the globe. These technological breakthroughs have further allowed pools of networked server warehouses filled with central processing units (CPUs) and graphics processing units (GPUs) around the globe to provide access to any software application from any device, from any location.

The rise of "cloud storage computing" has facilitated live multichannel video streaming, ideal not just for teaching and learning (as well as watching Netflix and playing games) but also for fast supervised and unsupervised training of machine-learning algorithms. Lastly, this ever-accelerating partnership between science and technology is allowing the artificial intelligence (AI) research community to start to envision true artificial sentience, affording expectations for an artificial general intelligence (AGI) model in the near future.

This chapter outlines a brief history and short survey of applications and future uses of single- and multilearner virtual immersive learning spaces, rendered possible by the next generation of networked virtual reality/augmented/mixed reality (MR) devices. A few use cases are provided, but because there is limited quantity (and quality) of scholarship in teaching and learning using MR methods, I speculate about the impact of wider adoption of MR in education and offer examples where it may enhance and improve upon current pedagogy.

The chapter continues with a short history and overview of evolving distributed ledgers, or blockchain models, and their application in teaching and learning. It concludes with an overview of Scriybium, an original education-related blockchain exercise. Finally, it proposes what an AGI teacher may look like, with caveats of course, including listing some of the cognitive models a great AI teacher would need to own in order to simulate, or indeed emulate, a great human educator.

VIRTUAL REALITY, AUGMENTED REALITY, AND MIXED REALITY

In 1987, the term *virtual reality* was first attributed to Jaron Lanier, an American programmer, author, and composer.[6] Lanier left Atari in 1985 to found VPL Research, the first commercial start-up to offer a 3-D immersive VR environment, experienced via a head-mounted display, data gloves, and even a full-body data suit. More importantly, Lanier and a cohort of VPL visionaries received a patent in 1990 that read in partial as follows:

> The virtual environment is displayed to the participants using sensory displays such as head-mounted visual and auditory displays, which travel with the wearer and track the position and orientation of the wearer's head in space. Participants can look at each other within the virtual environment and see virtual body images of the other participants in a manner similar to the way that people in a physical environment see each other. Each participant can also look at his or her own virtual body in exactly the same manner that a person in a physical environment can look at his or her own real body. The participants may work on a common task together and view the results of each other's actions.[7]

Even though the inventions never worked as described, as scientific and technology innovation needed to catch up with each other, Lanier and team predicted the true significance of VR, augmented reality (AR), and a combination of the two called *mixed reality*: the ability of more than one person to participate in an immersive environment and collaborate on a common task together.

The opposite of the instructor-led "passive learning" environment, mostly observed as one lecturer talking and a group of learners taking notes, is the "active learning" environment (or space) that requires learners to take the initiative in their learning process.[8] Simply defined, active learning is everything that requires anything greater than listening or recording what learners believe they heard. Active learning may still require the traditional lecture, but it augments the learner experience with complementary active analysis, calculations, debate, assessments, or reflections.[9]

Team-based learning, or collaborative learning (sometimes referred to as cooperative learning), is a special type of active learning that necessitates inclusion of ideas, beliefs, and active participation of a learning team to accomplish a given task. If active learning is "doing," then collaborative learning is "doing with others."[10] This is the power that new technologies like VR bring to the practice of teaching and learning. A learner doesn't need an interactive immersive 3-D environment to watch an instructor lecture, scroll through a video clip, or watch a demonstration of a scientific experiment. But if the learner is hundreds of miles away from the biochemistry lab in a college virtual learning space, and her assignment is to choose and mix the right chemical compounds as her contribution to the experiment, VR can be transformative.

There are essentially three forms of VR systems in use today for teaching and learning: immersive VR, non-immersive augmented AR, and mixed reality, or MR, defined as a combination of the two. Figure 5.1 provides examples of all three.

Immersive VR provides an interactive 3-D environment, 360 degree graphically modeled or video recorded, experienced generally via a headset or goggles coupled with hand controllers or gloves used for hand-eye interactivity. For true immersion, 3-D or binaural speakers or earplugs are essential as well. Streaming or live ambient sounds and specific content-associated sounds (clinking of glass) and speech are critical to suspended belief within a virtual space.

Lastly, many VR systems also employ large room body-motion trackers and sensors that calculate a scaled-down 3-D plane between VR users' actual tracked space and distance they move within. Motions and sounds are then synced to hand controllers, similar to the inversion of motion-capture suits worn by actual athletes used to replicate their body kinesis in sports video games.

Nonimmersive augmented VR, or today shortened to augmented reality (AR), was first described in 1990 by Thomas Caudell, a Boeing scientist, to describe how a project he was working on would allow Boeing electricians to use a head-mounted display to keep track of a multitude of colored wires assembled in harnesses with the aid of artificially overlaid images on a wiring peg board.[11] Generically speaking, unlike VR, AR is the application of artificially generated information overlaid on real-world imagery, generally superimposed 2-D or 3-D graphically generated images laid on top of real-time images or prerecorded video.

AR uses generally fall into four primary categories: presentation and visualization, industrial, entertainment, and education/training.[12] One of the earliest commercial applications of AR was the use of the automotive heads-

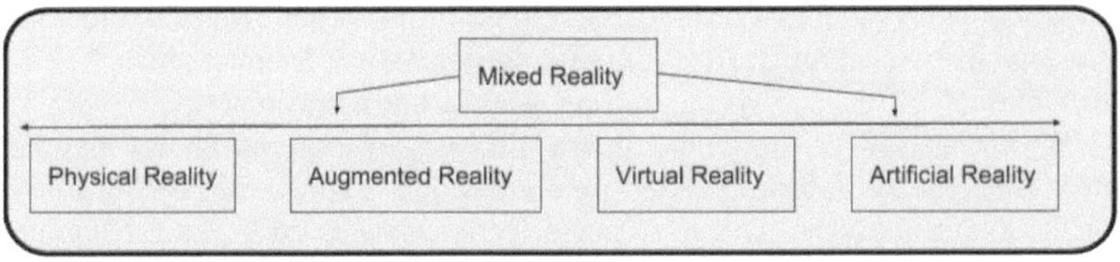

Figure 5.1. Three types of VR systems: 3-D immersive, augmented, and mixed

up displays seen in the GM 1989 Oldsmobile Cutlass Supreme. Following early aircraft cockpit designs, drivers could monitor the speed and other vital engine gauges projected onto the windshield of their vehicles.[13] Another unique early application of AR was and is the National Football League's overlaid yellow-stripe first down marker (1st & Ten, Sportvision) initially broadcast on national television in 1989.[14]

However, what truly solidified AR as a prospective useful technology to deploy for training and education was the release of the portable, hands-free, lightweight, and mobile phone–connected prototype device called Google Glass in 2013. Glass was initially only available to eight thousand people who applied to the Google Explorer Program and who proposed a unique project that Glass could be used for, or a problem that Glass could solve.[15] Figure 5.2 provides an illustration of the original beta Google Glass device.

One of the first class of early adopters were medical clinicians, where the glass camera and prism screen could be potentially ideal in patient records access, verbal note recording, and even diagnosis.[16] In education, Glass had the potential for learners to record lectures with a blink of the eye, quickly look up topics and view videos on the web during a class lecture, and even hear instantaneous language translations of lectures in a foreign tongue.[17]

Although the literature is full of unique applications and uses of Google Glass, it never made it past the beta version due to technical limitations and privacy concerns, and Google closed the semi-commercial division in 2015.[18] Even though scientific breakthrough and technological advancement needed to catch up with each other once again to match the promises of the Glass device, the scientific research and medical communities took note of the potential of AR to enhance and improve upon tasks required of their professions.

Lastly, the recent popularity of the game Pokémon Go (Nintendo) has demonstrated to everyone that they have a formidable AR device in their pocket, spotlighting another use of augmented reality for the general populace. Although many loose definitions abound, as figure 5.1 outlines above, mixed reality (MR) is the combination of functionality from both VR and

AR. Using an MR system, a person could be placed into a real-world physical space with virtual assets (objects), or placed in a virtual reality world with true physical world assets, or a combination of both.[19] So in essence, MR is the "mixing" of real and virtual objects, people, and environments.

Within an MR environment, where the lines of real and unreal may be more difficult to discern, perhaps we should now define what we mean by virtual and real assets. An early categorization developed by Paul Milgram and Fumio Kishino follows:

- Real objects are any objects that have an objective existence.
- Virtual objects are objects that exist in essence or effect but not formally or actually.
- Virtual objects cannot be viewed indirectly, but real objects can, such as through windows or air.
- Real objects have some luminosity at the location at which they appear to be located and occlude objects behind it.
- Virtual objects have no luminosity at the location at which they appear to be located and may or may not occlude other objects behind it.[20]

Although various forms of MR have existed for decades, what solidified MR as a potential advantageous technique to deploy for training and education

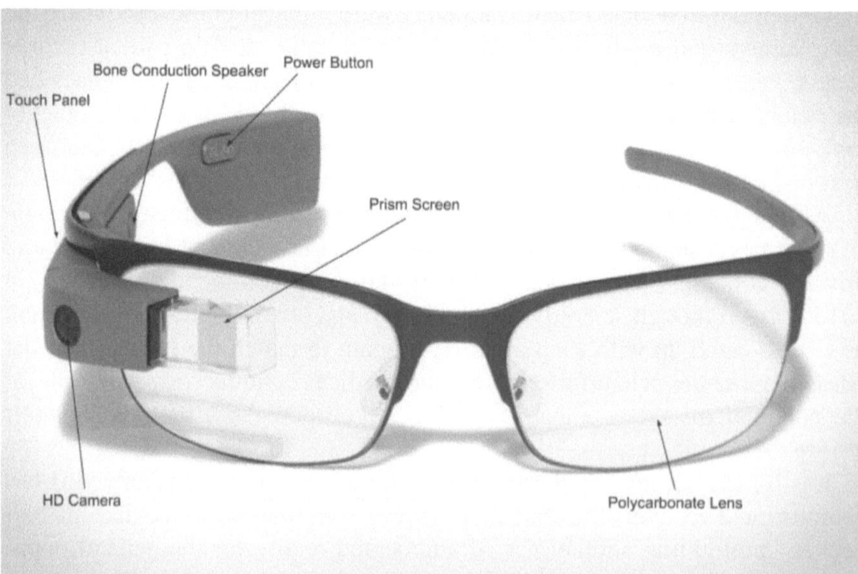

Figure 5.2. Beta version of Google Glass

was the 2016 preproduction beta release of Microsoft's HoloLens. The HoloLens is a tether-less, fairly lightweight, adjustable networked headset, with ear-placed speakers that can mimic sound spatial location, microphones, and multiple synthesized and synced cameras that can project an interactive artificial 3-D asset within a user's physical space—what Microsoft calls a hologram.[21] The external cameras essentially scan the space a user is in to place the desired artificial 3-D asset within the same space. Figure 5.3 provides an illustration of Microsoft HoloLens and an example of a generated hologram.

Although originally also requiring a project proposal and application, the HoloLens has been available to the general public since late 2016 as either a Development Edition, ideal for software tinkerers and developers, or as an Enterprise Suite, targeted toward larger organizations where multiple users may share a single headset for different purposes. To help expand the HoloLens into the more frugal teaching and learning space, Microsoft started to lease the HoloLens in 2018.[22]

Again, one of the first groups of early adopters originated from the medical profession. One novel example is using a slightly customized HoloLens to allow surgeons to differentiate between cancerous and healthy tissue by converting infrared fluorescence images into color-coded holograms over a patient's real tumor during real time during surgery.[23]

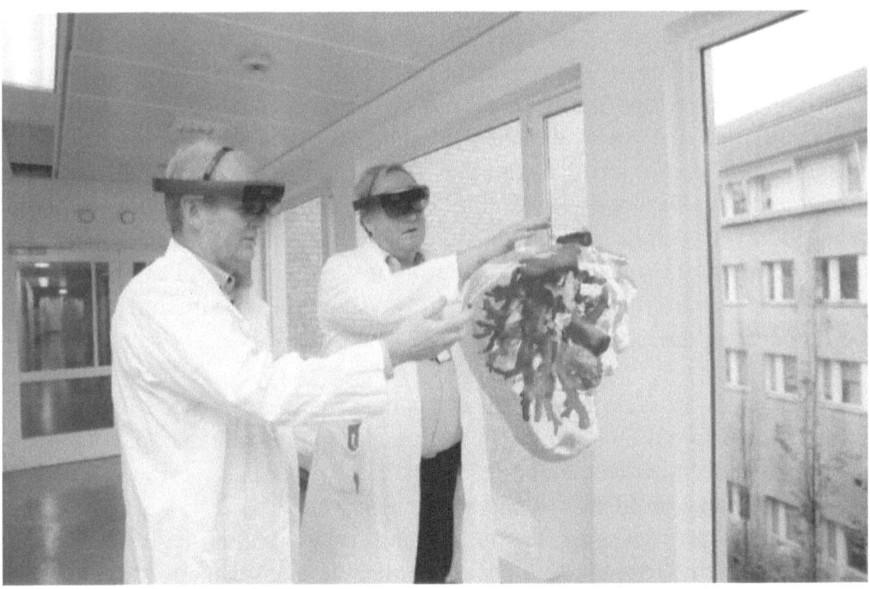

Figure 5.3. Microsoft HoloLens and hologram example

Another impressive medical field example was the use of the HoloLens to autopsy gross and acute 3-D scanned images of human organs as 3-D holograms. When the organs are scanned in 3-D, pathologists could rotate, examine, and annotate an organ, and share their annotated hologram with other pathologists globally.[24]

Lastly, in a small controlled study conducted in 2018 of three groups of Danish students using the HoloLens to study human anatomy, the results found that even though quiz scores were only slightly greater for students that used the HoloLens to examine and manipulate holograms of CT scans of the human body, their self-efficacy scores and the qualitative analysis of the MR student's spatial understanding were significantly higher.[25]

As impressive as these VR/AR/MR hardware systems may be, it's not the tech, the shiny bauble, that is transformative in teaching and learning; rather, it's what the learner sees and does within the virtual environment. After all, new iterations of headsets, glasses, eye tracking, sound transducers, and body tracking systems will continue to evolve and become more precise, lighter, and more affordable for colleges and universities in the near future. It's the design of the immersive content, the objects, environments, and new artificial geometric planes, that will be truly transformative.

The greatest power with MR is the ability to place a learner not in a familiar Newtonian immersive environment, one that replicates the real world, but in an atypical, more abstract one. These opportunities offer a learner new intellectual challenges and encourage active learning greater than anything that can be found in the traditional classroom.

In the past several years, the Virginia Serious Game Institute has subscribed to multiple partner programs to test and evaluate all the device types mentioned above, and many more not covered in the first section of this chapter. Every one we evaluated held immense potential for teaching and learning, and were a lot of fun to use, but all had a few technical issues or implementation limitations—whether that be limited battery life, tethered cables to PCs, weight, restricted "field of view,'" faulty hand sensors and tracking, or cost. However, one of the biggest issues with all of the devices we evaluated was their inability to fully interconnect with other learners using the same device, at the same time, within the same 3-D learning environment.

In addition, all were unable to interconnect with any other MR-type devices from different manufacturers. If you can't connect a group of learners that can tackle a project together, sharing best practices, critical thinking approaches, and problem solving strategies, you'll never be able to help foster peer-to-peer learning, active learning, or social learning. What about the exponentially growing number of online students displaced all over the globe who are supposed to participate in the same 3-D immersive biology or chemistry lab experiments and who own different devices?

Let's assume in a few years industry somehow agrees on a new interoperability and interconnectivity protocol so any VR/AR/MR device using the same protocol can connect together over a cloud network. Problem solved, right? What happens when you have a learner with a low-resolution mobile-phone-enabled VR headset from a poor community in West Virginia working on the same biology experiment in the same 3-D immersive laboratory with one from Long Island using next-gen AR glasses? Will each student receive the same level of engaging cohort experiential learning? Of course not.

So, with these new promising teaching and learning tools, we must stay vigilant to not allow a second wave of a digital divide, or more precisely, virtual immersive learning divide (VILD), to emerge, and ensure that technology remains the potential equalizer for educational opportunity for every learner, not the divider, again.

VIRTUAL IMMERSIVE LEARNING SPACES

In the arts, sciences, and engineering, learner success depends on critical thinking and problem-solving skills and the ability to work with abstract information and extract patterns and correlations from the information presented, and manipulate that information to solve a problem, engineer a new solution, or create a new work of art. To visualize the information is one method that will assist a learner to identify patterns that can hopefully disclose a solution.[26] Historically, methods of visualization of this information have been presented two-dimensionally on chalkboards, on screens, and in books. Although three-dimensional visualization is possible on a computer screen, the observation of that information is still delivered to users from a two-dimension pixel-per-inch (PPI) screen.

The ability to solve a complex problem, especially a complex abstract problem, is aided by taking different visual points of view, assuming different perspectives and angles. It has been argued that there are three basic human frames of reference: the exocentric, which allows a learner a view from the outside looking in (such as visualizations that appear in books or from a computer screen); the egocentric, inside the visualization looking out; and bicentric, which allows the dynamic movement between the two.[27]

Immersive virtual environments, such as those offered by VR/AR/MR (let's combine as just MX moving forward) can provide all three for a learner. Moreover, immersive environments do not need to conform to Newtonian physics or Euclidean or 3-D Cartesian geometry. Gravitationally heavy objects in a Newtonian environment can be as light in mass and density as found on our lunar or the Martian surface. Learners can not only pick up an object of previous heft and examine and measure the underbelly but also expand the objects or themselves, and virtually enter the object for further analysis, demonstrating the use of the three frames of reference noted above. Lastly, the learner could further interact with the object by dropping it or throwing the object against another, hearing aural cues from the events that produces appropriate sound effects that communicate weight, hardness, and distance.

Virtual immersive environments provide three general types of experiences:

1. the ability to change the dimension and size of a user and/or object representation;
2. the ability to use sensory cues to convince a user of their presence in an environment; and
3. the ability to create and visualize representation of objects and events that have no physical form in the real world.[28]

The ability to manipulate these variables within MX virtual learning spaces, by learners *or* instructors, offers immense potential to transfigure the practice of teaching and learning.

It even offers the opportunity to finally redefine the role of the "instructional designer," created to help traditional lecturers convert their course materials to the old online asynchronous learning management platforms (LMSs). Perhaps with so many MX learning approaches to trial, pedagogical options to test, and new assessment models to validate, an instructor will need the assistance of an expert MX instructional designer to help design and deploy their MX course. A new designer role that can assist an instructor to convert and transform their current course content into multilearner immersive 3-D learning materials and to help create new course content would be unimaginable in a traditional classroom or 2-D online platform. So, what would the job description of an MX instructional designer look like?

Description

The MX instructional designer will be an integral member of the teaching and learning instructional design team whose primary objective is to assist subject-matter experts (SMEs) and instructional faculty with developing highly immersive 3-D learning experiences across multiple domains and learning spaces. The ideal candidate will be a member of the instructional design team responsible for developing and deploying educational processes and new methodologies that enable SMEs and faculties to rapidly transfer and improve upon their standing course content and successful pedagogical approaches within a multilearner immersive environment.

The ideal candidate should possess intimate knowledge of all MX-related hardware, software, and middleware to help guide and assist SMEs and faculty members with implementing MX learning solutions and to inform about technical limitations, strengths, opportunities, and capabilities available in the conversion and transposition of course content.

Lastly, the candidate will also possess the knowledge and analytical skills to develop the assessment matrixes of learning outcomes that faculty members could employ to measure academic outcomes and success in full or partial MX learning spaces.

Essential Job Duties and Responsibilities

- Guide and inform SMEs and faculty members during initial review of their course content, schedule, learning outcomes, and performance needs. Conduct needs process and content and learner analysis to translate opportunities into teaching and learning solutions.
- Test and retest potential solutions, tools, platforms, and environments to better inform SMEs and faculty members about appropriate and optional MX solutions and learning environments.
- In close collaboration with SMEs and faculty members, develop assessment vehicles that match or improve upon standing matrixes, and integrate these vehicles into the learning experience.
- Build pilot test beds for the SMEs and faculty members to test and engage with their course content. Enlist quality assurance teams to debug any issues prior to launch of any MX learning experience.
- Guide, debug, advise, and assist the SMEs and faculty members during the early phases of their live MX learning environment experiences.
- Work on multiple projects of varying domains, scope, and complexity to ensure project timelines, learning objectives, assessment models, and budgets are met.
- Assist in the implementation of effective and efficient methodologies for designing, developing, and deploying immersive and interactive modular and full course materials.
- Create and maintain library of MX learning materials, and improve methodologies for transfer, conversion, transposition, and delivery of course content.
- Proactively build and implement assessment methodologies during the MX course design phase. Use SME, faculty, facilitator, and team feedback, hands-on experience, and analytical skills to analyze results and modify and improve MX course content. When possible, measure return on investment (ROI) through testing methods such as Kirkpatrick's Four-Level Model.
- Prepare comprehensive reporting on learning results to help identify opportunities to improve educational content and materials and methodologies.

- Create, maintain, and apply documentation as needed during the MX design and development processes.
- Monitor emerging MX development trends and standards, bring current best practices to the organization, and expand the boundaries of creativity and impact in teaching and learning.

Education and Experience Requirements

- Terminal degree in one science knowledge domain in addition to strong IT, CS, networking, or related technical field advance study, degrees, and/or certificates
- Three to five years' experience in learning science, learning engineering, and software development
- Knowledge of teaching and learning theories and principles, including first-time, adult, and underserved population learning theories and established educational and training models of assessment and evaluation
- Knowledge of standing instructional design methodology and development (e.g., ADDIE, SAM, action mapping)
- Proven technical writing experience
- Experience as instructor of domain-non-specific immersive education modules or courses a plus

Skills and Abilities

- Effective organizational skills to work on multiple projects, including the ability to prioritize tasks
- Strong written and verbal communication, listening, and analytical skills necessary to interact with instructional design team members, SMEs, instructional faculty members, topic experts, and learners of all ages and knowledge levels
- Advanced hardware and software technical skills, including experience with all commercially available MX goggles, glasses, controllers, trackers, and interfaces
- Familiarity with emerging technology and industry-related trends
- Ability to translate complex information to a wide range of audiences
- Demonstrated ability to identify and assess topic experts', SMEs', instructional faculty members', and learners' needs to achieve maximum satisfaction of MX learning experiences

Based on a review of scholarly literature and my own observations, beyond simple experiments and pilots, MX has but a small toehold in traditional academic institutions. However, it has been adopted and embraced at a much higher frequency in industry, especially in corporate training and manufacturing. MX allows industrial manufacturers to not just save time and money by using repetitive multiuser immersive environments to better train employees on tasks but also replicate an environment that negates the inherent dangers posed by swinging heavy automated arms and precise autonomous robots found on a modern factory floor.

One exemplary study led by the Airbus Group and funded by an Innovate UK grant used a customized and modified Oculus Rift goggle-type headset to allow simultaneous multiuser collaborative training of the assembly jig used in the manufacture of aircraft maintenance doors.[29] Twenty-four trainees observed a trainer inspect and operate the parts of a door assembly jig, both live in a training room and through the modified Oculus Rift headset. The study examined whether trainees could retain the information presented by the trainer better face-to-face using actual equipment pieces or through a 3-D immersive learning environment using virtual 3-D pieces of equipment. Figure 5.4 outlines the two conditions that occurred in the study.

The conclusion of the A/B study found that although both training methods produced nearly equal high knowledge-retention rates exhibited during the evaluation phase, the MX training value was greater, in that it reduced the costs of physical equipment and trainer time and increased safety.[30] This discovery was not part of the initial study hypothesis, but the ancillary findings ended up being of greater worth to the company, both in cost savings and in worker safety.

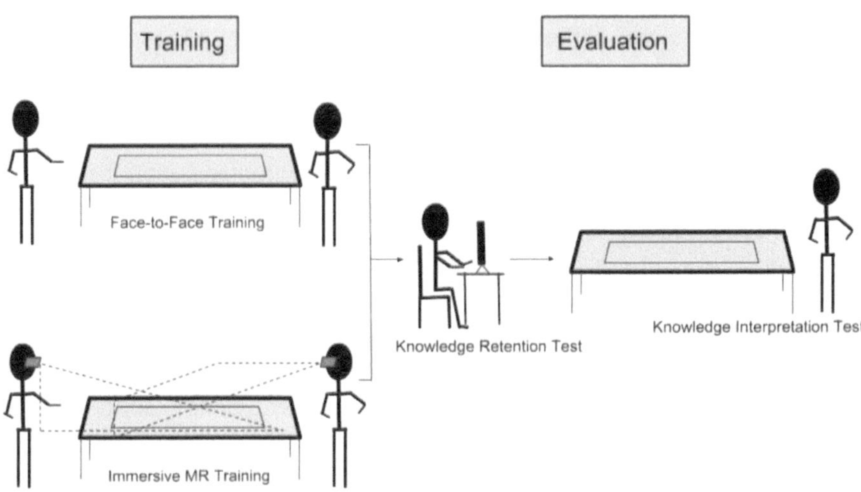

Figure 5.4. Contrasting types of training, on-site and MX, used in aircraft door assembly jig study

Another outstanding industrial MX training example outlines how Honeywell Connected Plant developed an immersive competency program to train manufacturing plant safety, operations, and maintenance personnel to plan and execute maintenance tasks virtually.[31] Technically headset agnostic, the Honeywell system is also designed to be used after training in the field to allow maintenance technicians to pull up repair and parts manuals in their MX HUD goggles, and virtually share in real time the diagram of the replacement part needed with a parts supplier. Their system also allows for overlay of machine assembly schematics to repair a broken machine when the part arrives, all within a multiuser MX environment.[32]

In early 2018, a team of five students and two faculty members in the Virginia Serious Game Institute (VSGI) in partnership with CHI Systems wrapped up a joint applied-research pilot of an MX project titled Interactive Mixed-Media Augmented Reality Simulation Engine (IMMERSE). IMMERSE was designed to help train and guide army medics in the classroom and in the field with emergency combat casualty medical care.

Funded by a federal Small Business Technology Transfer (STTR) grant, IMMERSE was designed to overlay virtual 3-D emergency surgical operational procedures through a tablet, phone, HUD, or MX Glasses to provide interactive training to lower field combat care mistakes, and to better guide army medics in the field to treat combat casualties. Figure 5.5 outlines what an army combat medic will see within the IMMERSE Environment.

A virtual 3-D hand and fingers demonstrates how to determine where an incision should occur for an emergency tracheotomy. Future versions of the IMMERSE solution will allow army medics to overlay their physical fingers above 3-D projected animation of virtual fingers guiding the medic through the operation on a live patient. The solution will even be able to critique the medic during the operation, correcting their performance in real time—the entire experience recorded for postoperation review and assessment.

Anecdotally, colleges and universities are a decade behind private industry in adopting MX solutions for training and education and even far behind industry and governments incorporating MX solutions within their courses, labs, and team projects.

Faculties and administrators are historically risk averse in their financial and reward models and see no short-term benefit to change. In many cases, this managerial philosophy eschews their mission, as grand and foresighted as most are, for financial predictability. Perhaps one day administrators and faculties will see that just a small financial investment, both to adopt an MX solution and to train faculty members to use it, will actually save money, increase student safety, and improve learning outcomes on the back end. Perhaps soon, teachers of history will work with MX instructional designers, animators, and videographers to help them re-create immersive environments

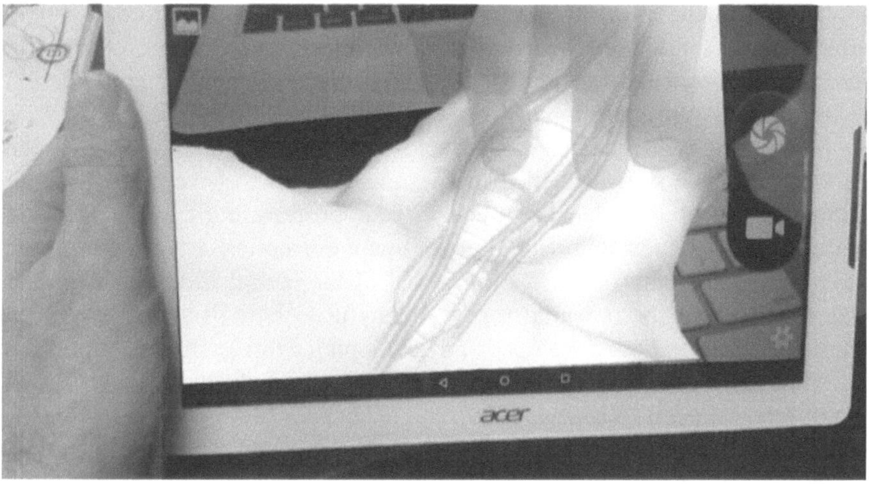

Figure 5.5. Overlaid instruction to perform a tracheotomy

of historical places and events to allow the learner to see, hear, and sense historical moments at the time and place they occurred.

As is mentioned multiple times in this book, a new paradigm is slowly enveloping higher education, a new archetype of teaching and learning that will require faculties to develop new scholastic methodologies, assessments tools, and learning environments to permit the learner to acquire the new knowledge, experiences, and skills that will be in demand tomorrow. This transfiguration is required not just for the learner to stay relevant in the fourth industrial revolution but also for the teacher to stay relevant as well.

BLOCKCHAIN EDUCATION MODELS

Besides immersive MX, and perhaps machine learning, few emerging innovations promise to disrupt and transform teaching and learning more than digital distributed ledgers, better known as blockchain technologies. The term *distributed ledger* is used as the original purpose of the technology was to function as a digital semipublic transaction log of the buying and selling of non-nation, non-state-backed, highly encrypted virtual coins or tokens, better known as crypto-currencies.

Originally made popular by the publication of a paper in 2008 titled "Bitcoin: A Peer-to-Peer Electronic Cash System" authored by Satoshi Nakamoto, a pseudonym used by an unknown person or people to this day, crypto-currencies were created to offer an alternative method of online payment to be sent directly from one person to another without going through an established financial institution.[33] Of course, financial transactions that are not routed to a financial institution for processing are not subject to that bank's governmental regulatory oversight and, therefore, could be susceptible to fraud and abuse. However, the lack of government oversight and regulation is also partially the attraction of some crypto-currency offerings.

It's not a coincidence that most crypto-currency coins and tokens over the past decade have been launched in countries known to have high levels of human rights abuses, lack of clear citizen protection from unwarranted searches and seizures, and overall government corruption. Crypto-currencies have provided a safe haven for the assets of the lawful in these dictatorial states, as well as the potential for the unlawful to hide ill-gotten assets via encrypted coins in both developed and developing democratic states.

Although blockchain technology protocols have evolved quite a bit, offering different models of tokens, coins, and exchanges between traders, buyers, and sellers, the original Bitcoin transaction scheme stands as the foundation. In the Bitcoin model, every user transaction is encrypted and stored on a serial virtual ledger as a block and is semipublicly time stamped so other users within the same ledger can "see" when the block was created by a hash, or a pointer. Within the Bitcoin scheme, every electronic coin is represented as a chain of user signatures. The first transaction in a block creates a new virtual coin that is owned by the block's creator. Each new subsequent block is "chained" to the previous block transaction. Each owner transfers the coin to the next by digitally signing a hash of the previous transaction and the public keys of the next owner and adding these to the end of the chain. A payee can verify the signatures to verify the chain of ownership.[34]

Even if an adversary could break the encryption, to change or alter one block by trying to hack or steal it, an attacker would destroy or "undo" all the blocks posted afterward, making the effort fruitless. Figure 5.6 provides a simplified diagram of the Bitcoin blockchain system. Lastly, in a traditional banking system, every transaction between two entities is required to go through a trusted third party, whereby except in public transactions (stock or commodity trades on public markets), the public has no knowledge of the transaction. In Bitcoin's model, the transactions are (semi-) public, but the identities of the parties are still protected. Meaning, another user on the blockchain can "see" that a transaction is taking place but has no idea who the parties are unless the parties elect to provide encryption keys to the user to unlock their identity.

As is the case with most currencies, the number of virtual coins or tokens produced are finite, so following Adam Smith's *Theory of Moral Sentiments* (1759), the value of the crypto-coins are subject to competition, supply and demand, and self-interest. With the rise of Bitcoin value per dollar, tying it to the major basket of real-world currencies, and the growing acceptance of many retailers (e.g., Tesla and Starbucks) to accept Bitcoin, so too did the

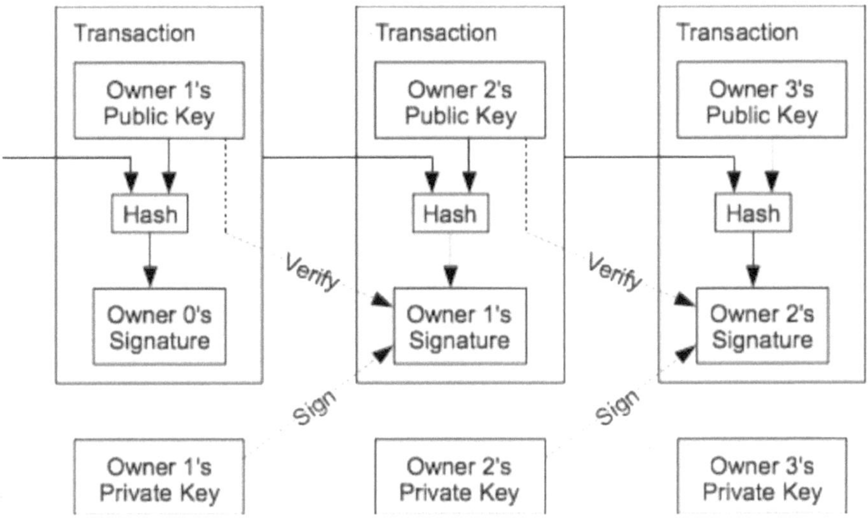

Figure 5.6. Bitcoin blockchain system

demand for the virtual currency rise. At one point, on December 17, 2017, Bitcoin's "price" reached an all-time high of $19,666 and then fell 70 percent to $5,920 on February 6, 2018,[35] demonstrating extreme volatility. However, as concerns about price manipulation and criminal activity mounted, more and more retailers started to drop Bitcoin as an acceptable currency, and the value stabilized and traded in a much narrower range.[36]

With the success and notoriety of the Bitcoin blockchain technology, additional crypto-currency technologies protocols were developed, some that improved upon the original schema. Ethereum was developed to serve more as an open-source platform, rather than just a virtual currency. Per the Ethereum white paper published in 2014, Ethereum is indeed another semipublic crypto-currency, but with the added protocol of *smart contracts* and the ability for outside developers to use the open-source software to create their own coins to sell products and "services" on a Ethereum platform.[37]

Smart contracts allow for the simultaneous secure exchange between a user and provider of goods, services, or coins. A few examples of smart contracts in use today include the exchange of loyalty rewards programs, digital IDs, real estate title transfers, medical record-keeping, weapons tracking, equity trading (and tracking), and notably, teaching and learning.[38] The concept of translating blockchain security and privacy protocols used in medical record-keeping to the protection of academic grades, transcripts, certificates, and other credentials, allowing a learner to provide access to one school or employer to review transcripts, and then post review, revoking the access privileges is unique.

To remedy the antiquated process of ordering, paying for, and waiting for a recipient to receive through the mail a stamped "official" copy of academic transcripts some weeks or months after the initial request, universities such as the Massachusetts Institute of Technology, the University of Nicosia, and the University of Birmingham have already turned to Blockcerts, a version of the Bitcoin schemata.[39] Using the same concept of trading secure tokens, blockchain could also be adapted as a tutoring or academic counseling peer-to-peer monitoring and payment platform, whereby learners can track their academic progress in real time, as a proof-of-progress scheme, and compensate the tutor or counselor accordingly with virtual tokens. How about an actual blockchain school, connecting colleges, teachers, and learners on a decentralized chain, including proof-of-course progress grading that includes automated administrative processes such as advising, registration, and token-funded financial aid and billing payments?

Woolf University was founded by a group of mostly Oxford University faculty members in 2018 as the "first" truly blockchain-powered university (online blockchain platform) with its own native token (coin) WOOLF.[40] As stated in its white paper (similar to a business plan for real-world startups), Woolf University is focused on lowering learner tuition costs, decreasing adjuncts while adding more full-time faculty members to the academy, and increasing overall faculty compensation.

The first college on the Woolf platform is called Ambrose, and it offers one-to-one tutoring, a peer-to-peer model using Ethereum-type smart contracts. A smart contract can be conducted using a blockchain protocol between a user and a service, or more applicably, between a learner and teacher, and third party that maintains the blockchain. If a learner and teacher agree a tutorial has begun, after completion a course credit transaction will occur from teacher to learner, and a payment transaction will occur from learner to teacher, with the blockchain "node," or third party transaction administrator Woolf University accrediting the trade. Although the actual tutorials may occur on any external unrelated platform, the administrative tasks of the teaching and learning process are administered simply and securely through the Woolf blockchain platform.

Another exciting blockchain education platform launched in 2018 is Education Ecosystem, or better known as LiveEdu. Again, the principal components consist of the learner and teacher functioning as the user and provider in blockchain parlance, and LiveEdu acting as the third party "node" administering the blockchain.

Per their white paper, one major difference between Woolf University and LiveEdu is that all LiveEdu courses are specifically offered on their proprietary live-streaming scalable platform. So even though the administrative aspects such as assignment of credits, certificates, grades, or payments to teachers are the same, one course offered on the LiveEdu platform can scale to hundreds or thousands of learners simultaneously. In addition, LiveEdu expands the peer-to-peer concept to offer project-quality moderators, content creators, and even instructional designer services to schools, colleges, and businesses, expanding the learner and provider paradigm on their blockchain model. Figure 5.7 provides a graph of the LiveEdu ecosystem network.

Lastly, Scriybium is an Ethereum-based blockchain smart-contract platform that I developed as an academic exercise for this chapter. Scriybium ensures the exchange of Scriybium tokens between the incentive creator (sponsor) and the incentive taker (learner). The incentive sponsor can be individuals, instructors, teachers, trainers, entire schools, colleges, or companies offering their content on the Scriybium platform. The incentive learner can be individuals, or learners originating from a sponsor, such as students already enrolled at a school or college, or employees of a company. Incentive learners are not just better engaged using the Scriybium platform; they are also motivated learners, as they can earn Scriybium tokens for successful

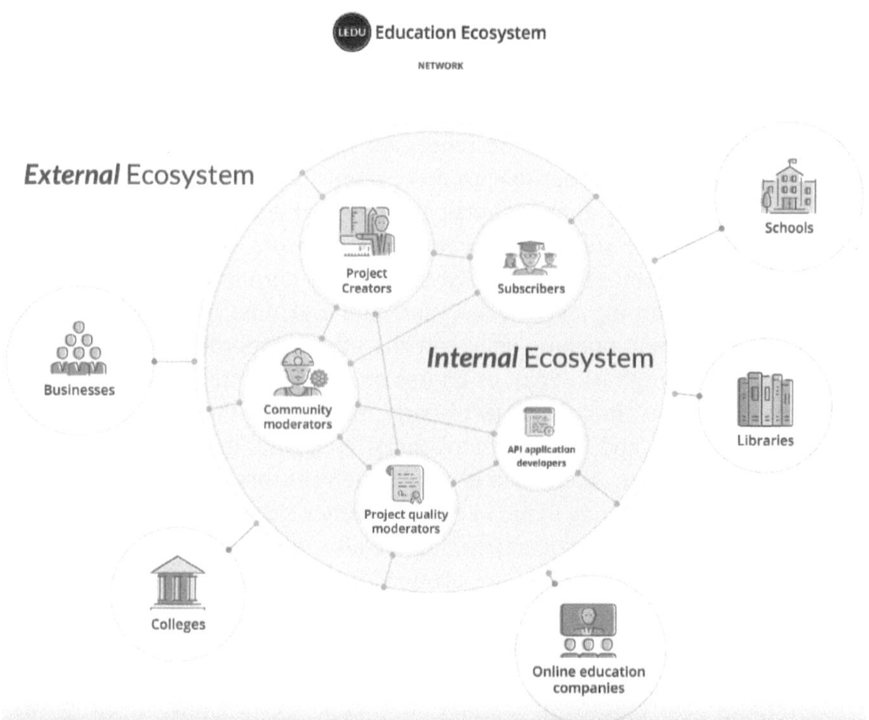

Figure 5.7. LiveEdu blockchain ecosystem

completion and automated verification of learning goals, tasks, courses, degrees, or certificates.

Sponsorship token amounts are indexed to points tied to learning content goals outlined in a gamified course syllabus. Points can be gained by completing a small piece of knowledge acquisition within a whole learning experience, say, a smaller identified task or goal such as reading a chapter from an entire book, or points can be tied to the completion of larger tasks such as completing a series of courses required to earn a certificate. Achievement points add up to credits, which in turn can be redeemed by a learner for Scriybium tokens. Provider credits are tiered as gold, silver, or bronze level credits, and earning them can be seen as learning slices of knowledge that form the pathway of a student's academic and professional journey. Provider credits can be easily mixed and matched for every learner, solely based on the learner's knowledge-acquisition goals, skills, experiences, and aptitude.

Sponsors set the amount of points (between 1 and 100) that a learner can earn for each learning task or goal accomplished: 100 points is equal to one gold credit, 50 points is equal to one silver credit, and 25 points is equal to one bronze credit. Therefore, a sponsor may assign 100 points for successful completion of a learning goal accomplished during a specific timeline. If one learner completes the goal on time, the learner receives 100 points, equal to one gold credit. However, if another learner completed only half the goal in the allotted time, that learner would receive one silver token.

Three gold credits can be redeemed for one Scriybium token. Six silver or twelve bronze credits can also be redeemed for one Scriybium token. This obviously motivates a learner to earn more points, which can be converted to credits, which not only demonstrates learning achievements, abilities, and skills but also can be redeemed for tokens. Sponsors will assign potential points to a Scriybium gamified syllabus, student enrollment minimum and maximum for a learning experience, start and end time of their session(s)/courses(s), enrollment opening date, and any other supporting materials associated with a learning task, goal, or course on the Scriybium platform. Scriybium, functioning as the "node" third-party manager of the blockchain, allocates points, credits, and Scriybium tokens offered from the sponsor.

Learners (incentive takers) can also become sponsors (incentive creators), by trading away or selling their tokens to another learner. Organic tutoring, peer-to-peer learning, and social learning are also major differentiators on the Scriybium platform, as learners are grouped in cohorts with similar interests and activities identified at registration for a Scriybium learning or tutoring experience. Figure 5.8 outlines the Scriybium provider and learner methodology.

Scriybium also allows all learners and sponsors to safely store points, tokens, and academic accomplishment (tasks, goals, course completions, certificates, and degrees), as well as professional, and even social, data that can

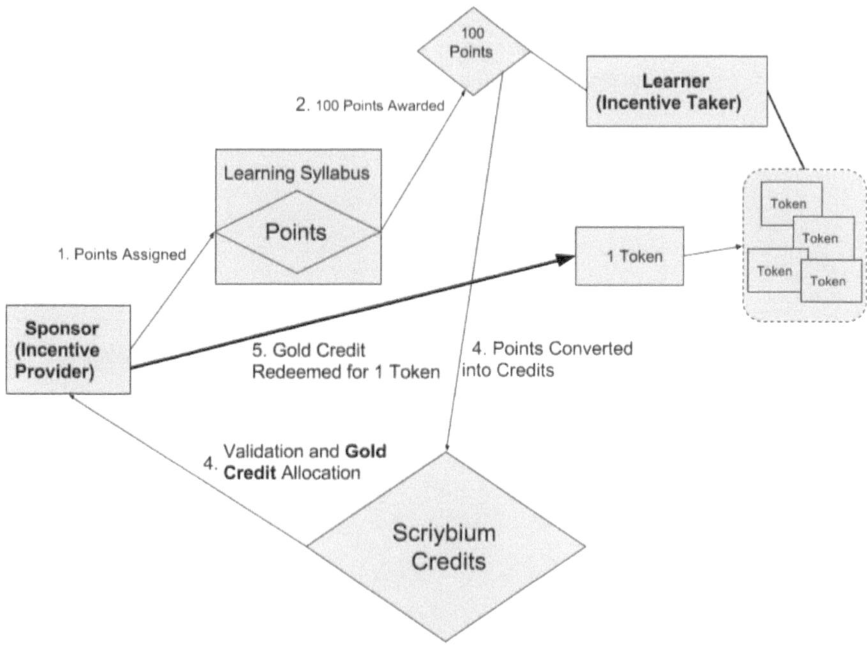

Figure 5.8. Scriybium incentive provider and incentive learner methodology

only be accessed by the learner but can be seen by whomever the learner chooses by providing a simple duel key.

A Scriybium smart contract will ensure that sponsors deposit and distribute their Scriybium tokens to learners as pledged, based on points earned and verified, and credits allocated and converted into tokens. The Scriybium platform methodology equalizes learning opportunities for anyone globally, as the pledged sponsor points, credits, and sponsor Scriybium tokens are not affected by any nation-state's economic condition, or political status. Figure 5.9 provides an example of the decentralized Scriybium blockchain token model.

All Scriybium users create a password-protected cryptographic pseudo-identity. Some sponsors, such as schools, colleges, or companies, may wish learners to link their pseudo-identity to an actual ID card, or may require additional information to become eligible for sponsored courses, certificates, or degrees. In these cases, learners can provide to the provider a specific crypto "keypair" that provides only the information required that is stored on the Scriybium platform. This access can be revoked at any time by a learner.

Sponsors will need to disclose their registered identities when sponsoring content on the Scriybium platform. If learners become sponsors, they can

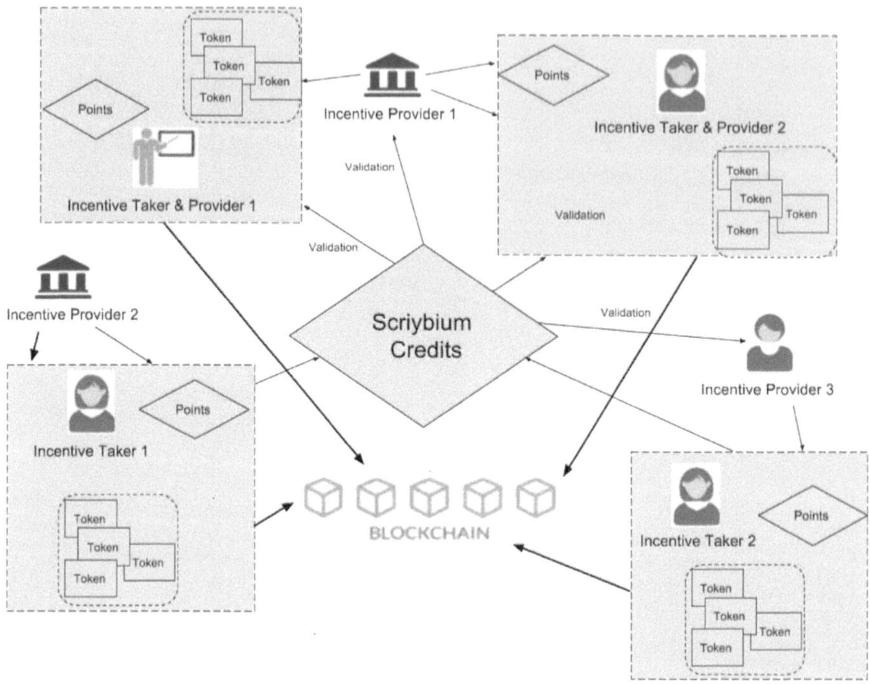

Figure 5.9. Scriybium blockchain model

choose if they want to disclose their government-issued identity to a new learner (incentive takers), but they still must designate to a new learner their point allocation schema that they can earn for each accomplished task or goal.

As lone wolf, organized criminal organizations, and state-sponsored hacking of data for theft, ransom, blackmail, and overall espionage becomes a daily and hourly occurrence in our internet-connected world, expect evolving and maturing blockchain technologies to assume a greater role in everyday transactions—from consumer banking, travel bookings, and retail purchases to requests for medical records or academic transcripts.

Moreover, the advancing iniquitousness of the internet of things (IoT) devices proliferating in our cars and homes, soon to be in our workplaces and schools, offers additional pathways for adversaries to purloin our personal data. In addition, with the continuing integration of AI machine-learning into these devices to personalize our user experiences, a breach of even greater personal information about our likes, dislikes, and daily life activities is now close to inevitable.

Lastly, as I have outlined in the previous chapter, with the advent of artificial cognitive learning memory maps, which over time mimic our actual biological memory-mapping process, our most intimate thoughts, emotions, and experiences are vulnerable to hacking without extremely secure encryption schemes. Although there are other powerful encryption protocols theoretically available, blockchain technologies, with their semipublic and private property keys, smart contract procedures, and third-party blockchain platform-management tools create an ideal secure system to offer not just a new virtual space for the exchange of knowledge but also the ability to secure the intimate practice of teaching and learning, and the simple automation of associated academic administrative tasks.

"LOOK MA, NO FACULTY": THE ARTIFICIAL GENERAL INTELLIGENCE TEACHER

As I asked in chapter 4, can interconnected AI deep-learning models be trained to actually teach subject-matter content to learners? And will learners grasp, comprehend the material taught, and learn from an AI teacher in the same fashion as they do from human teachers today? Will learners maintain the same motivation, level of engagement, and general inquisitiveness with an AI teacher as they do from a class taught by a great and engaging human teacher? After all, if well-trained Deep Academic Learning Intelligence (DALI) models can provide academic and counseling intervention recommendations, answer subject-matter-related questions, and "learn" whether discussions between students and teachers were correct and helpful, then certainly it's not a major leap for deep-learning models to assume the primary instructor role?

Theoretically, deep-learning models can be ingested and trained with all the textbook materials ever written about French history between 1700 and 1799, and then be further trained from a course syllabus about the French Revolution (1789–1799) within that timeframe that weights the deep-learning model's nodes stronger within the overall French history models and storage architecture. Therefore, again theoretically, can't an additional machine-learning model (let's call it the French Revolution Pedagogical Model) also be cross-trained with an instructor's lecture notes, slides, quizzes, and tests? Voila! We now have the AI architecture to actually "teach," assess, and evaluate learners about the French Revolution! Right?

Ah, but what about an instructor's teaching style and experience? Maybe the pedagogy we trained the model with will be incompatible with the learning style of the students in the class. Can the pedagogical model adjust itself if assessment results fall below previously trained performance levels? How do we quantify an instructor's personality traits, classroom management techniques, communication style, disciplinary approach, and even mannerisms? Does our French Revolution AI teacher even speak French?

In order for our AI French Revolution teacher to become a reality, these questions must be addressed, and we must also be able to finally quantify the dynamic criteria and attributes of a good and bad teacher, and bottle these elements somehow—a most difficult challenge not just technically but socially and politically as well.

In 2014, Georgia Tech launched the online master of science in computer science (OMSCS) degree program on the Udacity platform.[41] The degree, and many courses, specifically the knowledge-based artificial intelligence (KBAI) course offered by Dr. Ashok Goel, proved so popular that by fall 2016, five thousand students had enrolled from across the globe, and they flooded the course message boards with twelve thousand plus assignment questions, comments, and quips.[42]

Generally, participation of this magnitude in a course, either online or onsite, may indicate exceptional engagement and demonstrate motivation. On the other hand, this many questions may indicate the course content or delivery methods need revisions to improve comprehension for a larger more intellectually diversified group of learners. Either way, the large number of message board postings presented an immense problem for Dr. Goel and his small cadre of teaching assistants: how to possibly answer all the posted questions!

As many experienced teachers know, a large percentage of the learners in a class ask the same or similar questions, semester after semester. If Goel and his TAs could comb through past terms of posted questions and discover patterns of similar ones, perhaps they could develop a virtual teaching assistant that could categorize learner questions and retrieve a categorized stored answer from a database table (essentially a memory of question-answer pairs). In addition, this "Jill Watson" could check the message boards from morning to 11:00 p.m., imitating the average school day that course graduate teaching assistants (TAs) may be working. In the spring semester of 2016, although Jill Watson only answered a small number of learner-posted questions, more than 90 percent of them were correct.[43]

In subsequent KBAI courses (fall 2016, spring 2017), Goel developed actual AI versions of his virtual teaching agents, all producing similarly impressive question-answer accuracy. By the end of the 2017 spring semester, and bolstered by Goel's research publications, a 2016 Tedx talk, and Georgia Tech PR, Jill Watson was extensively covered by international mainstream and social media, and became a household name in the academic, AI, and business communities. The reality that Goel only divulged to his students that Jill Watson was an AI bot at the end of each semester he taught the KBAI course only added to the mass media intrigue, as most of his students never discovered their TA was in fact nonhuman.[44] Jill Watson became the first widely known successful deployment of an AI tool in the practice of teaching and learning.

It is understood that a consensus of philosophers, cogitative psychologists, neuroscientists, and evolutionary biologists believe that for machine-learning models to truly reach human brain parity, or reach artificial general intelligence (AGI), a complete human brain simulation of equal fidelity must be reached. In the last several years, various polls were taken by several prominent AI researchers and developers asking other AI researchers and developers when they thought AGI would be achieved. Vincent C. Müller and Nick Bostrom's groundbreaking 2013 survey results revealed 10 percent of AI experts believed the likelihood AGI would be reached in 2022, 50 percent believed the likelihood would be 2050, and 90 percent believed AGI could be accomplished by 2075.[45] Another 2013 survey conducted by James Barrat revealed similar results, with 42 percent of AI research respondents predicting AGI will be reached by 2030, 25 percent believing AGI will be reached by 2050, and 30 percent predicting 2100 or later.[46] Is there any way we can speed up the predictions of these expert prognosticators?

A large portion of the human brain is already hardwired from birth for specific purposes other than for cognitive learning. Although human brain functions tend to overlap spatially between the hemispheres, and are interconnected through billions of neurons, there are defined module portions for specific uses. For example, the occipital lobe dedicated to human sight, color, light, image recognition, and visual perception consumes 14 percent of our brain density. Essentially unconscious low-level neural processing occurs automatically outside of conscious cognitive focus.[47]

The auditory cortex, responsible for processing sound, amplitude, and frequency, sits inside our skull next to our ears, and although neural computational networks interconnect to the Brodmann area of the cerebral cortex to help interpret language, the sound-processing function takes up 5 percent (both hemispheres) of our brain mass.[48] There are also multiple interconnected overlapping portions of brain mass, such as the parietal lobe that is primarily responsible for taste and sensory perception.

To reach AGI, perhaps we could focus on designing replicas of only the modules and portions of our brain that we require for cognitive tasks that truly differentiate us from other mammals. Evolution certainly didn't grant us the best vision, nor the best hearing, in the mammalian kingdom. However, evolution, or a fortunate accident of evolution, did grant us a superior brain containing a cerebral cortex that provided us with the ability to emote, concentrate, plan, calculate, judge, reason, solve, speak, and create, along with exclusive memory processing, storage, and retrieval abilities of a supreme knowledge acquisition, storage, and retrieval system.

Perhaps machine-learning designers should concentrate on developing and bottling some of these superior human mind attributes and ignore the dedicated body function and regulation regions of the human brain. Why would an AGI teacher model require neural signals to message potential bodily injury, hunger, temperature, or voluntary muscle contractions? Whole brain simulation may not be necessary to achieve a successful machine-learning teacher model; human mind attributes coupled with extensive domain knowledge might be sufficient. Perhaps we can simulate the human mind by breaking up the useful human brain modules and their related functions, as understood today, into dedicated artificial neural cognitive modules that an AI teacher would actually need. We could interconnect only the applicable mind attributes, domain knowledge, and best human teaching traits to build an apex teaching cogitator deep-learning neural network model.

Over the ages, chess was considered the preeminent game that signified the apex of human intellectual dominance. Claude Shannon, the great Bell Labs and Princeton mathematician, calculated that chess held more potential moves at 10^{120} than atoms in the observable universe 10^{80}.[49] The Shannon number seemed to prove that chess was only a game that a human mind could invent and play, and that this game of the ages truly differentiated the human brain apart from the mammalian kingdom.

However, in 1997, using huge hardware towers holding thousands of massively parallel processors and thousands of algorithms calculating statistical probabilities of each move and countermove, IBM's Deep Blue eventually beat the world-reigning chess grand master Garry Kasparov.[50] Although Deep Blue utilized more of a lexicon look-up table methodology rather than what we would consider modern AI techniques, the results were still monumental. In late 2017, DeepMind, a London-based Google acquisition, utilized "transfer learning"[51] to create AlphaZero, an unsupervised reinforcement deep-learning technique, in hopes it could teach itself to play chess against Stockfish (self-play), the 2016 Top Chess Engine Champion (TCEC).

Not only did AlphaZero learn chess on its own (unsupervised learning), but also when it played, it drew or beat Stockfish 100 out of 100 matches![52] As remarkable as this feat is, AlphaZero is but a singularly designed deep-learning model created for one purpose, and one purpose only. It can't engage in dialog about any topic with either a human or another AI model. It has no ontological language map to understand dialog content or context. It can't reason in human terms. It can't create or replicate anything, or solve any problems presented to it outside of the chess game schema. It can accomplish only one grand complex task: win a chess game very well.

Perhaps that's the design approach we need to take in order to create an expert AGI teacher: parcel the best practices of a human teaching into bite-sized traits and mind modules into smaller artificially replicable pieces. In order to save time developing a new software application, say, a new image-editing application, programmers don't have to create things like the operating system drop-down menus, window frames, or icons for the trash can or hard drive. These preprogrammed modules reside in software libraries that usually come with the language compiler. The programmer can just imbed in the code or call when required, allowing the programmer to focus on new tasks and features of the new image-editing application being built.

This is very similar to how programmers today can license a pretrained natural language-processing model residing on a cloud server somewhere and connect it to their PC-based software platform through an application programming interface (API), or license a pretrained image-pattern-detection model to identify a black Labrador on your PC application from a series of dog pictures. Current cloud-based pretrained machine-learning models functionally serve the same purpose as traditional software libraries did—forming the basic building blocks of a new AI application being developed to accomplish new tasks.

An AGI teaching framework then could be fashioned the same way. Pretrained domain-knowledge neural network models could be stored in an asset library, alongside innate knowledge models and other human mind attributes in an AGI schematic library. An AI programmer could then build a framework for an AGI teacher to teach the French Revolution and embed calls in the framework for the pretrained entire French history domain model, the French language model when required for translations, and the best practices of the best French Revolution history teachers, to capture their best practices, pedagogical methodologies, and traits employed by human teachers of French history. What would result is a framework, or rulebook of sorts, that identifies the best of the best from proven efficacy studies that have stood the test of time, regardless of class size, learner demographics, or time period. But what would this rulebook actually contain?

> Ordinary teachers direct us along the right path, but great teachers inspire us to seek our own path.
>
> —Unknown

For purposes of this exercise, I'm only going to provide a summary of dynamic best practices for an imaginary rulebook that may represent the best higher education teacher, but not the best that may be found in K–12 education. Teachers in a public or private K–12 system must also contend with children and adolescent maturity issues—that offer the challenges of a much larger motivation span and narrower and more restricted domain guidelines that are tied to state-required standardized exams.

Although there are some parallel similarities and concerns between undergraduate and graduate studies, the limitations tend to be much smaller, so they do not generally exist in the same manner in higher education—which offers a teacher greater freedom to experiment with a classroom structure, adjust course content to match the classroom's abilities, and even modify assessment and evaluation criteria on the fly.

An Example AGI Teacher (Characteristics and Attributes) Rulebook

a. Expert Domain Knowledge: This is a given, as all great teachers require extensive knowledge about the subject matter that they teach.
b. Ability to Plan Clear Goals and Objectives for Each Class Meeting/ Session: Although the syllabus may outline the schedule for an entire semester or quarter, a great teacher must parcel the overreaching goals into smaller digestible segments of information offered over time that when combined, match the expected learning outcomes of the course.
c. Immense Curriculum Knowledge: A great teacher knows their course resides in a larger curriculum framework, and the information conveyed in their class must augment and continue the information that was taught before, and prepare the learner for what is to come in the course sequence.
d. Excellent Classroom Management Skills: Great teachers manage class time to meet session goals by guiding presentations, discussions, and questions accordingly. The best teachers can also detect when students are not engaged, or are lost, and may repeat the information using a different methodology or approach. They also may call on as many learners as possible, to engage the entire class during each session.
e. Great Communication and Engagement Skills: Great teachers maintain open communication channels with all of their learners and use effective engagement methods that are unbiased and impartial, and that promote positive behaviors and attitudes.
f. Dynamic Teaching Style and Engaging Personality Traits: A great teacher consistently engages the classroom through innovative, inspiring, and varying teaching methodologies. Moreover, a great teacher uses changing facial and body language or voice amplitude changes to provide emphasis when discussing important course content. Sometimes engagement may manifest through passionate expression, storytelling, or providing anecdotes and analogies related to the materials being taught.[53]

As was previously touched upon, machine-learning models that represent domain knowledge can be pretrained and added to an overall asset library. However, the other characteristics and attributes listed above may need to be first quantified theoretically and mathematically before they can artificially emulate actively trained neural-network black boxes residing in the AGI teacher library.

Imagine an English department chair contemplating his fall course offerings and weighing enrollments against teaching resources. For his oversubscribed freshman English 101 course, he may task his future full-time faculty machine-learning (ML) design staff to interconnect an AGI teacher that focuses on specific texts that emphasize writing skills and grammar (based on poor incoming summer literacy scores). Moreover, the AGI teacher may have a teaching style that is more energetic (speaks or types at a slightly faster pace but changes voice pitch and dynamic level to overemphasize salient points), but may also teach at a slower pace, sprinkled with humor and stories about the authors taught and other famous past learners who also struggled with English writing as freshmen.

For the next fall course, the chair requests the design of a different AGI to teach an upper-level undergraduate English literature course that possesses expert domain knowledge about William Shakespeare, Geoffrey Chaucer, William Wordsworth, and Virginia Woolf. This AGI teacher must also have a very low disciplinary schema and muted animated personality, focusing more on the course content, as the motivation of students in this class are higher than would be found in English 101.

Granted, some rulebook model assets outlined above may be difficult to create today, as the characteristics and attributes found in D and E are a challenge to theoretically, mathematically, and socially quantify, being in some cases behavioral in nature, and their expression depending on external stimuli that may define the learner experience. So, therefore, we may need to build an AGI teacher submodel strata of dedicated neural cognitive models that simulate partial cognition that can be seamlessly integrated together to define the AGI rulebook described above.

Let us break apart some of the larger AGI requirements outlined in our department chair scenario into smaller trained submodels that may represent separately standing library assets that can be pieced together in an AGI library architecture.

An Example AGI Teacher Submodel Rulebook

a. Expert Domain Knowledge: This is a given, as all great teachers require extensive knowledge about the subject matter that they teach.
b. Ability to Plan Clear Goals and Objectives for Each Class Meeting/Session: Although the syllabus may outline the schedule for an entire semester or quarter, a great teacher must parcel the overreaching goals into smaller digestible segments of information offered over time ($_1$), that when combined, match the expected learning outcomes of the course ($_2$).
c. Immense Curriculum Knowledge: A great teacher knows their course resides in a larger curriculum framework, and the information con-

veyed in their class must augment and continue the information that was taught before ($_1$), and prepare the learner for what is to come in the course sequence ($_2$).

d. Excellent Classroom Management Skills: Great teachers manage class time to meet session goals by guiding presentations, discussions, and questions accordingly. The best teachers can also detect when students are not engaged ($_1$), or are lost ($_2$), and may repeat the information using a different methodology or approach ($_3$). They also may call on as many learners as possible, to engage the entire class during each session.
e. Great Communication and Engagement Skills: Great teachers maintain open communication channels with all of their learners, and use effective engagement methods ($_1$) that are unbiased and impartial ($_2$), and that promote positive behaviors and attitudes ($_3$).
f. Dynamic Teaching Style and Engaging Personality Traits: A great teacher consistently engages the classroom through innovative ($_1$), inspiring ($_2$), and varying teaching methodologies ($_3$). Moreover, a great teacher uses changing facial and body language ($_4$), or voice amplitude changes ($_5$) to provide emphasis ($_{4,5}$) when discussing important course content. Sometimes engagement may manifest through passionate expression ($_6$), storytelling ($_7$), or providing anecdotes and analogies ($_8$) related to the materials being taught.

One could perceive these partial submodel cognitive simulations outlined above as singular cognitive elements that may sometimes overlap and even compete for activation with other interconnected submodels within a larger collective AGI teacher model architecture. This challenge may appear similar to the definition of collective intelligence, whereby group intelligence emerges from many learners trying to solve a collective problem—through competition and conflict, the group eventually agrees upon a group consensus of the best solution to solve a problem. Or it's similar to how we as teachers in near real-time consciously flip between various potential answers we may give at the same time that we are listening to a learner's question.

Other characteristics found in f above, such as "inspiring ($_2$)," are even more difficult to quantify being so subjective, such as a broad human traits that is ill definable. So even ingesting positive or good examples and negative or bad examples (conscious bias) into a machine-learning black box submodel may result in exaggerated AGI voice frequency and amplitude changes in hopes of focusing the learners, but instead producing laughter and irritation rather than the intended outcome.

Remember, even the programmer of deep machine-learning models doesn't actually know what is truly taking place in the training of the black box model, as the layers and nodes reprogram themselves through input and output data set corrections, even potentially changing intended tasks outside of a preprogrammed narrow band of optional outcomes! Figure 5.10 outlines a revised AGI teacher rulebook comprising an example of the humanlike machine-learning models and sub-models as described above.

Although artificial general intelligence is believed by many researchers to be anywhere from five to fifty years away or more, innovation fueled by financial investment from central government labs, large and small tech R & D efforts, and the deep-learning related research in the larger university research labs convince me we are closer than most prognosticators predict. Original cognitive-based mathematical algorithms, new unsupervised and transfer training techniques, and new approaches to cognitive modeling are being tested every week. Many recent redesigns of older techniques such as Bayesian Models of Cognition, Monte-Carlo decision trees and forests, and unique policy gradient reinforcement algorithms offer glimpses of how AGI submodels may be created in the near future to hopefully uncover more useful and precise submodel outcomes that ever closer approach human-level cognition.

In closing this section, we must also consider that future great AGI teachers may not act like and appear like a great human teacher that match our expected goals and outcomes. Their characteristics and attributes might be equally quite different than what we as academics and learners are used to observing and experiencing. A self-training machine-learning AGI model given the task of teaching a course, using a submodel asset library of pre-trained and self-training models, may ultimately offer a completely unfamiliar teaching pedagogy.

Similarly to how humans eventually learned how to swim for long distances underwater, we can't imitate nature. We don't possess gills like fish, and we will never evolve the lung capacity of water-based mammals such as dolphins and whales. So we developed underwater breathing systems such as the self-contained underwater breathing apparatus (SCUBA) so we could survive for great lengths of time underwater.

As Nick Bostrom notes, as much as we tried, we learned to fly not by imitating nature's flapping of wings but by the creation of a fixed curved wing designed for lift, a turning twisted propeller designed for pull, and a movable vertical tail fin designed for stability and direction—sometime imitating (human) nature is the wrong pathway.[54] Perhaps what we believe is our ideal interconnected submodel AGI teacher architecture may not resemble the rulebook that defines a great teacher of the future. The AGI teacher may not imitate us but learn and evolve to offer better and more precise teaching approaches, including nobler assessment and evaluation methodologies that we as educators and researchers have never considered or thought of.

The technical challenges of having thousands of interconnected AGI sub-models residing in a machine-learning library, self-ingesting and producing massive amounts of data sets that need to be stored and accessed, and the bandwidth necessary for instantaneous call of these stored data sets, will not be easy to overcome in the short term. The infrastructure and architecture to support the scenarios above does not yet exist but may be aided soon with the launch of the 5G cellular architecture and advanced edge computing which allows for machine-learning calculations on local devices, at great network speeds.[55]

Lastly, quantum computing also holds great promise as a new technique to process machine-learning data sets, using 1, 0, or both combined called *qubits*, estimated to compute tasks at 100M times faster than traditional 1 or

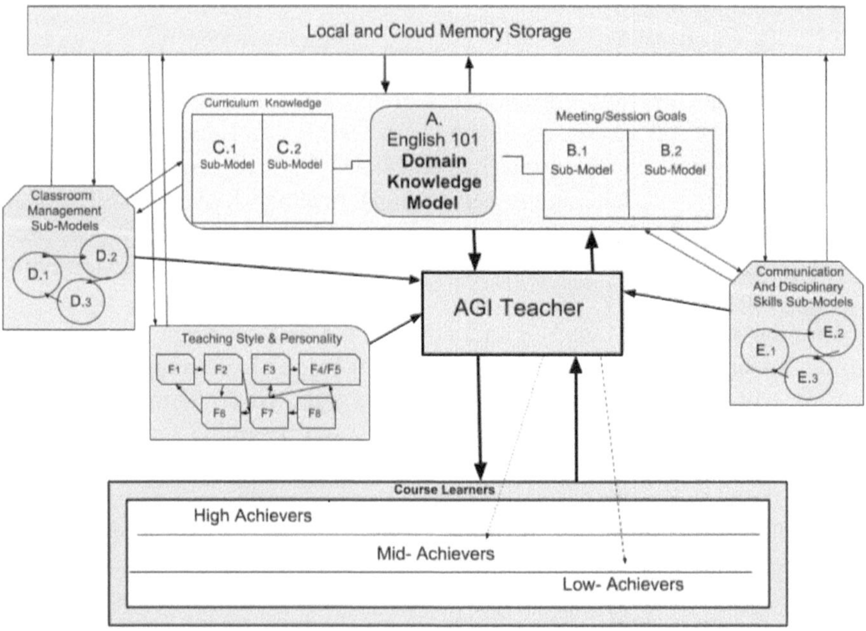

Legend:

Expert Domain Knowledge **[A]**
Ability to Plan Clear Goals and Objectives for Each Class Meeting/Session **[B]**
Immense Curriculum Knowledge **[C]**
Excellent Classroom Management Skills **[E[**
Great Communication and Engagement Skills **[F]**
Dynamic Teaching Style and Engaging Personality Traits **[G]**

Figure 5.10. Example AGI teacher rulebook designed to teach English 101

0 binary-based central and graphical processing units.[56] Soon, scientific research and technology will catch up with each other again.

WHY THIS MATTERS

Just like the examples of MX deployment cited above, many of the current innovations and research in next-gen machine-learning techniques are targeted not toward education at all but toward the tidier and more profitable endeavors of finance, retail, transportation, and logistics. In addition, most AI-related policy think tanks and research centers such as OpenAI, the Future of Humanity Institute (FHI) at Oxford, and even the Chan Zuckerberg Initiative either ignore or are not focused on exploring the impact AI could have on teaching and learning.

If they do examine AI's potential in education, it's usually in the realm of exploring AI's capacity for upending economies or unleashing irreparable harm. However, as discussed in this chapter and in chapter 4, MX and AI can have an immediate positive impact to not just enhance and improve upon the teaching and learning practice but also successfully scale a more engaging online classroom to more diverse learners globally.

Perhaps the reluctance to launch education research projects that may support the efficacy and adoption of MX in the classroom is due to technical Luddism, and if so, a new generation of digital native educators and researchers will resolve this blockade. Perhaps it's caused by lack of funding sources for educational research, and since public university and college budgets are tight, no one's going to have the funds to buy the MX headsets anyway, let alone take the time to integrate them into their curriculum and examine their efficacy.

It could be due to educator analysis paralysis, a type of consumer behavior formed when so many product promises fall short, and the reviews of the newest greatest gadgets are mixed; they just stop buying the next best thing. Educators and researchers need the support and advocacy from their department heads and central administration to overcome such apathy and provide the "cover" to launch a pilot to trial an MX platform within their syllabi, whether it's successful or not. And if successful, support should be provided to scale the discovery across applicable courses and curricula.

After all, as we read earlier in this chapter, some form of MX has been in use for more than forty years, and finally their technology has caught up to their promise—they are now mature enough and cheap enough for widespread adoption for at least experimentation and testing inside the sacrosanct classroom or lab. Administration needs to support and foster innovation in the classroom and across their institutions to facilitate an educational environment that embraces calculated risk and experimentation, all to better prepare our learners for the challenges that lie ahead.

On the machine-learning front, small steps can be taken now by university and college administrations to adopt AI bots that can assist learners with such mundane tasks as querying their next test date or current grades, providing campus-wide information such as location and times available for their campus academic advisor, and answering simple registration and bursar questions. There are now many commercially available AI bot authoring tools and open-source platforms available that can be developed for specific courses that can mimic the teacher assistance success of Goel's Jill Watson, although I would recommend letting the learners in on the plan!

It's up to administration to advocate and foster partnerships between academic disciplines that can realize such innovation, maybe between humanities and computer science professors and their graduate assistants to develop, test, and deploy course bots. The technology and tools are readily available to now deploy AI in academia, with the only impediment to adoption being leadership apprehension.

As we have outlined throughout this book, tools and tech—from the chalkboard, overhead projector, and handheld calculator to the computer—have all originated in industry but were slowly and successfully adopted and integrated into an academic curriculum by innovative administrators and educators to enhance and improve upon the practice of teaching and learning. So too must the next generation of innovative administrators and educators redefine the future classroom learning spaces to better prepare our graduates to succeed within the Fourth Industrial Revolution.

NOTES

1. Nat Levy, "PAX Panelists: It Won't Be Long before People Have Virtual Reality in Their Homes," *GeekWire*, September 7, 2016, https://www.geekwire.com.
2. Seth Feigerman, "Facebook Is Bigger than Amazon, by Market Cap," Mashable, February 14, 2014, https://mashable.com.
3. Erin Griffith, "How Zuck Met Oculus: The Story behind Facebook's Big Bet on Virtual Reality," *Fortune*, April 14, 2014, http://fortune.com.
4. Mark Zuckerberg, Facebook, March 25, 2014, https://www.facebook.com/zuck/posts/10101319050523971.
5. As quoted in Nic Fildes, "2016 Set to Be Year Virtual Reality Takes Off," *Raconteur*, December 17, 2015, https://www.raconteur.net.
6. "Who Coined the Term 'Virtual Reality'?" Virtual Reality Society, accessed December 16, 2018, https://www.vrs.org.uk.
7. Jaron Z. Lanier, Jean-Jacques G. Grimaud, Young L. Harvill, Ann Lasko-Harvill, Chuck L. Blanchard, Mark L. Oberman, and Michael A. Teitel, "Method and System for Generating Objects for a Multi-Person Virtual World Using Data Flow Networks," U.S. Patent 5588139, filed October 8, 1993, issued December 24, 1996.
8. Richard M. Felder and Rebecca Brent, "Navigating the Bumpy Road to Student-Centered Instruction," *College Teaching* 44 (Spring 1996): 43–47.

9. L. Dee Fink, *Creating Significant Learning Experiences: An Integrated Approach to Designing College Courses* (San Francisco: Jossey-Bass, 2003).
10. Patricia L. Machemer and Pat Crawford, "Student Perceptions of Active Learning in a Large Cross-Disciplinary Classroom," *Active Learning in Higher Education* 8, no. 1 (2007): 11–31.
11. Rachel Metz, "Augmented Reality Gets to Work," *MIT Technology Review*, February 24, 2014, https://www.technologyreview.com.
12. Christine Ludwig and Christian Reimann, "Augmented Reality: Information im Fokus," *Cooperative Computing and Communication Laboratory* 4, no. 1 (2005), https://www.c-lab.de.
13. M. Weihrauch, G. Meloeny, and T. Goesch, "The First Head Up Display Introduced by General Motors," SAE Technical Paper 890288, 1989, https://doi.org/10.4271/890288.
14. Bill Squadron, "The Story behind Football's Innovative Yellow First Down Line," *Sports Illustrated*, July 18, 2013, https://www.si.com.
15. See the Google Glass developer overview at "Design before You Develop," Glass Explorer Edition, accessed March 18, 2019, https://developers.google.com/glass.
16. Wendy Glauser, "Doctors among Early Adopters of Google Glass," *Canadian Medical Association Journal* 185, no. 16 (2013): 1385, http://www.cmaj.ca.
17. R. Sivakumar, "Google Glass in Education," *Conflux Journal of Education* 2, no. 2 (July 2014), http://www.cjoe.naspublishers.com.
18. "Design before You Develop."
19. Charles E. Hughes, Christopher Stapleton, Darin E. Hughes, and Eileen Smith, "Mixed Reality in Education, Entertainment, and Training," *IEEE Computer Graphics and Applications* 25, no. 6 (November 2005): 24–30.
20. Paul Milgram and Fumio Kishino, "A Taxonomy of Mixed Reality Visual Displays," *IEICE Transactions on Information and Systems* E77-D, no. 12 (December 1994): 1321–29.
21. See "HoloLens 2," Microsoft, accessed March 18, 2019, https://www.microsoft.com/en-us/hololens.
22. For an example of a leasing partner, see "Microsoft HoloLens," Abcomrents, accessed March 18, 2019, https://www.abcomrents.com/microsoft-hololens-rental.
23. Nan Cui, Pradosh Kharel, and Vikto Gruev, "Augmented Reality with Microsoft HoloLens Holograms for Near Infrared Fluorescence Based Image Guided Surgery," *Proceedings Volume 10049, Molecular-Guided Surgery: Molecules, Devices, and Applications III* (2017), https://doi.org/10.1117/12.2251625.
24. Michael G. Hanna, Ishtiaque Ahmed, Jeffrey Nine, Shyam Prajapati, and Liron Pantanowitz, "Augmented Reality Technology Using Microsoft HoloLens in Anatomic Pathology," *Archives of Pathology and Laboratory Medicine* 142, no. 5 (2018): 638–44.
25. Cita Nørgaard, Lotte Dyhrberg O'Neill, Kurt Gammelgaard Nielsen, Søren Juul, and John Chemnitz, "Learning Anatomy with Augmented Reality," *Proceedings: 10th Annual International Conference on Education and New Learning Technologies*, 2018, doi:10.21125/edulearn.2018.0445.
26. Douglas N. Gordin and Roy D. Pea, "Prospects for Scientific Visualization as an Educational Technology," *Journal of the Learning Sciences* 4, no. 3 (1995): 249–79.
27. Marilyn C. Salzman, Chris Dede, R. and Bowen Loftin, "VR's Frames of Reference: A Visualization Technique for Mastering Abstract Multidimensional Information," in *Proceedings of the SIGCHI Conference on Human Factors in Computing Systems*, 489–95 (New York: ACM, 1999).
28. William Winn, *A Conceptual Basis for Educational Applications of Virtual Reality* (Seattle: Human Interface Technology Laboratory, Washington Technology Center, 1993).
29. Mar Gonzalez-Franco, Rodrigo Pizarro, Julio Cermeron, Katie Li, Jacob Thorn, Windo Hutabarat, Ashutosh Tiwari, and Pablo Bermell-Garcia, "Immersive Mixed Reality for Manufacturing Training," *Frontiers in Robotics and AI* 4, no. 3 (February 2017): 1–8, doi:10.3389/frobt.2017.00003.
30. Ibid.
31. Rick Rys, "Increasing the Performance of the Human Asset," Arc Advisory Group, March 29, 2018, https://www.arcweb.com.
32. Ibid.

33. Adrian Chen, "We Need to Know Who Satoshi Nakamoto Is," *New Yorker*, May 9, 2016, https://www.newyorker.com; Satoshi Nakamoto, "Bitcoin: A Peer-to-Peer Electronic Cash System," Bitcoin.org, 2008, https://Bitcoin.org/Bitcoin.pdf.
34. Ibid.
35. Sally French, "Here's Proof that This Bitcoin Crash Is Far from the Worst the Cryptocurrency Has Seen," *Market Watch*, February 9, 2017, https://www.marketwatch.comcryptocurrenc.
36. Trunk, Aleš, and Jure Trunk. "Digital Currencies and Bitcoin." *Financial Literacy among the Young*, 91.
37. Vitalik Buterin, "On Bitcoin Maximalism, and Currency and Platform Network Effects," *Ethereum Blog*, November 19, 2014, https://blog.ethereum.org.
38. Sean Williams, "20 Real-World Uses for Blockchain Technology," *Motley Fool*, April 11, 2018, https://www.fool.com.
39. Alexander Grech and Anthony F. Camilleri, *Blockchain in Education* (Luxembourg: Joint Research Centre [JRC], European Union, 2017), http://publications.jrc.ec.europa.eu.
40. Joshua David Broggi, "Woolf Building the First Blockchain University," Woolf Development, April 3, 2018.
41. Visit http://www.omscs.gatech.edu/ to learn more about the degree program.
42. Ashok Goel, Terry Anderson, Jordan Belknap, Brian Creeden, William Hancock, Mithun Kumble, Shanu Salunke, Bradley Sheneman, Abhinaya Shetty, and Bryan Wiltgen, "Using Watson for Constructing Cognitive Assistance," *Advances in Cognitive Systems* 4 (2016), http://www.cogsys.org.
43. Ibid.
44. Ashok K. Goel and Lalith Polepeddi, "Jill Watson: A Virtual Teaching Assistant for Online Education," Georgia Tech, School of Interactive Computing Technical Reports, 2016, https://smartech.gatech.edu.
45. Vincent C. Müller and Nick Bostrom, "Future Progress in Artificial Intelligence: A Survey of Expert Opinion," in *Fundamental Issues of Artificial Intelligence*, ed. Vincent C. Müller, 553–71 (Berlin: Springer, 2016).
46. James Barrat, *Our Final Invention: Artificial Intelligence and the End of the Human Era* (New York: St. Martin's, 2013).
47. Nick Bostrom, *Superintelligence: Paths, Dangers, Strategies* (New York: Oxford University Press, 2016).
48. P. M. Grasby, C. D. Frith, K. J. Friston, J. Simpson, P. C. Fletcher, R. S. J. Frackowiak, and R. J. Dolan, "A Graded Task Approach to the Functional Mapping of Brain Areas Implicated in Auditory-Verbal Memory," *Brain* 117 (1994): 1271–82.
49. Claude Elwood Shannon, "Programming a Computer for Playing Chess," *London, Edinburgh, and Dublin Philosophical Magazine and Journal of Science* 41, no. 314 (1950): 256–75.
50. Read more about Deep Blue at "Deep Blue," IBM100, accessed March 19, 2019, http://www.ibm.com.
51. Transfer learning is reusing the same pretrained models, slightly altered to complete a different task, in this case, unsupervised models that were previously trained to learn to play and win the game Go.
52. David Silver, Thomas Hubert, Julian Schrittwieser, Ioannis Antonoglou, Matthew Lai, Arthur Guez, Marc Lanctot, Laurent Sifre, Dharshan Kumaran, Thore Graepel, Timothy Lillicrap, Karen Simonyan, and Demis Hassabis, "Mastering Chess and Shogi by Self-Play with a General Reinforcement Learning Algorithm," *arXiv Preprint arXiv:1712.01815* (2017), https://arxiv.org.
53. James H. Stronge, *Qualities of Effective Teachers* (Alexandria, VA: ASCD, 2018).
54. Bostrom, *Superintelligence*.
55. Federico Boccardi, Robert W. Heath, Angel Lozano, Thomas L. Marzetta, and Petar Popovski, "Five Disruptive Technology Directions for 5G," *IEEE Communications Magazine* 52, no. 2 (2014): 74–80. doi:10.1109/MCOM.2014.6736746; Weisong Shi, Jie Cao, Quan Zhang, Youhuizi Li, and Lanyu Xu, "Edge Computing: Vision and Challenges," *IEEE Internet of Things Journal* 3, no. 5 (October 2016): 637–46, doi:10.1109/JIOT.2016.2579198.

56. David Deutsch and Arthur Ekert, "Quantum Computation," *Physics World* 11, no. 3 (March 1998): 47–52.

Conclusion

At the dawn of my final semester as a student at Johns Hopkins University, I was walking down a corridor on my way to class in one of the academic buildings on the Homewood campus, and I noticed a flyer advertising opportunities to work in finance. Since finance and economics was a slight interest of mine ever since I read that my favorite famously eccentric pianist Glenn Gould was an avid equities trader, I applied on a whim. Days after being flown in first class and put up in a five-star hotel in New York City, and after four rounds of on-site interviews, many in upper-floor offices with beautiful but distracting views of the Hudson River, Morgan Stanley awaited an answer.

It seemed during the late 1980s/early 1990s, Morgan Stanley was searching for unique and a nontraditional type of talent to hire and train to differentiate themselves from the other investment banks. Students that majored in engineering, humanities, music, and math included several new categories of undergraduates that Morgan Stanley's managers believed they could shape into ideal technicians and future traders. Since I possessed knowledge in a few of those areas, it appeared I was an ideal candidate.

Shortly after my offer from Morgan Stanley arrived, I received a letter of interest requesting an interview for teaching combined with a low-level administrative role at Alabama State University (ASU), a historically black college and university (HBCU) in Montgomery, Alabama. After flying down to Montgomery in coach, staying in a subpar hotel for two days, and after several rounds of interviews, I was both disappointed but also intrigued. Several days after returning to Baltimore, I received a term-contract offer from Alabama State for less than half the pay offered by Morgan Stanley.

There should have been no dilemma to ponder; the choice was obvious. Coming from a single-parent household with limited financial means, I accumulated significant debt after six years at Hopkins. The upside, of course, was with several degrees under my belt, having acquired new knowledge and mastered new skills, and cultivating relationships with teachers and peers from the four corners of the globe, I then considered myself quite educated and cosmopolitan, cultured, and worldly.

At that time, Montgomery was as far away in cosmopolitanism and urbaneness from New York City as could be measured. Besides the oppressive spring and summer heat and humidity, everything seemed limited in Montgomery, from housing choices available on the small salary offered, narrow food and entertainment choices, and even slim vacation options (where the Gulf Shores, I learned during my interview visit, was tactlessly named the "Redneck Riviera"). But would another rags-to-riches story (Morgan Stanley) satiate the passions I deeply held to not just teach but also teach the next generation of learners that stem from familiar, less fortunate circumstances?

ASU offered the possibility to guide and mentor many first-time learners, the historically underserved, and indeed historically segregated and discriminated-against learners. All of these opportunities existed for me ironically within a segregated institution of learning, forged after the Civil War in the Deep South, originally founded to confer teaching credentials to mostly first-generation and discriminated-against black teachers to teach mostly first-generation and discriminated-against primary and secondary black school children.

Upon completing the course credits (and then some) required for conferral of my degrees from the Johns Hopkins University/Peabody Conservatory of Music, my now wife and I departed in a large rickety truck with all of our worldly possessions to Montgomery, Alabama, to teach and build a new undergraduate program at ASU.

ASU is a successor of the Lincoln Normal School, founded in 1867 in Perry County, Alabama, as the nation's first state-sponsored and partially state-funded teaching college for black Americans. In 1889, after multiple conflicts with the state legislature and with the state supreme court, Lincoln Normal School was reestablished and renamed the Normal School for Colored People in Montgomery. The name changed again and again to the State Teacher College (1929), Alabama State College for Negroes (1948), and then to Alabama State College in 1954, reflecting the college's President Harper Council Trenholm's vision to grow to serve all the families of Alabama.[1]

It was also during these transitions, although granted independently for "white" and "black" universities, when the esteemed Southern Association of Colleges and Schools (SACS) bestowed the college a class A accreditation. The civil rights movement, which included the infamous Montgomery Bus Boycott and other civil disobedience acts in the city, involved many Alabama State College faculty members and students, resulting in a retaliatory state legislative cut to their appropriated budget and a loss of their accreditation by SACS.[2]

President Levi Watkins and his new administrative team negotiated with the state legislature, the State Board of Education, and simultaneously with SACS, restoring the class A accreditation in 1966, and approval for the final name change to Alabama State University in 1969.[3] However, the original state budget full-time equivalent (FTE)–based funding formula that had been cut during the civil rights movement was not restored, leaving ASU with less state funding than their historically "white" state school competitors, such as Alabama and Auburn, with comparable student enrollments.[4]

After I adjusted to teaching a full-time 4-4 load, and finalized the finishing touches of a new music media technology bachelor of arts degree proposal to be submitted to the board of education for review, I petitioned my dean to adjunct teach elsewhere in the region to supplement my derisory salary. Within days, my petition was approved. Although unusual for a college or university to allow their faculty to teach at a competing university, ASU was overall underfunded so could not offer competitive full-time faculty salaries. I submitted an adjunct faculty application to the dean of Troy State University in Montgomery to teach courses in U.S. history and music appreciation, two academic domains required for every bachelor degree they offered. After a brief interview, I was hired.

Troy State University, headquartered in southern Troy, Alabama, also began as a normal school and had a branch campus situated on the Maxwell U.S. Air Force base in Montgomery. The site of the Maxwell base has a storied history, as its location, Wright Field, was originally established as the first flight school in the United States founded by Wilbur Wright in 1910, seven years after his brother Orville's and his historic Kitty Hawk flight in North Carolina.[5] Founded in 1918, and named after Second Lieutenant William C. Maxwell (who perished when he crash-landed his aircraft in the Philippines in 1920 to avoid a group of children), Maxwell Air Force Base hosted Troy State Montgomery campus until 2005, when the base needed the Troy facilities to expand their own air university programs.[6]

Besides the mandate that all my Troy courses began at the ungodly 0700 hour, and that the students appeared as sleepy as I was at the start of class, I also made several interesting observations: most of the students were in air force military fatigues, they were all enlisted, and their average age was in the upper twenties. These students were all nontraditional adult learners, and most of them were first in their family to pursue a college degree.

In addition, similar to what I came to discover at ASU, many of these learners were also raised by a single parent living in households at or slightly above the poverty line. Although on average the Troy students appeared a tad more motivated to learn, probably as a result of the strict behavior doctrine instilled in them from basic training onward, or from just being in uniform in class (or both), the teaching methods, instructional approaches, and classroom structure and management techniques I used were common to both sets of learners.

It was common for me to advise the adult and underserved learner alike about course choices, career options, and professional interests. And it was common for me to mentor and counsel the two sets of learners about productive professional and personal decision-making, positive relationship building, and self-actualization and esteem. Besides the average age differences and job responsibilities of Troy students, which lends a bit more maturity than an eighteen-year-old freshman, the student support services and intervention methods I was subconsciously deploying were also almost identical to the two sets of learners.

Although I taught a few courses as a teaching assistant in graduate school, these two institutes of higher education presented to me my first real professional teaching opportunities, so I had no other instructional experiences to compare them to. Meaning, I assumed these counseling and mentoring responsibilities, methods, and strategies were par for the course, along with domain knowledge and teaching abilities for the teaching profession.

It wasn't until many years after I returned to the East Coast and taught at the University of Maryland and at George Mason University, where I still reside, that I realized they were not just extraordinary services for a faculty member to provide; it was extraordinary for colleges and universities to offer such personalized support. While the learners from a financially stable, educated, two-parent household may require additional tutoring services or interventions from time to time, they don't require an entire support structure to be built around their degree plan in order for them to be academically successful.

As we have discovered in this book, the coming decade will flood community colleges and public universities with more first-time learners, historically underserved populations, and adult learners alike searching for new knowledge and skills. These enrollments will soon surpass traditional residential student enrollments. Some of these new learners will also arrive with language barriers, learning disabilities, and social and emotional divergences.

Moreover, most will arrive at a college's front door with limited financial resources, continuing the trend line of increasing student debt well into the future. As I have personally and professionally discovered, and a quick literature review will support, these nontraditional learners will require a massive expansion of student support services by colleges and public universities, from nontraditional advisors (not just the bean counters) to personal coaches, intervention counselors, and peer and professional mentors.

So, how will colleges and universities of the future increase their academic offerings and class sizes, massively expand their student support services, *and* lower their tuition rates to match the circumstances and prerequisites of their future learners? In short, under the current community college and public university business and financial models, they can't.

These first teaching experiences in Montgomery shaped my philosophy, methodology, and pedagogical approach to teaching, and indeed toward higher education as well. These early experiences have both informed and influenced my own classroom teaching practices, and my personal research activities, with a goal to offer other faculty members new approaches to improve upon their own teaching methods. Moreover, observing firsthand the discrepancy between the haves and have-nots in higher education, I have attempted not only to uncover and invent new solutions that can scale educational opportunities to a greater number of diverse learners but also to better support the act of teaching by providing the resources teachers need to improve their practices and truly personalize learning for every one of their students. And lastly, I hope I have offered several solutions to scale and expand nonacademic support structures to all learners, especially for special learners that require an extra helping hand to ensure academic success.

And finally, I hope I have instilled a sense of urgency within higher education board members, presidents, provosts, deans, and chairs about the shortcomings of the current education model and the great need for change. In all likelihood, community college and public university funding formulas will either stagnate or continue to fall in the foreseeable future. Therefore, they too must take risks and greenlight tests and pilot programs of new tools in their institutions to not just better prepare their typical pipeline of learners with new knowledge and skills required in this Fourth Industrial Revolution but also prepare for the coming wave of new special learners to ensure they succeed as well.

At the very least, higher education administrators need to reach beyond their own familiar academic structures and curricula framework and initiate equally beneficial partnerships with industry, and with other colleges, to discover and potentially adopt new applications of technologies, assessments and evaluations approaches, and job training and placement programs. Administrators should also plan more site visits abroad to study best practices of the oft-criticized, but mostly successful, guilds and apprenticeship programs in Europe and Asia.

For a student that has settled on a trade or craft, a community college could offer a solid humanities and sciences curriculum, as well as partner with industry to offer a "City and Guilds"–type apprenticeship model for the technical and workforce training.[7] For students interested in programming and the network information technology side, but not necessarily in a bachelor degree, community colleges could partner with Oracle, IBM, Google, and Apple to offer truly applicable online interactive streaming courses in all the relevant knowledge sets and skills the companies seek. (Note: I purposely don't recommend coding boot camps or programs here, due to their high costs and overall lack of success in placing graduates into meaningful employment. Even innovative programs like Make School, one of the first early coding camps in Silicon Valley, has pivoted and now offers a bachelor's degree in applied computer science.[8])

Administrators of universities with strong undergraduate and graduate program enrollments, even many with a Carnegie Research I (R1) rating, also need to explore and initiate partnerships with industry for the same reasons. Little do most of these R1 senior administrators know that the curriculum in many of their engineering and computer science schools and colleges are near two decades old and don't even offer courses in modern machine-learning or deep-learning algorithm design and development.

The overwhelming majority of the innovative artificial intelligence and machine-learning research and published papers originate from the technology industry, and from a few faculty on leave working for that industry. The technology titans have mostly picked the academic winner and losers in the Fourth Industrial Revolution already, and odds are if you don't know who they are, you weren't chosen. That's not to say a second wave of innovative universities can't crack into the nobility of distinction, but they must now enter through intermarriage, namely, forming new partnerships and consortia whereby the top achievers help the lower achievers with similar interests, activities, and goals.

Lastly, although it may appear this book was constructed as a treatise on technology as a savior of the academy, it is the traditional arts and humanities that actually has the most to gain by teaching with and through technology. Yes, the humanities are most credited with offering critical-thinking and problem-solving skills. However, machine-learning and virtual-learning spaces may usher in an explosion of new research, offering new insights and discovery in the arts and letters, and a renewal of importance and appreciation of the humanities and liberal arts in the age of the Fourth Industrial Revolution.

Imagine American literature students applying a new NLP (neuro-linguistic programming) model to detect gradients of depression within the late works and letters of Sylvia Plath or Ernest Hemingway that may predict their eventual suicides. How about the knowledge gained by European medieval history students donning virtual reality devices to duel an artificial-intelligence-armored avatar to learn and study the body movements of the sixteenth-century Italian martial arts? Moreover, how educational would it be for the student of Native American history to wear a device walking along the Trail of Tears seeing and hearing re-creations of the inhuman experiences of Creek and Cherokee tribes at specific points along the actual route?

Hopefully this book has provoked the college and university administrator, board member, or teacher to singularly or jointly develop a plan to embrace some of the newly discussed and outlined teaching and learning technology-driven pedagogies, platforms, and tools. Developing small, albeit potentially disruptive, plans that will allow their institution to jump to the front of the line may attract ambitious and inspired faculty members, better engage staff members, and an expanding number of excited and motivated learners.

Yes, challenges lie in wait for the first- and even second-tier early adopters who are most adventurous, but thrilling rewards also await for the most pioneering and persistent administrators and teachers who forge ahead and find or build innovative technologies, curricula, course content, delivery methods, and assessment processes just right for their institution and their future learners. After all, technology will always change and evolve, but the importance of effective successful teaching and learning, whether offered artificially or by the next great human Nobel laureate sage, never will.

NOTES

1. For more information about the history, see "History of Alabama State University," Levi Watkins Learning Center, Archives and Special Collections, accessed March 19, 2019, http://www.lib.alasu.edu.
2. A. L. Evans, V. Evans, and A. M. Evans, "Historically Black Colleges and Universities (HBCUS)," *Education* 123, no. 1 (Fall 2002): 3–18.
3. "History of Alabama State University."
4. In 1995, the year after I departed ASU for the East Coast, the U.S. District Court for the Northern District of Alabama declared that many of the state's historical practices and laws facilitated segregation in their colleges and universities, and indeed were historically discriminatory in their funding formulas, and thus violated the U.S. Constitution. The court ordered mandatory changes to some of these practices, including correcting the funding formula going forward, but also to make up for past unconstitutional funding inadequacies. In essence, even though further lawsuits would persist for decades, ASU now had a funding base to not just renovate its facilities, offer a greater number of student scholarships and financial aid, and raise faculty salaries but also ensure its survival in perpetuity. Read more in an article by Kym Klass, "Historic ASU Discrimination Suit Changed Education in Alabama," *Montgomery Adviser*, January 23, 2014, https://amp.montgomeryadvertiser.com.
5. For more information about the Maxwell-Gunter Air Force Base, see "Maxwell-Gunter AFB: History," My Base Guide, last updated October 8, 2018, http://www.mybaseguide.com.
6. For more information about the history of Troy University, see "History of Troy University," Troy University, accessed March 19, 2019, https://www.troy.edu.
7. For more information, see City and Guilds, accessed March 19, 2019, https://www.cityandguilds.com.
8. For more information, see Make School, accessed March 19, 2019, https://www.makeschool.com.

Bibliography

Abdous, M'hammed, and Cherng-Jyh Yen. "A Predictive Study of Learner Satisfaction and Outcomes in Face-to-Face, Satellite Broadcast, and Live Video-Streaming Learning Environments." *Internet and Higher Education* 13, no. 4 (2010): 248–57.

Abrams, Helene G., and Louise Podojil Jernigan. "Academic Support Services and the Success of High-Risk College Students." *American Educational Research Journal* 21, no. 2 (1984): 261–74.

Accuray Research. "Global E-Learning Market Analysis and Trends: Industry Forecast to 2025." Research and Markets, September 2017. Accessed December 2, 2018. https://www.researchandmarkets.com.

Allen, Elaine, and Jeff Seaman. *Making the Grade: Online Education in the United States*. Needham, MA: Sloan Consortium, 2007. https://immagic.com.

Altman, Irwin, and Dalmas A. Taylor. *Social Penetration: The Development of Interpersonal Relationships*. New York: Holt, Rinehart and Winston, 1973.

Altschuler, Glenn C. "College Prep; The E-Learning Curve." *New York Times*, August 5, 2001.

Ames, Carole. "Classrooms: Goals, Structures, and Student Motivation." *Journal of Educational Psychology* 84, no. 3 (1992): 261–71.

Anderson, Terry. "Getting the Mix Right Again: An Updated and Theoretical Rationale for Interaction." *International Review of Research in Open and Distributed Learning* 4, no. 2 (2003). https://auspace.athabascau.ca.

Asendorpf, Jens B. "Recommendations for Increasing Replicability in Psychology." *European Journal of Personality* 27, no. 2 (April 18, 2013): 108–19. https://doi.org/10.1002/per.1919.

Atkinson, Richard C., and R. M. Shiffrin. *Mathematical Models for Memory and Learning*. Stanford, CA: Stanford University, Institute for Mathematical Studies in the Social Sciences, 1965.

Atwood, Brett. "That's Edutainment: Software Developers Provide Education and Entertainment for Young Minds." *Billboard Magazine*, May 13, 1995.

Azevedo, Richard, and Vincent Aleven. "Metacognition and Learning Technologies: An Overview of Current Interdisciplinary Research." In *International Handbook of Metacognition and Learning Technologies*, edited by Roger Azevedo and Vincent Aleven, 1–16. New York: Springer, 2013.

Babad, Elisha. *The Social Psychology of the Classroom*. New York: Routledge, 2009.

Baddeley, Alan. *Essentials of Human Memory (Classic Edition)*. Hove, UK: Psychology Press, 2013.

Baddeley, Alan D., and Graham Hitch. "Working Memory." *Psychology of Learning and Motivation* 8 (1974): 47–89.

Bandura, Albert, and Richard H. Walters. *Social Learning and Personality Development*. New York: Holt, Rinehart and Winston, 1963.

Barrat, James. *Our Final Invention: Artificial Intelligence and the End of the Human Era*. New York: St. Martin's, 2013.

Bengio, Yoshua, Réjean Ducharme, Pascal Vincent, and Christian Jauvin. "A Neural Probabilistic Language Model." *Journal of Machine Learning Research* 3 (February 2003): 1137–55.

Bennett, Daniel L., Adam R. Lucchesi, and Richard K. Vedder. *For-Profit Higher Education: Growth, Innovation and Regulation*. Washington, DC: Center for College Affordability and Productivity (NJ1), 2010.

Berners-Lee, Tim, and Mark Fischetti. *Weaving the Web: The Original Design and Ultimate Destiny of the World Wide Web by Its Inventor*. London: Orion Business, 1999.

Bersin, Josh. *HR Technology Disruptions for 2018: Productivity, Design, and Intelligence Reign*. Deloitte Development, 2017. Accessed June 3, 2018, http://marketing.bersin.com.

Bhargava, Anjuli. "Our Main Interest Is to Ensure Education Is Available Free to All: Mike Feerick." *Business Standard*, June 11, 2016. http://www.business-standard.com.

Blake-Plock, Shelly. "Learning Engineering: Merging Science and Data to Design Powerful Learning Experiences." Getting Smart. Last updated January 29, 2018. http://www.gettingsmart.com.

Blumenstyk, Goldie. "Should the Future of Education Include a 'Personalized Prescription' of Video Games?" *Chronicle of Higher Education*, July 5, 2017. https://www.chronicle.com.

Boccardi, Federico, Robert W. Heath, Angel Lozano, Thomas L. Marzetta, and Petar Popovski. "Five Disruptive Technology Directions for 5G." *IEEE Communications Magazine* 52, no. 2 (2014): 74–80. doi:10.1109/MCOM.2014.6736746.

Boettcher, Judith V. "The Changing Landscape of Distance Education: What Micro-Market Segment Is Right for You?" *Syllabus* 15, no. 12 (July 2002): 22–24, 26–27.

Bohannon, John. "Who's Afraid of Peer Review?" *Science* 342, no. 6154 (October 4, 2013): 60–65. https://doi.org/10.1126/science.342.6154.60.

Boli, John, Francisco O. Ramirez, and John W. Meyer, "Explaining the Origins and Expansion of Mass Education." *Comparative Education Review* 29, no. 2 (May 1985): 145–70.

Bonk, Curtis J. "The World Is Open: How Web Technology Is Revolutionizing Education." In *EdMedia: World Conference on Educational Media and Technology*, 3371–80. Chesapeake, VA: Association for the Advancement of Computing in Education (AACE), 2009.

Borich, Gary D. "A Needs Assessment Model for Conducting Follow-Up Studies." *Journal of Teacher Education* 31, no. 3 (1980): 39–42.

Bostrom, Nick. *Superintelligence: Paths, Dangers, Strategies*. New York: Oxford University Press, 2016.

Bowles, Samuel, and Herbert Gintis. "The Problem with Human Capital Theory: A Marxian Critique." *American Economic Review* 65, no. 2, Papers and Proceedings of the Eighty-Seventh Annual Meeting of the American Economic Association (May 1975): 74–82.

Boyles, Brian. *Virtual Reality and Augmented Reality in Education*. West Point, NY: U.S. Military Academy, Master Teacher Program, Center for Teaching Excellence, 2017.

Bradley, Margaret M., Maurizio Codispoti, Bruce N. Cuthbert, and Peter J. Lang. "Emotion and Motivation I: Defensive and Appetitive Reactions in Picture Processing." *Emotion* 1, no. 3 (2001): 276–98. http://dx.doi.org/10.1037/1528-3542.1.3.276.

Breslow, Lori, David E. Pritchard, Jennifer DeBoer, Glenda S. Stump, Andrew D. Ho, and Daniel T. Seaton. "Studying Learning in the Worldwide Classroom Research into edX's First MOOC." *Research and Practice in Assessment* 8 (2013): 13–25.

Broggi, Joshua David. "Woolf Building the First Blockchain University." Woolf Development, April 3, 2018.

Brophy, Jere. "Synthesis of Research on Strategies for Motivating Students to Learn." *Educational Leadership* 45 (1987): 40–48.

Brown, Malcolm, Joanne Dehoney, and Nancy Millichap. "The Next Generation Digital Learning Environment: A Report on Research." EDUCAUSE Learning Initiative (ELI), April 27, 2015. https://library.educause.edu.

Bryan, Janet, Saskia Osendarp, Donna Hughes, Eva Calvaresi, Katrine Baghurst, and Jan-Willem van Klinken. "Nutrients for Cognitive Development in School-Aged Children." *Nutrition Reviews* 62, no. 8 (2004): 295–306.

Bunderson, C. Victor, and Margaret Martinez. "Building Interactive World Wide Web (Web) Learning Environments to Match and Support Individual Learning Differences." *Journal of Interactive Learning Research* 11, no. 2 (2000): 163–95.

Bureau of Labor Statistics, U.S. Department of Labor. "Foreign-Born Labor Force Nearly Half Hispanic and One-Quarter Asian in 2017." *Economics Daily*. Accessed December 2, 2018. https://www.bls.gov.

Burnett, Keith. "Using Blogger to Get Teachers Started with e-Learning." Seb Schmoller, May 25, 2006. http://fm.schmoller.net.

Buterin, Vitalik. "On Bitcoin Maximalism, and Currency and Platform Network Effects." *Ethereum Blog*, November 19, 2014. https://blog.ethereum.org.

Butler, Andrew C., Elizabeth J. Marsh, Michael K. Goode, and Henry L. Roediger III. "When Additional Multiple-Choice Lures Aid versus Hinder Later Memory." *Applied Cognitive Psychology* 20, no. 7 (2006): 941–56. https://doi.org/10.1002/acp.1239.

Campus Technology. "Interactive Media in Education: An Interview with Chris Dede." Accessed June 3, 2018. https://campustechnology.com.

Carnevale, Anthony P., Nicole Smith, and Jeff Strohl. *Recovery: Job Growth and Education Requirements through 2020*. Washington, DC: Georgetown University, Center on Education and the Workforce, June 2013. http://cew.georgetown.edu.

Carnevale, Dan. "Justice Department Sees No Antitrust Concerns in Blackboard's Plan to Take Over WebCT." *Chronicle of Higher Education* 52, no. 24 (February 7, 2006): 37.

Carson, Colin. "How Much Data Does Google Store?" Cirrus Insight. Last updated November 18, 2014. https://www.cirrusinsight.com.

Carter, Dennis. "eSchool News: How to Create a Successful Virtual Campus." UMass Online. Last updated January 6, 2009. http://www.umassonline.net.

Cassidy, Simon. "Learning Styles: An Overview of Theories, Models, and Measures." *Educational Psychology* 24, no. 4 (2004): 419–44.

Charkins, R. J., Dennis M. O'Toole, and James N. Wetzel. "Linking Teacher and Student Learning Styles with Student Achievement and Attitudes." *Journal of Economic Education* 16, no. 2 (1985): 111–20.

Cheal, Catheryn. "Student Perceptions of a Course Taught in Second Life." *Innovate: Journal of Online Education* 5, no. 5 (July 1, 2009).

Chen, Adrian. "We Need to Know Who Satoshi Nakamoto Is." *New Yorker*, May 9, 2016. https://www.newyorker.com.

Chen, Zhuojun Joyce. "The Impact of Teacher-Student Relationships on College Students' Learning: Exploring Organizational Cultures in the Classroom." *Communication Quarterly* 48, no. 2 (2000): Q76.

Cini, Marie, and Matthew Prineas. "Scaling Online Learning: Obstacles on the Way to the Summit." Program Planning and Design, Evolllution, February 12, 2016. http://evolllution.com.

Clay, Rebecca A. "SMOCs: The Next 'Great Adventure.'" *American Psychological Association* 46, no. 7 (July/August 2015). http://www.apa.org.

Cleveland, William. "Data Science: An Action Plan for Expanding the Technical Areas of the Field of Statistics." *International Statistical Review* 69, no. 1 (May 21, 2007): 21–26. https://doi.org/10.1111/j.1751-5823.2001.tb00477.x.

Cohen, Neal J., and Larry R. Squire. "Preserved Learning and Retention of Pattern-Analyzing Skill in Amnesia: Dissociation of Knowing How and Knowing That." *Science* 210, no. 4466 (October 10, 1980): 207–10.

Coltheart, Max. "Iconic Memory and Visible Persistence." *Perception and Psychophysics* 27, no. 3 (1980): 183–228. https://doi.org/10.3758/BF03204258.

Conaway, Roger N., Susan S. Easton, and Wallace V. Schmidt. "Strategies for Enhancing Student Interaction and Immediacy in Online Courses." *Business Communication Quarterly* 68, no. 1 (2005): 23–35.

Conway, Martin A. "Episodic Memories." *Neuropsychologia* 47, no. 11 (2009): 2305–13. https://doi.org/10.1016/j.neuropsychologia.2009.02.003.

Corbeil, Joseph Rene, and Maria Elena Corbeil. "E-Learning: Past Present and Future." In *International Handbook of e-Learning*, vol. 1, edited by Badrul H. Khan and Mohamed Ally, 51–64. Abingdon, UK: Routledge, 2015.

Corcoran, Betsy. "Blackboard's Jay Bhatt Strikes Up the Brass Band." *EdSurge*, July 23, 2014.

Crane, Valerie, et al. *Informal Science Learning: What the Research Says about Television, Science Museums and Community-Based Projects* . Epharata, PA: Science Press, 1994.

Croft, Nicholas, Alice Dalton, and Marcus Grant. "Overcoming Isolation in Distance Learning: Building a Learning Community through Time and Space." *Journal for Education in the Built Environment* 5, no. 1 (2010): 27–64.

Cui, Nan, Pradosh Kharel, and Vikto Gruev. "Augmented Reality with Microsoft HoloLens Holograms for Near Infrared Fluorescence Based Image Guided Surgery." *Proceedings Volume 10049, Molecular-Guided Surgery: Molecules, Devices, and Applications III* (2017). https://doi.org/10.1117/12.2251625.

Cukier, Kenneth. "Big Data Is Better Data." Filmed June 2014 at TEDSalon Berlin 2014, Berlin, Germany. Video, 14:44. https://www.ted.com.

Cuseo, Joseph B., Viki Sox Fecas, and Aaron Thompson. *Thriving in College and Beyond: Research-Based Strategies for Academic Success and Personal Development*. Dubuque, IA: Kendall Hunt, 2010.

Davidson, Cathy N., and David Theo Goldberg. *The Future of Learning Institutions in a Digital Age*. Cambridge, MA: MIT press, 2009.

Dede, Chris, and Andrew Ho. "Big Data Analysis in High Education: Promises and Pitfalls." *EDUCAUSE Review*. Last updated August 5, 2016. http://er.educause.edu.

Delpit, Lisa. *Other People's Children: Cultural Conflict in the Curriculum*. New York: Springer, 1995.

Dennen, Vanessa Paz, and Kristina Wieland. "From Interaction to Intersubjectivity: Facilitating Online Group Discourse Processes." *Distance Education* 28, no. 3 (2007): 281–97.

Deshmukh, Neha V., Surbhi G. Atal, and Pushpanjali Chauragade. "Big Data Mining: An Overview." *International Journal for Engineering Applications and Technology* 7, no. 1 (January 2015): 76–79. http://www.ijfeat.org.

Deterding, Sebastian, Dan Dixon, Rilla Khaled, and Lennart Nacke. "From Game Design Elements to Gamefulness: Defining 'Gamification.'" In *Proceedings of the 15th International Academic MindTrek Conference: Envisioning Future Media Environments*, 9–15. New York: ACM, 2011. https://doi.org/10.1145/2181037.2181040.

Deutsch, David, and Arthur Ekert. "Quantum Computation." *Physics World* 11, no. 3 (March 1998): 47–52.

Dixson, Marcia D. "Creating Effective Student Engagement in Online Courses: What Do Students Find Engaging?" *Journal of the Scholarship of Teaching and Learning* 10, no. 2 (2010): 1–13. https://www.iupui.edu.

Djaouti, Damien, Julian Alvarez, Jean-Pierre Jessel, and Olivier Rampnou. "Origins of Serious Games." In *Serious Games Edutainment Application*, edited by Minhua Ma, Andreas Oikonomou, and Lakhmi C. Jain, 25–43. New York: Springer, 2011.

Docebo. "Elearning Market Trends and Forecast 2017–2021." Accessed December 2, 2018. https://eclass.teicrete.gr.

Dolog, Peter, Nicola Henze, Wolfgang Nejdl, and Michael Sintek. "Personalization in Distributed e-Learning Environments." In *Proceedings of the 13th International World Wide Web Conference on Alternate Track Papers and Posters*, 170–79. New York: ACM, 2004.

Drew, Paul, Geoffrey Raymond, and Darin Weinberg. *Talk and Interaction in Social Research Methods*. London: Pine Forge Press, 2006.

Dumbill, Edd, Elizabeth D. Liddy, Jeffrey Stanton, Kate Mueller, and Shelly Farnham. "Educating the Next Generation of Data Scientists." *Big Data* 1, no. 1 (March 2013): 21–27. https://doi.org/10.1089/big.2013.1510.

Earle, Rodney S. "The Integration of Instructional Technology into Public Education: Promises and Challenges." *Educational Technology* 42, no. 1 (2002): 5–13.

Earp, Brian D., and David Trafimow. "Replication, Falsification, and the Crisis of Confidence in Social Psychology." Frontiers. Last updated May 19, 2015. https://www.frontiersin.org.

Eichenbaum, Howard. "A Cortical-Hippocampal System for Declarative Memory." *Nature Reviews Neuroscience* 1, no. 1 (2000): 41–50.

Elementary and Secondary Education Act of 1965, Public Law 89-10, H.R. 2362, 89th Cong., 1st Sess., April 11, 1965. Accessed December 3, 2018. https://www.gpo.gov.

Empson, Rip. "Education Giant Blackboard Buys MyEdu to Help Refresh Its Brand and Reanimate Its User Experience." *TechCrunch*, January 16, 2014.

Engle, Randall W., Stephen W. Tuholski, James E. Laughlin, and Andrew R. A. Conway. "Working Memory, Short-Term Memory, and General Fluid Intelligence: A Latent-Variable Approach." *Journal of Experimental Psychology: General* 128, no. 3 (1999): 309–31.

Entertainment Software Association. "2018 Essential Facts about the Computer and Video Game Industry." Accessed June 3, 2018. http://www.theesa.com.

Evans, A. L., V. Evans, and A. M. Evans. "Historically Black Colleges and Universities (HBCUS)." *Education* 123, no. 1 (Fall 2002): 3–18.

Fayyad, Usama, Gregory Piatetsky-Shapiro, and Padhraic Smyth. "From Data Mining to Knowledge Discovery in Databases." *AI Magazine* 17, no. 3 (1996): 37–54.

Feigerman, Seth. "Facebook Is Bigger than Amazon, by Market Cap." Mashable, February 14, 2014. https://mashable.com.

Felder, Richard M., and Rebecca Brent. "Navigating the Bumpy Road to Student-Centered Instruction." *College Teaching* 44 (Spring 1996): 43–47.

Fildes, Nic. "2016 Set to Be Year Virtual Reality Takes Off." *Raconteur*, December 17, 2015. https://www.raconteur.net.

Fink, L. Dee. *Creating Significant Learning Experiences: An Integrated Approach to Designing College Courses*. San Francisco: Jossey-Bass, 2003.

Flemming, Arthur S. "The Philosophy and Objectives of the National Defense Education Act." *Annals of the American Academy of Political and Social Science* 327, no. 1 (1960): 132–38.

Freeland, Julia, and Alex Hernandez. "Schools and Software: What's Now and What's Next." Clayton Christensen Institute. Accessed April 28, 2017. https://www.christenseninstitute.org.

French, Sally. "Here's Proof that This Bitcoin Crash Is Far from the Worst the Cryptocurrency Has Seen." *Market Watch*, February 9, 2017. https://www.marketwatch.com.

Fuks, Hugo, Mariano Pimentel, and Carlos José Pereira De Lucena. "RU-Typing-2-Me? Evolving a Chat Tool to Increase Understanding in Learning Activities." *International Journal of Computer-Supported Collaborative Learning* 1, no. 1 (2006): 117–42.

Gabrieli, John D. E. "Cognitive Neuroscience of Human Memory." *Annual Review of Psychology* 49, no. 1 (1998): 87–115.

Gathercole, Susan E. "Cognitive Approaches to the Development of Short-Term Memory." *Trends in Cognitive Sciences* 3, no. 11 (1999): 410–19.

Geske, Joel. "Overcoming the Drawbacks of the Large Lecture Class." *College Teaching* 40, no. 4 (1992): 151–54.

Gibson, James J. "The Visual Perception of Objective Motion and Subjective Movement." *Psychological Review* 61, no. 5 (1954): 304–14.

———. *The Senses Considered as Perceptual Systems*. Boston: Houghton Mifflin, 1966.

Gill, Christopher. "The Death of Socrates." *Classical Quarterly* 23, no. 1 (1973): 25–28.

Glauser, Wendy. "Doctors among Early Adopters of Google Glass." *Canadian Medical Association Journal* 185, no. 16 (2013): 1385. http://www.cmaj.ca.

Goel, Ashok, Terry Anderson, Jordan Belknap, Brian Creeden, William Hancock, Mithun Kumble, Shanu Salunke, Bradley Sheneman, Abhinaya Shetty, and Bryan Wiltgen. "Using Watson for Constructing Cognitive Assistance." *Advances in Cognitive Systems* 4 (2016). http://www.cogsys.org.

Goel, Ashok K., and Lalith Polepeddi. "Jill Watson: A Virtual Teaching Assistant for Online Education." Georgia Tech, School of Interactive Computing Technical Reports, 2016. https://smartech.gatech.edu.

Goldberg, Lewis R. "An Alternative 'Description of Personality': The Big-Five Factor Structure." *Journal of Personality and Social Psychology* 59, no. 6 (1990): 1216–29.

Gonzalez-Franco, Mar, Rodrigo Pizarro, Julio Cermeron, Katie Li, Jacob Thorn, Windo Hutabarat, Ashutosh Tiwari, and Pablo Bermell-Garcia. "Immersive Mixed Reality for Manufacturing Training." *Frontiers in Robotics and AI* 4, no. 3 (February 2017): 1–8. doi:10.3389/frobt.2017.00003.

Goodell, Jim, Liz Glowa, and Brandt Redd. "The Implications of Gartner's Top 10 Tech Trends of 2018 for Education." Getting Smart, February 2, 2018. http://www.gettingsmart.com.

Gopnik, Alison, Clark Glymour, David M. Sobel, Laura E. Schulz, Tamar Kushnir, and David Danks. "A Theory of Causal Learning in Children: Causal Maps and Bayes Nets." *Psychological Review* 111, no. 1 (January 2004): 3–32. https://doi.org/10.1037/0033-295X.111.1.3.

Gordin, Douglas N., and Roy D. Pea. "Prospects for Scientific Visualization as an Educational Technology." *Journal of the Learning Sciences* 4, no. 3 (1995): 249–79.

Grasby, P. M., C. D. Frith, K. J. Friston, J. Simpson, P. C. Fletcher, R. S. J. Frackowiak, and R. J. Dolan. "A Graded Task Approach to the Functional Mapping of Brain Areas Implicated in Auditory-Verbal Memory." *Brain* 117 (1994): 1271–82.

Grech, Alexander, and Anthony F. Camilleri. *Blockchain in Education*. Luxembourg: Joint Research Centre (JRC), European Union, 2017. http://publications.jrc.ec.europa.eu.

Green, Denise. "Historically Underserved Students: What We Know, What We Still Need to Know." *New Directions for Community Colleges*, no. 135 (2006): 21–28.

Griffith, Erin. "Facebook Can Absolutely Control Its Algorithm." *Wired*, September 26, 2017.

———. "How Zuck Met Oculus: The Story behind Facebook's Big Bet on Virtual Reality." *Fortune*, April 14, 2104. http://fortune.com.

Grob, Gerald N. *Mental Institutions in America: Social Policy to 1875*. London: Collier-Macmillan, 1973.

Groom, Jim, and Brian Lamb. "Reclaiming Innovation." *Educause Review* 49, no. 3 (2014): 29–30. Accessed April 25, 2017. http://www.educause.edu.

Grünewald, Franka, Christoph Meinel, Michael Totschnig, and Christian Willems. "Designing MOOCs for the Support of Multiple Learning Styles." In *European Conference on Technology Enhanced Learning*, 371–82. Berlin: Springer, 2013.

Gunning, David. "Explainable Artificial Intelligence (XAI)." DARPA. Accessed December 21, 2018. https://www.darpa.mil.

Guri-Rosenblit, Sarah. "Eight Paradoxes in the Implementation Process of e-Learning in Higher Education." *Distances et saviors* 4, no. 2 (2006): 155–79.

Hafner, Katie. "The Epic Saga of the Well." *Wired*, May 1, 1997.

Hanford, Emily. "The Story of the University of Phoenix." American Public Media. Accessed June 3, 2018. http://americanradioworks.publicradio.org.

Hanna, Michael G., Ishtiaque Ahmed, Jeffrey Nine, Shyam Prajapati, and Liron Pantanowitz. "Augmented Reality Technology Using Microsoft HoloLens in Anatomic Pathology." *Archives of Pathology and Laboratory Medicine* 142, no. 5 (2018): 638–44.

Harris, Stacey. "Should You Break Up with Your LMS?" Chief Learning Officer, April 12, 2013. http://www.clomedia.com.

Hartley, David. *Education and the Culture of Consumption: Personalisation and the Social Order*. New York: Routledge, 2012.

Harvard University. "History." Accessed December 2, 2018. https://www.harvard.edu.

Hiltz, Starr Roxanne. *Online Communities: A Case Study of the Office of the Future*. Norwood, NJ: Ablex, 1985.

Hinton, G. E., and R. J. Williams. "Representation by Back Propagation Errors." *Nature* 3, no. 6 (1986): 899–905. doi:10.1038/323533a0.

Hochreiter, Sepp, and Jürgen Schmidhuber. "Long Short-Term Memory." *Neural Computation* 9, no. 8 (1997): 1735–80.

Hofstein, Avi, and Sherman Rosenfeld. "Bridging the Gap between Formal and Informal Science Learning." *Studies in Science Education* 28, no. 1 (1996): 87–112. https://doi.org/10.1080/03057269608560085.

Holguin, Jaimie. "Army Recruits Video Gamers." *CBS Evening News*, March 30, 2004. https://www.cbsnews.com.

Hood, Leroy, and Lee Rowen. "The Human Genome Project: Big Science Transforms Biology and Medicine." *Genome Medicine* 5, no. 9 (September 2013): 1–8. https://doi.org/10.1186/gm483.

Horrigan, John B. "Online Communities." Pew Research Center, October 31, 2001. http://www.pewinternet.org.

Hoxby, Caroline M., and Gretchen Weingarth. *Taking Race out of the Equation: School Reassignment and the Structure of Peer Effects*. Working paper 7867. Palo Alto, 2005. https://www.pausd.org.

Hua, Karen. "Education as Entertainment: YouTube Sensations Teaching the Future." *Forbes*, June 23, 2015. https://www.forbes.com.

Hughes, Charles E., Christopher Stapleton, Darin E. Hughes, and Eileen Smith. "Mixed Reality in Education, Entertainment, and Training." *IEEE Computer Graphics and Applications* 25, no. 6 (November 2005): 24–30.

Hussar, William J., and Tabitha M. Bailey. "Projections of Education Statistics to 2022: NCES 2014–051." National Center for Education Statistics, 2014. Accessed April 5, 2017. https://nces.ed.gov.

Illeris, Knud. *How We Learn: Learning and Non-Learning in School and Beyond*. New York: Routledge, 2007.

Internet World Stats. "Internet Growth Statistics." Accessed December 2, 2018. https://www.internetworldstats.com.

Jefferson, Thomas. "79: A Bill for the More General Diffusion of Knowledge, 18 June 1779." Founders Online, National Archives. Last updated June 13, 2018. https://founders.archives.gov. [Original source: Papers of Thomas Jefferson, vol. 2, 1777–18 (June 1779), edited by Julian P. Boyd, 526–35. Princeton, NJ: Princeton University Press, 1950.]

Jenkins, Henry. "Game Theory." *MIT Technology Review*, March 29, 2002.

Jennings, Christopher P. "SimCity 1900: Virtuality and Spectatorship at the Turn of the Twentieth Century." Master's thesis, University of Texas, 2000.

Jones, Donald K. *The Making of the Education System, 1851–81*. London: Routledge/Thoemms Press, 1977.

Jones, Gregory V. "A Fragmentation Hypothesis of Memory: Cued Recall of Pictures and of Sequential Position." *Journal of Experimental Psychology: General* 105, no. 3 (1976): 277–93. http://dx.doi.org/10.1037/0096-3445.105.3.277.

Kalaivani, Karuppiah, and K. AmuthaPrabaker. "Analysis of Big Data with Data Mining Using HACE Theorem." *Journal of Recent Research in Engineering and Technology* 2, no. 4 (April 2015). https://docplayer.net.

Katz, Michael B. "The Origins of Public Education: A Reassessment." *History of Education Quarterly* 16, no. 4 (1976): 381–407.

Kelly, Declan, and Brendan Tangney. "Predicting Learning Characteristics in a Multiple Intelligence Based Tutoring System." In *International Conference on Intelligent Tutoring Systems*, 678–88. Berlin: Springer, 2004.

Kensinger, Elizabeth A., and Suzanne Corkin. "Memory Enhancement for Emotional Words: Are Emotional Words More Vividly Remembered than Neutral Words?" *Memory and Cognition* 31, no. 8 (2003): 1169–80. https://doi.org/10.3758/BF03195800.

Kesner, Raymond P., and Jason Rogers. "An Analysis of Independence and Interactions of Brain Substrates that Subserve Multiple Attributes, Memory Systems, and Underlying Processes." *Neurobiology of Learning and Memory* 82, no. 3 (2004): 199–215.

King, Alison. "From Sage on the Stage to Guide on the Side." *College Teaching* 41, no. 1 (Winter 1993): 30–35. http://www.jstor.org/stable/27558571.

Kizilcec, René F. "Collaborative Learning in Geographically Distributed and In-Person Groups." *AIED 2013 Workshops Proceedings* 67 (2013).

Kizilcec, René F., and Emily Schneider. "Motivation as a Lens to Understand Online Learners: Toward Data-Driven Design with the OLEI Scale." *ACM Transactions on Computer-Human Interaction* (*TOCHI*) 22, no. 2 (April 2015).

Klass, Kym. "Historic ASU Discrimination Suit Changed Education in Alabama." *Montgomery Adviser*, January 23, 2014. https://amp.montgomeryadvertiser.com.

Klopfer, Eric, Scot Osterweil, and Katie Salen. *Moving Learning Games Forward: Obstacles, Opportunities and Openness*. Cambridge, MA: Education Arcade, 2009.

Knight, Will. "The Dark Secret at the Heart of AI." *MIT Technology Review*, April 11, 2017. https://www.technologyreview.com.

Krause, Jackie, Laura Portolese Dias, and Chris Schedler. "Competency-Based Education: A Framework for Measuring Quality Courses." *Online Journal of Distance Learning Administration* 18, no. 1 (Spring 2015). https://www.westga.edu.

Kronk, Henry. "Goldman Sachs Launches Their 10,000 Women Entrepreneurial Course as a Coursera MOOC." *Elearning Inside*, May 22, 2018. https://news.elearninginside.com.

Lang, Leah, and Judith A. Pirani. "The Learning Management System Evolution: CDS Spotlight Report." EDUCAUSE Research Bulletin, May 20, 2014, https://library.educause.edu.

Lanier, Jaron Z., Jean-Jacques G. Grimaud, Young L. Harvill, Ann Lasko-Harvill, Chuck L. Blanchard, Mark L. Oberman, and Michael A. Teitel. "Method and System for Generating Objects for a Multi-Person Virtual World Using Data Flow Networks." U.S. Patent 5588139, filed October 8, 1993, issued December 24, 1996.

Lave, Jean, and Etienne Wenger. *Situated Learning: Legitimate Peripheral Participation*. Cambridge: Cambridge University Press, 1991.

Lawrence, J., S. Volet, A. Dodds, and B. McGaw. "Students' Representations of Problems." *Problem-Based Learning in Education for the Professions*. Sydney: Higher Education Research and Development Society of Australasia, 1985.

Leckart, Steven. "The Stanford Education Experiment Could Change Higher Learning Forever." *Wired*, March 20, 2012. https://www.wired.com.

Lederman, Doug. "Who Is Studying Online (and Where)." *Inside Higher Ed*, January 5, 2018. https://www.insidehighered.com.

Lee, Nick. *Childhood and Society: Growing Up in an Age of Uncertainty*. Oxford, UK: McGraw-Hill Education, 2001.

Lee-Post, Anita. "e-Learning Success Model: An Information Systems Perspective." *Electronic Journal of e-Learning* 7, no. 1 (2009): 61–70.

Lehman, Rosemary. "The Role of Emotion in Creating Instructor and Learner Presence in the Distance Education Experience." *Journal of Cognitive Affective Learning* 2, no. 2 (Spring 2006): 12–26.

Leitch, Alexander. "The Founding of Princeton." In *A Princeton Companion*. Princeton, NJ: Princeton University Press, 1978. https://etcweb.princeton.edu.

Levy, Nat. "PAX Panelists: It Won't Be Long before People Have Virtual Reality in Their Homes." *GeekWire*, September 7, 2016. https://www.geekwire.com.

Lobo, Freia. "My Favorite College Professor Was YouTube." Mashable, May 12, 2017. https://mashable.com.

Locker, Melissa. "Google Is Working with Community Colleges to Train Future IT Professionals." Fast Company, June 25, 2018. https://www.fastcompany.com.

Loring Brace, Charles. *The Dangerous Classes of New York and Twenty Years' Work among Them*. New York: Wynkoop & Hallenbeck, 1872.

Lowenthal, Patrick R. "The Evolution and Influence of Social Presence Theory on Online Learning." PhD diss., University of Colorado Denver, 2009.

Ludwig, Christine, and Christian Reimann. "Augmented Reality: Information im Fokus." *Cooperative Computing and Communication Laboratory* 4, no. 1 (2005). https://www.c-lab.de.

Machemer, Patricia L., and Pat Crawford. "Student Perceptions of Active Learning in a Large Cross-Disciplinary Classroom." *Active Learning in Higher Education* 8, no. 1 (2007): 11–31.

Makel, Matthew C., and Jonathan A. Plucker. "Facts Are More Important than Novelty: Replication in the Education Sciences." *Educational Researcher* 43, no. 6 (August 1, 2014): 304–16.

Makel, Matthew C., Jonathan A. Plucker, and Boyd Hegarty. "Replications in Psychology Research: How Often Do They Really Occur?" *Perspectives on Psychological Science* 7, no. 6 (November 7, 2012): 537–42.

Malone, Thomas W., and Mark Lepper. "Making Learning Fun: A Taxonomy of Intrinsic Motivations for Learning." In *Aptitude, Learning, and Instruction*. Vol. 3, *Conative and Affective Process Analyses*, edited by Richard E. Snow and Marshall J. Farr, 223–53. Hillsdale, NJ: Lawrence Erlbaum, 1987.

Marshall, Hermine H., and Rhona S. Weinstein. "Classroom Factors Affecting Students' Self-Evaluations: An Interactional Model." *Review of Educational Research* 54, no. 3 (1984): 301–25.

Marsick, Victoria J., and Karen E. Watkins. *Informal and Incidental Learning in the Workplace*. New York: Routledge, 1990.

Martin, Scott McKay. "System and Method for Providing Group Learning via Computerized Student Group Assignments Conducted Based on Student Attributes and Student-Variable-Related Criteria." U.S. Patent 9,691,291, issued June 27, 2017.

Martin, Scott McKay, James R. Casey, and Christopher Etesse. "Deep Academic Learning Intelligence and Deep Neural Language Network System and Interfaces." U.S. Patent Application 15/901,476, filed August 30, 2018.

Martin, Scott McKay, Peter Joseph Chick, Daniel Sovanndara T. E., and Brandon Parker Williams. "Networked Activity Monitoring via Electronic Tools in an Online Group Learning Course and Regrouping Students during the Course Based on the Monitored Activity." U.S. Patent Application 15/265,579, filed March 15, 2018.

Martin, Scott McKay, Prescott Henry Martin, Matthew Luu Trang, Rachel Naidich, and Emad Mohamed. "Artificial Cognitive Declarative-Based Memory Model to Dynamically Store, Retrieve, and Recall Data Derived from Aggregate Datasets." U.S. Patent Application 15/686,144, filed August 23, 2018.

Martinez, Margaret A. *An Investigation into Successful Learning: Measuring the Impact of Learning Orientation, a Primary Learner-Difference Variable, on Learning*. Provo, UT: Brigham Young University, 1999. http://www.trainingplace.com.

———. "Key Design Considerations for Personalized Learning on the Web." *Educational Technology and Society* 4, no. 1 (2001): 26–40.

Massaro, Dominic W., and Geoffrey R. Loftus. "Sensory and Perceptual Storage: Data and Theory." In *Memory*, edited by Elizabeth L. Bjork and Robert A. Bjork, 67–99. San Diego: Academic Press, 1996.

Matthews, Doris B. "An Investigation of Learning Styles and Perceived Academic Achievement for High School Students." *Clearing House* 69, no. 4 (1996): 249–54.

Mayadas, A. Frank. "Asynchronous Learning Networks: A Sloan Foundation Perspective." *Journal of Asynchronous Learning Networks* 1, no. 1 (March 1997). https://onlinelearning-consortium.org.

Mayer, Richard E. "Multimedia Learning." *Psychology of Learning and Motivation* 41 (2002): 85–139.

Mayer, Richard E., and Roxana Moreno. "Nine Ways to Reduce Cognitive Load in Multimedia Learning." *Educational Psychologist* 38, no. 1 (2003): 43–52.

McElheran, Kristina, and Erik Brynjolfsson. "The Rise of Data-Driven Decision Making Is Real but Uneven." *Harvard Business Review*, February 3, 2016. https://hbr.org.

McFarland, Matt. "I Spent 53 Minutes in Amazon Go and Saw the Future of Retail." *CNN Business*, October 3, 2018. https://www.cnn.com.

McKenzie, Lindsay. "The 100K Club." *Inside Higher Ed*, April 23, 2018. https://www.insidehighered.com.

McLoughlin, Catherine Elizabeth. "The Pedagogy of Personalised Learning: Exemplars, MOOCS and Related Learning Theories." In *EdMedia: World Conference on Educational Media and Technology*, 266–70. Chesapeake, VA: Association for the Advancement of Computing in Education (AACE), 2013.

Metz, Cade. "In Two Moves, AlphaGo and Lee Sedol Redefined the Future." *Wired*, March 16, 2016. https://www.wired.com.

Metz, Rachel. "Augmented Reality Gets to Work." *MIT Technology Review*, February 24, 2014. https://www.technologyreview.com.

Meyer, Katrina. "The Closing of the U.S. Open University." *Educause Review*, January 1, 2006.

Michaelsen, Larry K., and Michael Sweet. "The Essential Elements of Team-Based Learning." *New Directions for Teaching and Learning*, no. 116 (2008): 7–27. doi:10.1002/tl.330.

Michaelson, Peter. "The Invisible Wall of Psychological Resistance." WhyWeSuffer.com. Accessed December 2, 2018. https://www.whywesuffer.com.

Milgram, Paul, and Fumio Kishino. "A Taxonomy of Mixed Reality Visual Displays." *IEICE Transactions on Information and Systems* E77-D, no. 12 (December 1994): 1321–29.

Miller, C. Chet, and Laura B. Cardinal. "Strategic Planning and Firm Performance: A Synthesis of More than Two Decades of Research." *Academy of Management Journal* 37, no. 6 (1994): 1649–65.

Mitchell, Michael, Michael Leachman, and Kathleen Masterson. "Funding Down, Tuition Up: State Cuts to Higher Education Threaten Quality and Affordability at Public Colleges." Center on Budget and Policy Priorities, 2016. Accessed April 15, 2017. http://www.cbpp.org.

Moon, Jae Yun, and Lee Sproull. "Essence of Distributed Work: The Case of the Linux Kernel." *First Monday* 5 (2000). https://firstmonday.org.

Moore, Anne H. "Lens on the Future: Open-Source Learning." *Educause Review*, September/October 2002. https://www.educause.edu.

Moore, Michael Grahame. "The Theory of Transactional Distance." In *Handbook of Distance Education*, edited by Michael Grahame Moore, 84–103. New York: Routledge, 2013.

Morat, Daniel. *Sounds of Modern History: Auditory Cultures in 19th- and 20th-Century Europe*. Oxford, UK: Berghahn Books, 2014.

Moreno, Roxana, and Richard Mayer. "Interactive Multimodal Learning Environments." *Educational Psychology Review* 19, no. 3 (2007): 309–26.

Morgan, Josh. "How Podcasts Have Changed in Ten Years: By the Numbers." *Medium*, September 2, 2015. https://medium.com.

Muensterera, Oliver J., Martin Lacher, Christoph Zoeller, Matthew Bronstein, and Joachim Kübler. "Google Glass in Pediatric Surgery: An Exploratory Study." *International Journal of Surgery* 12, no. 4 (2014): 281–89.

Müller, Vincent C., and Nick Bostrom. "Future Progress in Artificial Intelligence: A Survey of Expert Opinion." In *Fundamental Issues of Artificial Intelligence*, edited by Vincent C. Müller, 553–71. Berlin: Springer, 2016.

Nakamoto, Satoshi. "Bitcoin: A Peer-to-Peer Electronic Cash System." Bitcoin.org, 2008. https://bitcoin.org/bitcoin.pdf.

National Academies of Sciences, Engineering, and Medicine. *How People Learn II: Learners, Contexts, and Cultures*. Washington, DC: National Academies Press, 2018.

Newell, Allen. "Unified Theories of Cognition." 1987. William James Lectures, Harvard Library Archives, 1990.

Nørgaard, Cita, Lotte Dyhrberg O'Neill, Kurt Gammelgaard Nielsen, Søren Juul, and John Chemnitz. "Learning Anatomy with Augmented Reality." *Proceedings: 10th Annual International Conference on Education and New Learning Technologies*, 2018. doi:10.21125/edulearn.2018.0445.

O'Connor, Mary Catherine, and Sarah Michaels. "Aligning Academic Task and Participation Status through Revoicing: Analysis of a Classroom Discourse Strategy." *Anthropology and Education Quarterly* 24, no. 4 (1993): 318–35.

O'Keefe, P., S. Kerr, V. K. Johnson, S. E. Gans, J. Krumrine, and V. Tinto. "Leaving College: Rethinking the Causes and Cures of Student Attrition." *College Student Journal* 45, no. 4 (1993): 195–99.

Onah, Daniel F. O., Jane Sinclair, and Russell Boyatt. "Dropout Rates of Massive Open Online Courses: Behavioural Patterns." *EDULEARN14 Proceedings* (2014): 5825–34.

O'Neil, Cathy. *Weapons of Math Destruction: How Big Data Increases Inequality and Threatens Democracy*. New York: Broadway Books, 2016.

Oremus, Will. "University Suspends Online Classes after More than Half the Students Fail." *Slate: Future Tense*, July 19, 2013. https://slate.com.

Paivio, Allan. *Mental Representations: A Dual Coding Approach*. Oxford: Oxford University Press, 1990.

Pankseep, Jaak, and Lucy Biven. *The Archaeology of Mind: Neuroevolutionary Origins of Human Emotions*. New York: Norton, 2012.

Paris, Scott, and Peter Winograd. "Promoting Metacognition and Motivation of Exceptional Children." *Remedial and Special Education* 6, no. 11 (1990): 7–15.

Park, Vicki, Alan J. Daly, and Alison Wishard Guerra. "Strategic Framing: How Leaders Craft the Meaning of Data Use for Equity and Learning." *Educational Policy* 27, no. 4 (2012): 645–65.

Pew Internet and American Life Project. "Online Communities: Networks that Nurture Long-Distance Relationships and Local Ties." Accessed June 3, 2018. http://www.pewinternet.org.

Pew Research Center, Social and Demographic Trends. "America's Shrinking Middle Class: Close Look at Changes within Metropolitan Areas." May 11, 2016. Accessed April 15, 2017. http://www.pewsocialtrends.org.

Popper, Karl. *The Logic of Scientific Discovery*. London: Hutchison, 1959.

Porter, Eduardo. "A Smart Way to Skip College in Pursuit of a Job." *New York Times*, June 17, 2014. https://www.nytimes.com.

Powers, Elia. "Latest Twist in Distance Ed." *Inside Higher Ed*, August 9, 2007. https://web.archive.org.

Quartz, Steven R., and Terrence J. Sejnowski. "The Neural Basis of Cognitive Development: A Constructivist Manifesto." *Behavioral and Brain Sciences* 20, no. 4 (December 1997): 537–56. https:doi.org/10.1017/S0140525X97001581.

Ralph, John, and Richard Rubinson. "Immigration and the Expansion of Education in the United States." *American Sociological Review* 45 (December 1980): 943–54.

Rashed, Roshdi. "A Polymath for the 10th Century." *Science* 297, no. 5582 (August 2, 2002): 773. http://d2ufo47lrtsv5s.cloudfront.net/content/sci/297/5582/773.full.pdf.

Rauh, Virginia A., and Amy E. Margolis. "Research Review: Environmental Exposures, Neurodevelopment, and Child Mental Health: New Paradigms for the Study of Brain and Behavioral Effects." *Journal of Child Psychology and Psychiatry* 57, no. 7 (2016): 775–93.

Redden, Elizabeth. "The Engaged E-Learner." *Inside Higher Ed*, November 13, 2006. https://web.archive.org.

Reiser, Robert A. "Instructional Technology: A History." In *Instructional Technology: Foundations*, edited by Robert Gagne, 11–48. New York: Routledge, 1987.

Rheingold, Howard. *The Virtual Community: Homesteading on the Electronic Frontier*. Reading, MA: Addison Wesley, 1993.

Riipinen, Markku. "Extrinsic Occupational Needs and the Relationship between Need for Achievement and Locus of Control." *Journal of Psychology* 128, no. 5 (1994): 577–87.

Robinson, Matt, and Tom Schoenberg. "Bitcoin-Rigging Criminal Probe Focuses on Tie to Tether." Bloomberg, November 20, 2018. https://www.bloomberg.com.

Rogoff, Barbara. *The Cultural Nature of Human Development*. New York: Oxford University Press, 2003.

Ross, Brian H., and Gordon H. Bower. "Comparisons of Models of Associative Recall." *Memory and Cognition* 9, no. 1 (1981): 1–16. https://doi.org/10.3758/BF03196946.

Ross, Tanya. "Making Reflective Practice Visible: Supporting Shifts in Practice towards Personalized Learning." Master's thesis, University of Victoria, 2016.

Rothman, David J. *The Discovery of the Asylum: Social Order and Disorder in the New Republic*. Boston: Little, Brown, 1971.

Rustici, Mike. "Opinion: The LMS Isn't Dead . . . Yet." Chief Learning Officer, July 21, 2017. http://www.clomedia.com.

Rys, Rick. "Increasing the Performance of the Human Asset." Arc Advisory Group, March 29, 2018. https://www.arcweb.com.

Saettler, Paul. *A History of Instructional Technology*. New York: McGraw-Hill, 1968.

Salzman, Marilyn C., Chris Dede, and R. Bowen Loftin. "VR's Frames of Reference: A Visualization Technique for Mastering Abstract Multidimensional Information." In *Proceedings of the SIGCHI Conference on Human Factors in Computing Systems*, 489–95. New York: ACM, 1999.

Sandeen, Arthur. "Educating the Whole Student: The Growing Academic Importance of Student Affairs." *Change: The Magazine of Higher Learning* 36, no. 3 (2004): 28–33. Accessed April 25, 2017. https://my.queens.edu.

Scanlan, Christopher. *Reporting and Writing: Basics for the 21st Century*. Oxford: Oxford University Press, 2000.

Schamer, Toni, and Michael Johns. "Converging Evidence that Stereotype Threat Reduces Working Memory Capacity." *Journal of Personality and Social Psychology* 85, no. 3 (2003): 440–52.

Scharf, Erwin R. *Martin Luther Reformer in the Making*. Milwaukee: Northwestern, 2016.

Schiefele, Ulrich, and Mihaly Csikszentmihalyi. "Motivation and Ability as Factors in Mathematics Experience and Achievement." *Journal for Research in Mathematics Education* (1995): 163–81.

Schiff, Judith. "A Brief History of Yale." Yale University Library. Last updated July 2, 2018. https://guides.library.yale.edu.

Schmidt, Jan. "Social Software: Facilitating Information-, Identity- and Relationship Management." In *BlogTalks Reloaded: Social Software; Research and Cases*, edited by Thomas N. Burg and Jan Schmidt, 31–49. Norderstedt, Germany: Books on Demand, 2006.

Schuler, Douglas. *New Community Networks: Wired for Change*. Reading, MA: ACM Press and Addison-Wesley, 1996.

Scriven, Michael. "The Methodology of Evaluation." In *Perspectives of Curriculum Evaluation*, edited by Ralph W. Tyler, Robert M. Gagné, and Michael Scriven, 39–83. Chicago: Rand McNally, 1967.

Serpell, Robert, and A. Wade Boykin. "Cultural Dimensions of Cognition: A Multiplex, Dynamic System of Constraints and Possibilities." In *Thinking and Problem Solving*, edited by Robert J. Sternberg, 369–408. New York: Academic Press, 1994.

Shanks, David R., and Mark F. St. John. "Characteristics of Dissociable Human Learning Systems." *Behavioral and Brain Sciences* 17, no. 3 (1994): 367–95.

Shannon, Claude Elwood. "A Mathematical Theory of Communication." *Bell System Technical Journal* 27, no. 3 (1948): 379–423.

———. "Programming a Computer for Playing Chess." *London, Edinburgh, and Dublin Philosophical Magazine and Journal of Science* 41, no. 314 (1950): 256–75.

Sharma, Gireesh. "Top 10 Learning Management Systems (LMS) of 2018." eLearning Carnival, February 22, 2018. https://elearningcarnival.com.

Shi, Weisong, Jie Cao, Quan Zhang, Youhuizi Li, and Lanyu Xu. "Edge Computing: Vision and Challenges." *IEEE Internet of Things Journal* 3, no. 5 (October 2016): 637–46. doi:10.1109/JIOT.2016.2579198.

Shumski, Daniel. "6 Colleges that Flipped STEM Classrooms." EducationDive, February 20, 2014. https://www.educationdive.com.

Silver, David, Thomas Hubert, Julian Schrittwieser, Ioannis Antonoglou, Matthew Lai, Arthur Guez, Marc Lanctot, Laurent Sifre, Dharshan Kumaran, Thore Graepel, Timothy Lillicrap, Karen Simonyan, and Demis Hassabis. "Mastering Chess and Shogi by Self-Play with a General Reinforcement Learning Algorithm." *arXiv Preprint arXiv:1712.01815* (2017). https://arxiv.org.

Sivakumar, R. "Google Glass in Education." *Conflux Journal of Education* 2, no. 2 (July 2014). http://www.cjoe.naspublishers.com.

Sproull, Lee, and Sara Kiesler. *Connections: New Ways of Working in the Networked Organization*. Cambridge, MA: MIT Press, 1991.

Squadron, Bill. "The Story behind Football's Innovative Yellow First Down Line." *Sports Illustrated*, July 18, 2013. https://www.si.com.

Squire, Larry R. "Memory Systems of the Brain: A Brief History and Current Perspective." *Neurobiology of Learning and Memory* 82, no. 3 (2004): 171–77.

Stark, Harold. "Carter Wilkerson: The Nuggets Guy Who Broke Twitter." *Forbes*, May 3, 2017. https://www.forbes.com/.

Stern, Joanna. "Jeff Bezos: A Down-to-Earth CEO Reaching for the Stars." *ABC News*, September 25, 2013. https://abcnews.go.com.

Stipek, Deborah, and Denise H. Daniels. "Declining Perceptions of Competence: A Consequence of Changes in the Child or in the Educational Environment?" *Journal of Educational Psychology* 80 (1988): 352–56.

Stockdale, Susan L., and Robert L. Williams. "Cooperative Learning Groups at the College Level: Differential Effects on High, Average, and Low Exam Performers." *Journal of Behavioral Education* 13, no. 1 (2004): 37–50.

Stronge, James H. *Qualities of Effective Teachers*. Alexandria, VA: ASCD, 2018.

Talley, Susan, and D. Hollinger Martinez, eds. "Tools for Schools: School Reform Models Supported by the National Institute on the Education of At-Risk Students." U.S. Department of Education. Last updated April 1998. https://www2.ed.gov.

Tamhane, Deepak S., and Sultana N. Sayyad. "Big Data Analysis Using HACE Theorem." *International Journal of Advanced Research in Computer Engineering and Technology (IJARCET)* 4, no. 1 (January 2015): 18–23.

Teloh, Henry. "Socratic Education in Plato's Early Dialogues." *International Journal for Philosophy of Religion* 26, no. 1 (1986): 60–61.

Teranishi, Robert, Carola Suarez-Orozco, and Marcelo Suarez-Orozco. "Immigrants in Community Colleges." *Future of Children* 21, no. 1 (2011): 153–69.

Thompson, Mary J., and Terrance P. O'Brien. "Learning Styles and Achievement in Postsecondary Classrooms." Annual Conference of the American Educational Research Association, Chicago, 1991 (ERIC No. ED 331 554).

Thyagharajan, K. K., and Ratnamanjari Nayak. "Adaptive Content Creation for Personalized E-Learning Using Web Services." *Journal of Applied Sciences Research* 3, no. 9 (2007): 828–36.

Tinto, Vincent. "Building Community." *Liberal Education* 79, no. 4 (1993): 16–21.

Tukey, John W. "The Future of Data Analysis." *Annals of Mathematical Statistics* 33, no. 1 (March 1962): 1–67, JSTOR.

Tulving, Endel. "Episodic Memory: From Mind to Brain." *Annual Review of Psychology* 53, no. 1 (2002): 1–25.

Turian, Joseph, Lev Ratinov, and Yoshua Bengio. "Word Representations: A Simple and General Method for Semi-Supervised Learning." In *Proceedings of the 48th Annual Meeting of the Association for Computational Linguistics*, 384–94. Stroudsburg, PA: Association for Computational Linguistics, 2010.

Turian, Joseph, Lev Ratinov, Yoshua Bengio, and Dan Roth. "A Preliminary Evaluation of Word Representations for Named-Entity Recognition." In *NIPS Workshop on Grammar Induction, Representation of Language and Language Learning*, 1–8. 2009. http://www.iro.umontreal.ca.

Türker, Mustafa Ali, and Stefan Zingel. "Formative Interfaces for Scaffolding Self-Regulated Learning in PLEs." Slideshare. Last updated July 2008. https://www.slideshare.net.

Tyler-Smith, Keith. "Early Attrition among First Time eLearners: A Review of Factors that Contribute to Drop-out, Withdrawal and Non-completion Rates of Adult Learners Undertaking eLearning Programmes." *Journal of Online learning and Teaching* 2, no. 2 (2006): 73–85.

Urdan, Trace, and Cornelia C. Weggen. *Corporate E-Learning: Exploring a New Frontier*. Berwyn, PA: Hambrecht, 2000.

U.S. Department of Education, National Center for Education Statistics. Digest of Education Statistics, 2016 (NCES 2017-094). 2018. https://nces.ed.gov.

Vassileva, Julita. "Toward Social Learning Environments." *IEEE Transactions on Learning Technologies* 1, no. 4 (2008): 199–214.

Wagner, Anthony D., Daniel L. Schacter, Michael Rotte, Wilma Koutstaal, Anat Maril, Anders M. Dale, Bruce R. Rosen, and Randy L. Buckner. "Building Memories: Remembering and Forgetting of Verbal Experiences as Predicted by Brain Activity." *Science* 281, no. 5380 (1998): 1188–91.

Waldrop, M. Mitchell. "Massive Open Online Courses, aka MOOCs, Transform Higher Education and Science." *Scientific American*, March 13, 2013. https://www.scientificamerican.com.

Wang, Yingxu. "On Cognitive Mechanism of the Eyes: The Sensor vs. the Browser of the Brain." In *Proceedings of the Second IEEE International Conference on Cognitive Informatics, 2003*, 225. Piscataway, NJ: IEEE, 2003.

———. "The OAR Model of Neural Informatics for Internal Knowledge Representation in the Brain." *International Journal of Cognitive Informatics and Natural Intelligence (IJCINI)* 1, no. 3 (2007): 66–77.

Wang, Yingxu, Ying Wang, Shushma Patel, and Dilip Patel. "A Layered Reference Model of the Brain (LRMB)." *IEEE Transactions on Systems, Man, and Cybernetics, Part C (Applications and Reviews)* 36, no. 2 (2006): 124–33.

Warlick, David. "Curriculum Is Dead." *2¢ Worth Blog*, May 22, 2006. http://2cents.onlearning.us/?p=420.

Webster, Noah. "On the Education of Youth in America." In *A Collection of Essays and Fugitiv Writings on Moral, Historical, Political and Literary Subjects*. Boston, 1790. Reprint, Federalist Papers Project, 2013. https://www.thefederalistpapers.org.

Weihrauch, M., G. Meloeny, and T. Goesch. "The First Head Up Display Introduced by General Motors." SAE Technical Paper 890288, 1989. https://doi.org/10.4271/890288.

Weiss, Kenneth R. "California Virtual University Has a Collision with Reality." *Los Angeles Times*, April 8, 1999. http://articles.latimes.com.

Weller, Chris. "A Top Futurist Predicts the Largest Internet Company of 2030 Will Be an Online School." *Business Insider*, December 27, 2016. https://www.businessinsider.com.

Wenger, Etienne. *Communities of Practice: Learning, Meaning, and Identity (Learning in Doing: Social, Cognitive and Computational Perspectives)*. Cambridge: Cambridge University Press, 1998.

Werker, Janet F., and Richard C. Tees. "Speech Perception as a Window for Understanding Plasticity and Commitment in Language Systems of the Brain." *Developmental Psychobiology* 46, no. 3 (April 2005): 233–51. https://doi.org/10.1002/dev.20060.

Whitmer, John. "How Successful Students use LMS Tools—Confirming Our Hunches." *Blackboard Blog*, September 7, 2016. http://blog.blackboard.com.

William & Mary. "History and Traditions." Accessed December 2, 2018. https://www.wm.edu.

Williams, Sean. "20 Real-World Uses for Blockchain Technology." *Motley Fool*, April 11, 2018. https://www.fool.com.

Wilson, James. *The Principles of Psychology*. New York: Henry Holt, 1890.

Wilson, Margaret. "Six Views of Embodied Cognition." *Psychonomic Bulletin and Review* 9, no. 4 (2002): 625–36.

Wing-yi Cheng, Rebecca, Shui-fong Lam, and Joanne Chung-yan Chan. "When High Achievers and Low Achievers Work in the Same Group: The Roles of Group Heterogeneity and Processes in Project-Based Learning." *British Journal of Educational Psychology* 78, no. 2 (2008): 205–21.

Winn, William. *A Conceptual Basis for Educational Applications of Virtual Reality*. Seattle: Human Interface Technology Laboratory, Washington Technology Center, 1993.

Winograd, Terry. "Frame Representations and the Declarative/Procedural Controversy." In *Representation and Understanding: Studies in Cognitive Science*, edited by Daniel G. Bobrow and Allan M. Collins, 185–210. New York: Academic Press, 1975.

Winters, Charles H. "Theological Education in the Next Decade." In *Realities and Visions: The Church's Mission Today*, edited by Furman C. Stough and Urban T. Holmes III, 125–33. New York: Seabury, 1976.

Young, Jeffrey R. "Blackboard Announces New MOOC Platform." *Chronicle of Higher Education*, July 10, 2013. https://www.chronicle.com.

About the Author

Scott M. Martin is an inventor, a mentor, an educator, an entrepreneur, and an author. He is the founding director of the Virginia Serious Game Institute (VSGI), former (founding) director of the Computer Game Design Programs, and is currently a professor at George Mason University in Fairfax, Virginia. Previously, he formed and led the School of Art and Visual Technology by integrating the art studio department with digital arts, resulting in one of the largest academic programs at Mason. Prior to his arrival at Mason, Martin founded the music media technology program at Alabama State University in Montgomery.

Martin earned undergraduate and graduate degrees from Johns Hopkins University, and his DMA from the University of Maryland, College Park. For the past six years, Martin's research focus has been designing new technological solutions and deep-learning algorithmic models applied to teaching and learning, combining the fields of data science and the social sciences of human knowledge acquisition. He also recently developed a new blockchain algorithm paradigm designed to secure and protect online user data sets.

In the last thirty years, Martin has taught courses on the undergraduate and graduate levels as distinct as philosophy, theory and criticism, cyberculture, music composition, digital arts, business entrepreneurship and management, business finance, acoustics, audio engineering, and software development. Martin has a catalog of more than one hundred musical compositions—from sonatas, chamber works, and operettas to experimental interactive stage dramas incorporating MIDI hardware devices he personally built and programmed. His music has been heard in concert halls, broadcast television shows, advertisements, movies, and games.

Martin has founded multiple institutes, research centers, schools, and businesses, and he is the founder of PSTH LLC, a business consultancy, and previously cofounder of Scriyb LLC, a machine-learning education technology platform company.

* * *

Christopher Jennings has more than fifteen years' experience in instructional design and educational technology. He has built online courses for the University of Texas, directed the Center for Innovation in Teaching and Learning at NYU, and for the past ten years, worked as an instructional designer and learning manager at Google. He managed the building of DoubleClick's first global online training and certification program for Google advertisers and publishers including curriculum, as well as registration and certification systems. Now he manages the Analytics Academy, a custom learning platform built on the Google Analytics stack that has trained more than one million students globally on Google marketing products such as Google Analytics, Google Tag Manager, and Google Ads.

Jennings has a bachelor's degree in creative writing from San Diego State, a master of arts in American studies from the University of Texas at Austin, and a master's of professional studies in interactive telecommunications from New York University. His interests include fiction and nonfiction writing, the history of virtual spaces and spectatorship, physical prototyping and user-centered design, and designing and coding apps for learning and information management.

Jennings is also interested in the future of educational technology. This includes the potential for machine learning to personalize and intuit educational experiences, open courseware to democratize education, virtual reality to create more compelling learning experiences, and data analysis to inform learning engineering for better instructional design. He has spoken on these themes at conferences that include DevLearn, EdTechX in London, and Learning Analytics and Knowledge (LAK) in Sydney. He has also contributed a chapter to *Learning Engineering for Online Education: Theoretical Contexts and Design-Based Examples* (2018) sponsored by the Harvard Extension School, and published articles about instructional design and educational technology in *E-learn Magazine* and *Learning Solutions Magazine*.

www.ingramcontent.com/pod-product-compliance
Ingram Content Group UK Ltd.
Pitfield, Milton Keynes, MK11 3LW, UK
UKHW012040150926
475560UK00001B/114

9 781475 847277